CROYDON AIRPORT
THE BATTLE FOR
1939~1940

1. The Control Tower at Croydon in wartime dress, covered in camouflage netting. The building equipment may relate to repairs after damage suffered in the air-raid of August 15th, 1940.

CROYDON AIRPORT AND
THE BATTLE FOR BRITAIN
1939 ~ 1940

DOUGLAS CLUETT

JOANNA BOGLE (NASH)

BOB LEARMONTH

London Borough of Sutton Libraries and Arts Services

ILLUSTRATIONS ACKNOWLEDGEMENTS

1. Derek Wood
2, 14, 22, 25, 28, 41, 42, 43, 44, 45, 46, 48, 49, 53, 55, 57: photographs taken by the late Albert E. Jessop; reproduced by kind permission of Mr. L. Jessop
3, 4, 5, 6: Lettice Curtis
7. Mr. L. Pepper
8, 10, 11, 12, 13, 15, 18, 19, 21, 40, 59: the late Leslie W. L. Penfold
9, 16, 17, 20, 23, 24, 27, 50, 54: Brian Haimes
26, 73, 76, 89, 92, 93, 94, 95: Colin Brown
29, 30, 31, 32, 33, 34: the late Peter W. Moss, via John Bagley, Science Museum.
35, 36, 37: Public Record Office, Kew. Crown copyright reserved.
38, 39, 68: Peter G. Cooksley
51, 52: Popperfoto/Winston G. Ramsey, *After the Battle* magazine
56, 78, 79, 80: Imperial War Museum
58. Lloyd C. Ifould

60, 61, 62: Victor J. Wood
63, 64, 65: Surrey Press
66. Based on O.S. maps 1933 and 1941, with the sanction of the Controller of H.M. Stationery Office. Crown Copyright reserved
67. BBC Hulton Picture Library
69. Unidentified newspaper photograph
70, 71, 77: Ministry of Defence. Crown Copyright reserved
72. Keystone Press Agency
74, 75: Science Museum
81, 83, 84, 90: Christopher Currant
82. Photo: Douglas Cluett
85, 86. Robert Foster
88. Robert Hall, redrawn by Shirley Edwards
91. Albert Hodson
96. Tom Samson
97. Aerodrome Hotel (photo: George Jenkinson)

Copies of the above are now in Sutton Libraries' collection.

Many thanks to all the other people who have given or lent for copying photographs and other material which have not been used in this book.

GRAPHICS AND DESIGN — SHIRLEY EDWARDS

First Published 1984

ISBN 0 907335 11 X

Printed by
John Bentley (Printers) Ltd, Todmorden
A member of the Dunn & Wilson Group

CONTENTS

Chapter   *Page*

Foreword by Wing Commander
R. R. Stanford-Tuck, DSO, DFC (2 bars) RAF Ret'd   vi

Authors' Preface   vii

1. *London's Airport becomes RAF Croydon*   1

2. *Civil Aviation Goes to War*   15

3. *Croydon and the 'Phoney War'*   33

4. *Croydon and the Fall of France*   45

5. *Black Thursday*   69

6. *The Battle Rages*   83

7. *The Battle is Won*   99

References   142

Appendices   146

Index   156

FOREWORD

By Wing Commander R.R. Stanford-Tuck, DSO, DFC (2 bars)
RAF Retd., Vice-President, Croydon Airport Society.

When I first read through the manuscript of this book it brought back to me a flood of memories of my short period at Croydon in early 1940, when I joined 92 Squadron, recently re-equipped with Spitfires, to take over command of a Flight under the leadership of Squadron Leader Roger Bushell, who after being shot down and captured in Germany was later, in 1944, shot by the Gestapo when yet again he was recaptured by the Germans, having master-minded and organised what has become known as The Great Escape (from a book written by Paul Brickhill), which is an epic in itself.

Sadly, many of the pilots mentioned in *Croydon Airport and the Battle for Britain* were later shot down and killed, and to my knowledge, of the original members of the Squadron when it was at Croydon, there are probably only four or five of us living today.

Being the most experienced Spitfire pilot in 92 Squadron, I was flying continually in order to impart to them as much as I could, and as quickly as I could, the tactics of air combat. It was an intensive experience for all of us, and fortunately they were an excellent bunch of pilots and cottoned on to the intricacies of high altitude fighter combat very quickly, and it was not long before the Squadron Commander, Roger Bushell, on my advice, was able to report to Fighter Command that he considered 92 Squadron fully operational with its new aircraft.

We were then moved to R.A.F. Northolt, where we engaged in daily routine patrols, with the occasional excitement of shooting down barrage balloons which had broken loose and were floating around at high altitude, usually with a nasty long length of wire cable dangling below them.

After a fairly short period we were moved East to Hornchurch in Essex at the start of the Dunkirk campaign, which proved for us to be a most gruelling and taxing period of combat over the beaches of Dunkirk, during which time, whilst our losses were heavy (we lost five pilots and I myself was wounded in the thigh) we inflicted considerably more losses on the assorted German aircraft attacking our troops on the beaches.

However, back to our days at dear old Croydon, which we all loved. I remember the wonderful evenings which we used to have in our Mess, which was the old Aerodrome Hotel; the wonderful days of flying which we used to put in; and lastly jumping in our cars and roaring up to London for a party, and then back to Croydon for some more intensive flying.

Lastly, I should just like to say that I consider this book should be read by all amateur and professional air historians, as I think a lot of the wonderful history contained in this story is little known and I congratulate all who are involved in the compilation and production of it. Well done.

(signed) Bob Stanford-Tuck

AUTHORS' PREFACE

When we published *Croydon Airport: The Great Days 1928-1939* in May 1980, we said that the rest of the story would be published in a subsequent volume, and we set out to do this. It soon became clear that so much material existed relating to Croydon Airport in the Second World War that this merited treatment on its own, and we began to write "Croydon Airport: The Years of War". However, it then became obvious that the war period fell into two distinct parts: the first, Croydon's role as a fighter base, up to and including the Battle of Britain; the second, a gradual return to the Airport's more normal function as a centre of air transport services, albeit in unusual circumstances and with abnormal hazards. This book, therefore, covers the relatively short period until the Battle of Britain was won. This does not mean that we have abandoned writing-up the rest of Croydon Airport's war, or of dealing with the post-war period, and we are grateful to those people who have supplied us with information and material relevant to later periods, of which we still intend to make good use. We would, in fact, be very glad to hear from people stationed at, or with interesting experiences of, Croydon Airport in the remainder of its wartime, and immediately post-war, periods. Particularly, we need photographs relevant to Croydon Aerodrome from 1941 to 1946 (which would be copied and returned).

In the meantime, there are many people to whom thanks are due for this volume. First, we are very much indebted to Wing Commander Robert Stanford-Tuck for his excellent foreword, and for reading our book in draft and making helpful comments. Then we must thank, for help and advice throughout the preparation of the book, especially on technical matters; for sharing their research; and for reading and commenting on drafts of the book: Colin Brown, Peter G. Cooksley, E. J. H. (Ted) Crawforth and Brian Haimes.

Major contributions to the book have come from Squadron Leader Christopher Currant, Wing Commander Robert Foster, Brian Haimes and Robert Hall. We are very much indebted for hitherto unpublished photographs which they took at the time, to the late Albert E. Jessop and the late Leslie Penfold, the latter of whom also helped with written information.

Warm thanks for information and help of many kinds are also due to: John Bagley, Mary Batchelor, Keith Belcher, Evelyn Boyd, Arthur W. Bridger, June Broughton, Derek Card, Margaret Cunningham, Lettice Curtis, M. A. Deverell, Alan E. le G. Gillett, Norman Griffiths, Albert Hodson, Lloyd C. Ifould, George Jenkinson, Mr. L. Jessop, Ernest Jones, John King, Phyllis Lane, Flight Lieutenant David J. Looker, Norman Parker, Major Basil Peacock, Colin A. Perry, Rosalind Prest, Arthur Quin-Harkin, O.B.E., Winston G. Ramsey, Tom Samson, Ewart Sanders, Cyril Smith, Joss G. Spiller, Kenneth Steel, Eric Wheatley, Bill Whitehead, Eileen Whiteing, Viscount Whitelaw, Bill Wood Jnr., Derek Wood and Victor J. Wood. We would also wish to thank all members of the Croydon Airport Society, and others, who helped but have not been mentioned by name.

In addition, for information, material and illustrations, we are indebted to the Public Record Office (Kew); the Air Historical Branch of the Ministry of Defence; the Imperial War Museum; the Science Museum; and the RAF Museum, Hendon.

Particular thanks are due to Roy Smith, Borough Librarian, for his support for the whole project, without which none of the books could have been published. Our renewed thanks too, go to Valary Murphy for patiently typing and re-typing drafts of the text, and helping in many different ways throughout the production of the book.

Finally, we would like to pay tribute to all those connected with Croydon Airport who lost their lives during the Second World War, either in the air or on the ground. This book may serve, a little, to commemorate them.

Sutton Central Library   Joanna Bogle, Douglas Cluett
July 1984   and Bob Learmonth

2. Three Hurricanes, probably of No. 3 Squadron, come in over the south-west corner of the Aerodrome Hotel in November 1939. Note the camouflage netting of the Control Tower in the left foreground. The picture appears to have been taken from the roof of the Terminal Building.

Return of Sir Neville Henderson on 26th August 1939, with Hitler's final proposals "for good relations between Britain and Germany". The aircraft was later the last German air-liner to leave Croydon before the declaration of war.

3. *ABOVE:* Sir Neville leaving the aircraft.

4. *BELOW:* Entering the official car.

CHAPTER ONE

London's Airport becomes RAF Croydon

> There was no crisis panic in Wallington and Carshalton during the week-end. People went to football matches on Saturday afternoon; in the evening they enjoyed themselves as usual at the cinema. On Sunday they went to church, took the dogs for a walk, mowed the back lawns and did a little weeding. Some of them spent the day at the seaside or in the country. Everything seemed much as normal.
>
> Yet between these normal activities they were busy measuring the windows for black-out curtains, checking over the children's clothes in case of evacuation, fixing up air-raid shelters, counting up the tins in the food cupboard.

Thus began the main story on the front page of the last peace-time edition of the *Wallington and Carshalton Times*, August 31st 1939.

Despite the cheering words aimed at boosting morale, the reality of the final anxiety-ridden days was being reflected nearby at Croydon Airport, where a flurry of activity was taking place. On August 26th,[1] the British Ambassador to Germany, Sir Neville Henderson, arrived from Berlin on a Deutsche Luft Hansa flight, bringing a message from Hitler. The aeroplane was a Junkers Ju 52, D-AXOS, *Oswald Boelcke*; a few days later it was to be the last German aeroplane to leave Croydon, and therefore possibly Britain, before hostilities commenced.

Hitler's message insisted on Germany's rights to deal with Poland as she saw fit, whilst including some ritual phrases about the importance of maintaining peace with Britain and France.

Miss Lettice Curtis, later to be a pilot with the Air Transport Auxiliary and to write a book about her experiences[2] - was on the tarmac to witness Sir Neville's arrival: "When he arrived at Croydon all the press were turned off the airfield, but for some reason, although I was standing quite close with a camera, they didn't think I was worth bothering about." Miss Curtis was therefore able to take the photographs reproduced opposite.

On August 28th, Sir Neville (flying this time from Heston), book back to Germany the British Government's reply, which reaffirmed the pledge to Poland; whilst, naturally, suggesting that in happier times nothing would stand in the way of Anglo-German understanding.

All this was taking place against a background of crowds and confusion as British holidaymakers returned hurriedly from Europe, anticipating the coming conflict. *The Times* reported that the number of passengers passing through the airport was three times that for a normal day.

Prospective passengers at Le Bourget were prepared to pay more than four times the usual fare in order to get across the Channel. In the other direction, Germans hurried from Britain: at Croydon, all but one of the normal Luft Hansa staff of twelve had left by August 28th; only Herr Starke, the manager, remained to the end.

There was, however, still a Luft Hansa aircraft in the hangar in the first few days of war. This was the little Messerschmitt Bf 108B-1 Taifun (the type was later renamed Aldon), D-IJHW, used as a liaison machine with Luft Hansa's headquarters in Hamburg and by German Embassy officials. The story of its failure to leave is told in the words of Peter Moss:

As zero hour approached instructions came through to Croydon stating that while no one was to prevent the Taifun being moved, no one was to assist in any way. Soon after dawn on September 3rd [sic - we think this must have been earlier], German mechanics arrived and began preparing the aircraft for take-off. They uttered a few Teutonic curses when they found one of the tyres punctured, but a spare wheel was produced and they got down to the job of changing it. Later on it was realised that the tyre valve had disappeared and they went off to look for another, leaving the aircraft unguarded. A huge packing case was promptly lowered in front of the hangar doors and the crane whisked smartly away. Not to be defeated, the Germans started moving it out of the way, but in the middle of their exertions an ominous hissing emitted from one of the Taifun's tyres; rushing over they found a six inch nail sticking out of it! With no further stock of spare wheels and before they could repair the puncture, the balloon went up and the Germans hurriedly left in one of their Junkers transports and the Taifun was ours.

A few days later, two senior R.A.F. Officers were detailed to collect the Taifun and fly it to an R.A.F. airfield complete with its Swastika and German marks. Engine trouble developed en route and they force-landed in a field near the coast. While the two Officers were trying to locate the trouble, a zealous soldier 'captured' them and proudly marched them into custody. It was several days before this misunderstanding could be cleared up, while the Taifun was delivered by road to No. 10 M.U. on 6.12.39. [3]

Mr. Norman Griffiths, then an engine fitter, confirms this story - he was one of the Imperial Airways staff detailed to 'keep an eye' on the machine - except that he thinks the 'six-inch-nail' was a rivet or bolt. He also remembers that, by the time Imperial Airways evacuated Croydon, Luft Hansa's equipment stores had been mysteriously emptied. (So, too, we are told, had their offices.)

On a different note, Mr. Griffiths recalls the friendliness of the son of the German Ambassador, von Ribbentrop, who gave welcome lifts to and from Croydon in his large, comfortable car.[4]

One person at Croydon in September 1939 with an ideal opportunity of witnessing history was Brian Haimes, then a teenage Air Cadet in the newly-formed Croydon Squadron of the Air Defence Cadet Corps. In *Croydon Airport: The Great Days* we quoted his description of how he came to be at the aerodrome during that memorable August, when Squadron Leader Fox, in charge of the cadets, proposed that a detachment might perform useful work there.

Mr. Haimes, as a Cadet Sergeant, was in charge of the enthusiastic group of boys in their newly-acquired uniforms (Air-Force blue):

We used generally to muck-in at anything that was needed. I think he [Fox] felt that we might function rather like Boy Scouts had done in the air raids in the First World War. You know, they used to help the police, running round, helping old ladies into air raid shelters and that sort of thing . . . and we amounted, really, to sort of messenger boys, but there wasn't really a lot to do. [5]

The Royal Air Force itself had arrived at Croydon on August 25th, in the shape of Flight Lieutenant Geoffrey Cooper, who acted as Liaison Officer with the civil authorities. Four days later, two more senior officers - Squadron Leader Seidenburg-Seymour and Wing Commander Wray - visited, to start discussions on the use of the Aerodrome Hotel as an officers' mess. On August 30th, RAF Croydon was formally established as a satellite aerodrome to Kenley, with Flight Lieutenant Cooper as Camp Commandant. It formed part of No. 11 Group, Fighter Command, and immediately received a visit from the Air Officer Commanding No. 11 Group, Air Vice Marshal (later Sir Leslie) Gossage.

Mr. Haimes remembers Flight Lieutenant Cooper, a pilot with 615 "County of Surrey" Squadron, as a "tall, dark fellow" who seemed very much in charge of everything that was going on. He was later to rise to the rank of Wing Commander and to be mentioned in despatches. After the war he became a Labour M.P. He now lives in the Bahamas.

The RAF men and equipment arrived in lorries driven by members of the Women's Auxiliary Air Force. Brian Haimes remembers most of these as being "rather older ladies; I think a nucleus of volunteers who may have seen service in the First World War", rather than young girls; and also recalls that the RAF officers included "a lot of what I regarded as elderly chaps wearing First World War ribbons". Even many of the younger men had an old-fashioned appearance, however, because they were reservists who had been issued with old-style uniforms buttoning up to the neck, instead of the collar and tie style which soon became universal.

On September 1st, the civil function of London's airport ceased, when the aircraft of Imperial Airways were moved out of Croydon; most going to Whitchurch, near Bristol, where they were joined by the aircraft of British Airways Ltd. The two companies were in the process of amalgamation following the recommendations of the Cadman Report.[6]

None of the major Imperial Airways aircraft was to survive the Second World War. The end was particularly sad for the famous fleet of Handley Page H.P.42s. The private companies based at Croydon were dispersed to various airfields in the west of England as part of the pre-arranged plan drawn up in 1938 - of which more in Chapter Two.

Thus, at Croydon, as September 1939 began, all the civilians had gone except for a few in the aircraft repair organisation and in the various factories operating in the buildings of the First World War National Aircraft Factory No. 1 - or on their sites (see *The First Croydon Airport 1915-1928*).

Rollason Aircraft Services Ltd.* were still overhauling airframes and doing other aircraft repair and servicing work: for instance, on the ninth of January, 1940, 235 Squadron collected the airframe of a Fairey Battle (L 5379) from Rollason's and took it by road to Manston.[7]

Rollason's are also known to have been working on the DWI Wellington conversions in the early months of 1940. DWI stood for 'Directional Wireless Installation'; or, more colloquially, 'Down with 'Itler'! The conversion involved the fitting to four Mark I Wellington bombers of a huge - forty-nine feet nine inches in diameter - ring, containing an aluminium electro-magnetic coil, suspended below the aircraft from nose to tail, and from struts below the wings.

* Rollason's, since 1938, had been part of the Hunting Group of Companies. In 1941 it was renamed Field Consolidated Aircraft Services. Field's are still working on the Croydon site. Bill Rollason, having left the company, was by now in the RAF. He came back to Croydon at the end of the war, and formed a new company there, W.A. Rollason Ltd.; and it is this second Rollason's which still operates now at Shoreham Aerodrome (see *Croydon Airport: The Great Days*, p.93).

It was modified to detonate German magnetic mines from the air, and was developed in the Vickers Experimental Department at Weybridge, where the first four conversions using a Ford V-8 engine as the DWI Mk.1 were made. Subsequent conversions, however, were turned over to Rollason's at Croydon, who converted a further eleven Mk.1s in 1940 as DWI Mk. 2s, using a D.H. Gipsy 6 engine; twice as efficient, with a greater saving on weight. The first Mk. 2 was test-flown on March the 2nd. The system was successful. It was superseded, in British waters, by degaussing coils on board ships; but continued until March 1943 in the Middle East: maintaining the vital route through the Suez Canal.

A twelfth aircraft was converted in August 1942: Wellington HX 682, a Mk. 1c, was converted by Field Services to replace L 4374 lost in January 1942; and two new rings were built to replace one damaged in service as well as the one for HX 682.[8]

A personal account of life at Rollasons in those days was given by Mr. A. Deverell. Writing in 1968, as an Inspector at Rollason Aircraft and Engines Ltd., he recalled:

"We are now only a small Company and no one on our staff was actually on the job of fitting the 'magic rings' on the Wellingtons. However, two of our staff, and myself, were with Rollasons at the time (1940) and can remember this, although none of us was actually on the job, being still busily involved on Hawker Harts, Audaxes and Demons.

Everything was so 'hush hush'; the Wellingtons arrived mysteriously, and hangar doors were firmly closed and locked. No one knew how the 'rings' arrived - they just as mysteriously appeared. The rings were assembled in the hangar on trestles, and electrical experts arrived to install the multitude of wiring. Most of the fittings were made at Rollasons, and one at a time, a Wellington was fitted up. A few drawings were available, but merely to show the attachments. Weird-looking strangers did most of the work . . .

As far as we can remember, only about a dozen aircraft were fitted up - but our memories are a bit hazy. No records of this historical event were ever seen and certainly there are no records in our possession. Indeed, we have no records at all of this era and assume any that did exist were destroyed when we were bombed out, or in the fire that followed.

We remember all the rumours going round at the time as to what these rings were for, the most popular rumour was (that they were) to protect the aircraft from balloon cables. [9]

A further activity of Rollasons at this time is mentioned by Mr. Ken Steel, a former employee there, in a letter in 1983:

I returned to Croydon in 1940 and joined the Inspection Department of Rollasons. The work was on the inspection of overhauls and repairs of military aircraft and aero-engines. Some of it was in 'D' hangar which had been built at the end of the apron of 'C' hangar. We are working under a military guard on a secret project. It was the preparation of large gliders and their tugs to drop our troops behind the enemy lines.[10]

At Croydon in the autumn of 1939, however, the atmosphere was very much that of a military establishment, softened by the attentions of the local populace. Mr. Haimes recalls: "At night, there were always hordes of girls there, and tremendous conversations and negotiations going on through the camp. It was now an RAF camp and they weren't allowed out - and the girls weren't allowed in".[5]

Mr. Haimes and his fellow cadets, overlooked in the general bustle, continued to go to the place every day, merging with the other personnel in their RAF uniforms: "We were tolerated because we wore a blue uniform and nobody quite knew who we were".

The airport had now officially become Royal Air Force Station, Croydon.

As Wilf Nicoll wrote in *The Battle of Britain - Then and Now:*

The airfield was chosen to be a semi-permanent base within No. 11 Group Fighter Command to which squadrons could be withdrawn for short periods from the sector and forward aerodromes for tactical or logistical reasons. Its parent station was Kenley and squadrons from there used it on a rotational basis or when that aerodrome became unusable for any reason whatsoever. Officially, it had accommodation for two fighter squadrons. Four landing areas had been specifically laid out on the grass surface of the aerodrome, the two longest, each of 1,200 yards running N-S and NE-SW. The E-W runway had a length of 1,120 yards and that from SE-NW a total distance of only 966 yards. The terminal building had now become the administration block and the thirty-bedroom Aerodrome Hotel was taken over for pilots' accommodation and messing.

Storage was available for 46,000 gallons of aviation fuel, 2,000 gallons of MT [mechanical transport] fuel and 2,000 gallons of oil . . . Later in the war a concrete perimeter track 35 feet 6 inches wide was constructed around the grass together with a number of fighter pens and hard-standings, all of which were situated on the west side of the aerodrome. [11]

Two ammunition stores were established in the south-west corner of the Terminal Building. According to Wilf Nicoll 1,500,000 rounds of small arms ammunition were in store.

The arrival of the RAF aeroplanes at Croydon made a dramatic prelude to the outbreak of war. At 10.30 on the morning of Saturday September 2nd, they flew in from a clear blue sky, an impressive sight. Mr. Haimes recalls: "There were these aeroplanes, these great fighters, going round and round, and they began to come in from the Highview area, going across Stafford Road from the north and landing on the airfield". [5]

They were Gloster Gladiators of 615 "County of Surrey" Auxiliary Squadron, commanded by Squadron Leader A.V. Harvey, and previously based at Kenley. Arthur Vere Harvey (now Lord Harvey of Prestbury) had founded the squadron in 1937. After the war - he became an Air Commodore in 1943 - he was elected as Conservative MP for Macclesfield. He continued to represent this seat until 1971 when he was made a life peer.

On landing in the sunshine, the twelve Gladiators were dispersed to the perimeter of the airfield, with four reserve machines being placed in the former Imperial Airways hangars - where they shared accommodation with the airmen! These airmen ate in relays in the Imperial Airways canteen, in the Aerodrome Hotel, about five minutes' walk from the hangars.

An airman of 615 Squadron, Mr. Leslie Penfold, recalled moving in to Croydon:

Our dispersal point was near the Stafford Road and we were just about settled in when the Chamberlain speech came over the radio with its declaration of war . . . Imperial Airways workshops became our billets, and our beds were three planks on trestles, straw palliasses, and blankets. With old bedsteads, sandbags and a World War I machine gun, we made a ground defence gun-pit. Its close proximity to Croydon town made the camp very popular in spite of its inconveniences: plenty of pubs, cinemas, dance halls and, of course, the Davis Theatre tea-dances, all within bus or walking distance. There was another big attraction - on the north side of the airport, on the other side of the boundary railings, was the Croydon Gas Company's Sports and Social Club. Just a squeeze through the railings and we were there. Some of us became very friendly with the club members - were invited into their homes and were even allocated a tennis court for our exclusive use. This period - usually referred to as 'the Phoney War' - was a very pleasant time for us at Croydon. [12]

Mr. Keith Belcher, then a rigger with 615 Squadron, also recalls the arrival of the Gladiators:

They were dispersed all around the Foresters Drive area, with the tailplanes inside the back gardens of the houses. Our particular aircraft's tailplane was not more than six feet away from a little girl's rabbit hutch, and she was so distressed by this that the engine fitter and myself moved and rebuilt the hutch up by the house, which made her very happy.

The army formed the guard on the airfield, and at nights when we had finished duty we would stroll across the tarmac to the NAAFI which was in the Terminal Building. I can't remember what regiments were there, but I can say that one of the more easy-going regiments was very quickly replaced by the Honourable Artillery Company, and they took it very seriously. Going to the NAAFI I was challenged and had a bayonet stuck in my chest, and had to show my identity disc. This meant removing my tie and collar, and I'm sure the guard even checked the colour of my braces! Yes, the HAC were very enthusiastic.

I think I hold the record for running across Croydon Aerodrome. Our C.O., Squadron Leader Harvey, could be a little bit irascible, and one of his pet fetishes was that if you ever let go of a wing tip before he waved you off, then you were in serious trouble.

Our particular aircraft had the Squadron Leader's flag on the side of the cockpit, although the regular pilot was Pilot Officer Murton-Neile. One particular day, Squadron Leader Harvey flew the aircraft and was asked by the Flight Sergeant to taxi the aircraft to 'D' hangar at the end of his flight. He must have had a lapse of memory however, for at the end of the flight the Squadron Leader brought the aircraft back to us. He stopped the engine and asked where his car was, so the Flight Sergeant told him that it had been taken to 'D' hangar, where the Squadron Leader was supposed to have taken the Gladiator.

'I suppose I'd better take it over there now, then', said the Squadron Leader. Trying to start a hot Bristol Mercury engine is not the easiest of tasks, especially for a pilot who was out of practice. We wound ourselves silly getting that engine started with the starter handle. Eventually we did, and with the fitter (who, I think, was Fred Prosser) holding one wing-tip, and myself the other, away we went.

Its being autumn, we wore gum boots and oilskins, with a gas mask and tin hat. The speed got faster and faster - he must have stoked the thing up to about 25 miles per hour. We were looking at the Squadron Leader like dogs, pleading with him to let us off . . . This went on right across the airfield to within 200 yards of 'D' hangar, then I gave up the ghost. I thought to hell with it. If I'm on a fizzer, well I'm on a fizzer, and that's that.'

I just lay there on the ground. I've never been so exhausted in all my life. When I had recovered slightly I looked back, and there, twenty yards away, was the still form, all crumpled up and absolutely stationary, of the poor fitter. He was absolutely out. Eventually we both limped into the hangar. The C.O. had parked his 'plane and gone . . . [13]

615 Squadron was allocated a hut behind the houses along Foresters Drive, near the junction with Sandy Lane South, as a squadron headquarters. Slit trenches were dug alongside the aeroplanes. This squadron, later also to be known as "Churchill's Own", was an auxiliary squadron officially incorporated into the RAF when all such units were mobilised on 24th August.

The Squadron's log gives the composition of 615 at the outbreak of war. It also notes, which the Station Operations Record Book does not, the names of those running RAF Croydon:

Camp Commandant	Flight Lieutenant G.A.B. Cooper
Equipment Officer	Flight Lieutenant E.P. Dampier
Medical Officer	Flying Officer R.S. Cromie
Messing Officer	Pilot Officer F.G. Bowling [14]

Flight Lieutenant Dampier was the brother of the well-known comedian, Claude Dampier.

On that last day before war was declared, the Gladiators of 615 Squadron had just dispersed around the perimeter when Croydon was assailed by the roar of nineteen Merlin engines mounted in the Hurricane Is of No. 17 Squadron, arriving from North Weald. The Hurricanes, and two Miles Magisters belonging to the Squadron, were dispersed to the west side of the airport, where they were greeted by their ground crews who had arrived by road earlier that morning.

Accommodation for the officers was found in the Aerodrome Hotel, whilst the other ranks again were billeted in the Imperial Airways hanger; with one of the sub-managers' offices being used as the Squadron HQ.

17 Squadron was commanded by Squadron Leader C. Walter, who, together with his eighteen pilots, flew the fixed-pitch propeller Hurricane Is with which they had been re-equipped in May; although, as their Squadron log[15] points out, they were formerly the aircraft of No. 56 Squadron.

To complete Croydon's complement of fighter aircraft, the Hurricane Is of No. 3 Squadron arrived from Biggin Hill, commanded by Squadron Leader H. H. Chapman. These aircraft were dispersed to the south end of the airport, whilst the personnel made themselves at home in the hangars of K.L.M., S.A.B.E.N.A., and Air France.

The transformation to a military aerodrome was now complete; with over 50 fighting aircraft, together with their pilots, ground crews, and administrative staff, Croydon was once more ready to defend London, just as it had done twenty-three years before, in 1916.

But the war had still not quite officially started. Brian Haimes recalls standing at the gate near the airport's terminal building, adjacent to the Aerodrome Hotel, on that Saturday evening, watching the traffic stream down Purley Way from the South Coast. He remembers that it was a beautiful evening and the traffic unusually heavy: many people had been enjoying their last day of peace at the seaside, or in the country.

The next morning, the solemn voice of Britain's Prime Minister, Mr. Neville Chamberlain, informed the nation that Germany had failed to give an undertaking to withdraw troops from Poland, and that a state of war now existed between Britain and Germany.

A variety of different reasons have been given for the air-raid warning that blared out shortly after he had finished speaking; and a number of myths have collected around it. Certainly it is clear that there were no hostile aircraft of any kind and that the warning was the result of an unidentified aeroplane appearing on a radar screen. Often this aeroplane is described as ferrying refugees from the Continent at the very moment of the outbreak of war. One version of the legend holds that the machine landed at Croydon, but no evidence of any kind substantiates this.

In Derek Wood's book *Attack Warning Red*, a history of the Royal Observer Corps, the incident is reported thus:

The first sirens were sounded at 11.15 a.m. on September 3rd 1939, but to no useful purpose. A French aircraft had not filed a flight plan, and was therefore considered hostile when picked up by radar. The offender had passed over No. 1 Observer Group, Maidstone and 19 Group, Bromley, but as no one was supposed to be able to recognise aircraft by type it was only reported as a 'plane'.[16]

However, another, and perhaps the definitive, story of this false alarm, has been given to the authors by Mr. Eric Wheatley, now European Regional Manager for Hawaiian Air; but then an Imperial Airways Traffic Assistant.

Mr. Wheatley recalls that he had been going to work at Croydon Airport with a case ready-packed for the whole week before war was declared. He was one of those who would be working with the National Air Communications organisation, under RAF orders, should the expected war begin (see Chapter Two).

On Saturday the 2nd September, he and some colleagues were ordered to take the Armstrong Whitworth Ensign, *Explorer*, G-ADSV, to RAF Benson, in Oxfordshire. (He never, incidentally, returned to work at Croydon after this flight.) Mr. Wheatley says:

> On Saturday we had flown in from Croydon to Benson in an Ensign, G-ADSV. As soon as we got there, the RAF boys came out with buckets of paint and camouflaged the aircraft, working with brooms. The Ensign was loaded overnight, and we took off at dawn for Amiens, where we discharged our cargo [this was equipment and spares for a Squadron of Fairey Battles then at Benson, but transferring to France]. On our way back over the Channel it was about 11 o'clock, the time war was declared. There were battleships in the Channel, and we identified ourselves with Very pistols. We made landfall over Shoreham. On our return to Benson we were told that we had been the cause of an air-raid warning in London. [17]

Mr. Wheatley remained with G-ADSV, flying similar missions (but never from Croydon) until he was taken into the RAF after Dunkirk. He has another memory of events connected with the outbreak of war - the departure of the German Ambassador, Herr von Ribbentrop, from Croydon: "There was no fuss - it was all as unobtrusive as possible." Ribbentrop left in a Junkers Ju 52/3m.

Despite the declaration of war, followed so closely by the air-raid warning, local people in the vicinity of Croydon prided themselves on the calmness they displayed on that memorable morning. The writer of the "Mitcham and Tooting Notes" in the *Wallington and Carshalton Advertiser* of 7th September, 1939, pointed out that, in one local church, although the service had been cut short, the collection had still been taken: "It is that calmness of spirit and close attention to the things that matter which will win the war."

At Croydon Aerodrome, the siren produced no visible effect at all: itself rather disconcerting to a young Air Defence cadet standing alone on the tarmac. Brian Haimes can remember it vividly:

> Goodness knows why, but I was standing on the corner of the tarmac, by the tower, where the passengers used to come out to the aeroplanes. And the sirens went off . . . I wasn't exactly frightened or terrified, but I was distinctly nervous. It was a bit like being on the edge of a very steep cliff or a very high building with nothing between you and the ground. I was sixteen, and lived in what I thought was a secure world. I had a closed mind for politics, and the First World War was twenty years before, and twenty years is a long time; I hadn't even been on earth that long. And what seemed like a secure world had already begun to quiver and shake, and suddenly, perhaps, it was going to blow up fast. [5]

With newspaper stories of the bombing of Warsaw fresh in his mind, he imagined the worst. And yet, nothing happened. The sun shone, it was Sunday lunchtime; and on this, one of Britain's leading fighter airfields, no one bothered to do anything in response to the screaming siren. Perhaps they had better knowledge and knew that nothing was really yet happening.

The next day, Monday the 4th, No. 3 Squadron was scrambled following an air-raid alarm early in the morning; but no German aeroplanes were seen. 615 Squadron was called to readiness, but did not take off. Two days later, on the 6th, a third air-raid warning was received. "A" Flight of 615 were in readiness, and were ordered into the air at 8 am; but after orbiting at Kenley were ordered to land again.

The next week was to be a quiet one; culminating, however, in two significant visits: from the Rt. Hon. Winston Churchill, MP (at that stage a hasty new addition to Chamberlain's war cabinet: this visit was possibly the first time Churchill appeared in RAF uniform) on the 10th; and Captain H.H. Balfour,

Under Secretary of State for Air, on the 11th. Captain Balfour, once an RFC pilot, had, as director of the old British Airways Ltd., been involved in high-level negotiations on the reorganisation of civil aviation in the late 1930s. He later became Lord Balfour of Inchrye.

One of the pilots of 615 Squadron was Pilot Officer, later Flight Lieutenant, David J. Looker. David Looker remembers an odd thing from the first days of the war at Croydon. He was talking one day to another officer in the control tower when he noticed two telephones, which his colleague told him had been directly connected with Le Bourget and Templehof aerodromes. Picking one up, he dropped it hastily when he found himself greeted in German. "It was disconnected after that", he said in 1984. [18]

Meanwhile, the whole local area had taken on a wartime appearance. Wallington Town Hall and other public buildings were protected by sandbags; a sentry was posted each night at the 'Territorial Drill Hall' in Carshalton High Street (Carshalton Hall); and workmen painted white lines down the sides and centres of roads to assist drivers in the black-out. Air-raid shelters in Wallington included one in Roundshaw Park, just off the edge of the airfield, approached from Foresters Drive.

A mile or two away, at Hackbridge, on the banks of the River Wandle, the early nineteenth century house known as Hackbridge House had been taken over before the war by a Company of the 31st Regiment, Royal Engineers, commanded at the outbreak of the war by Major Basil Peacock. [19] The Company, which totalled some 550 men, operated a searchlight and anti-aircraft battery. By the time of the Munich crisis they had three searchlights and three guns.

Kennards of Croydon issued a statement which appeared in the local newspapers. It bristled with suitable slogans such as "Carry on Croydon" and "Courageous Croydon, the Spirit which Can't be Crushed" and went on to say:

When the news first came that this country would honour its obligations to the fullest extreme, this town, like every other city, village and hamlet on this island, was numbed with shock. And the first week of the war left many people still unable, fully, to grasp the fact that it would be necessary to readjust their lives completely.

Last week, however, an onlooker would have observed that all that is characteristic of the British race, courage, fortitude and the will-to-win was rapidly awakening within the heart and throughout the length and breadth of Croydon.

It was as though an unknown and unseen propagandist machine had instilled into the hearts of all Croydonians the thought that *they* must be the people to play their part in the formation of a resolute and unassailable home front of good cheer and good comfort.

The town became alive again with shoppers, bargain hunters, frequenters of their favourite cafes and restaurants, and towards the end of the week (we were glad to observe) people in search of a good cinema show. All carrying their gas masks, and all with smiles on their lips. The spirit of sunshine was rejuvenated and with it the flood-gates of cheerfulness were re-opened in Croydon.

That is why we want to say to everyone in the borough, WELL DONE!

The advertisement urged shoppers to carry on spending; offering blankets, black-out material, and other "ARP supplies" for purchase, in addition to the usual furniture, fabrics, and general goods. The store also ran a blood transfusion centre: "There is nothing painful or weakening in blood transfusion and by volunteering you will be doing a great service to yourselves and to your country."[19]

At the aerodrome, all three Squadrons now based there suffered casualties during these first days of the war, but not from enemy action.

At one o' clock on the morning of the 8th of September, a young New Zealand pilot, Flight Lieutenant Minden Vaughan Blake, was leading his two companions, Pilot Officer Harper and Sergeant Steward, back from patrol. They were members of No. 17 Squadron, returning to Croydon. With a heavy ground-mist obscuring the airfield, Blake's Hurricane (L1976) overshot the flare path. As he put on more throttle the engine at first picked up, but a few seconds later stopped completely. His altitude being too low for him to return to the airfield, he made a turn to what he thought looked like open ground. His selected target was, in fact, the grounds of Purley War Memorial Hospital.

He did not make a good landing. The Hurricane ripped into the top of the adjacent nurses' home, turned over, and crashed to the ground on its back. Blake, who had hit his head on the dashboard in the initial impact, had a very lucky escape from death. The cockpit of the aircraft came to rest over a deep trench, recently dug by the A.R.P.

Nurses rushed to the scene; but by the time they had arrived Blake had managed to free himself from the wreckage. He was, however, admitted to the hospital, where he spent the remainder of the night. [20]

No. 17 Squadron log records that, on the same morning, Pilot Offficer Whittaker hit a tree with his undercarriage when taking off, but fortunately managed to avoid any serious damage. Pilot Officer Meredith, however, did manage to damage a main-plane when he taxied his Hurricane into an unmarked flood-light. "It was not a successful night's flying", records the log. [15]

That day saw the departure from Croydon of No. 17 Squadron, transferred to Debden.

No. 3 Squadron, although based at Croydon, were spending a lot of their time at Manston Aerodrome, which was serving as a forward base. This meant making frequent journeys between those airfields.

At dawn on the morning of the 10th September, both 'A' and 'B' flights were returning to Croydon from Manston when, according to the Squadron log, [21] "they encountered low cloud and very poor visibility". The effect of this poor visibility seems to have been devastating to the Squadron. Flying Officer Vickery and Sergeant F. Howell made forced landings in a field, which unfortunately proved too small to take off from. Sergeant A.F. Butterick crashed his Hurricane and was admitted to Faversham Cottage Hospital with a broken ankle and injuries to his spine. Pilot Officer Lines-Roberts and Sergeants Ramsey and P.A. Sims also crashed their Hurricanes, though without any apparent damage to themselves.

With six aircraft lost in just one flight, hasty replacements had to be found from the Command Reserve, so that the Squadron could comply with its order to move back to Manston at 1600 hours.

On the next day, September the 11th, it fell to No. 615 to suffer the first fatal casualty of a Croydon-based Squadron in the Second World War. At 10 o'clock that evening, Pilot Officer Anthony Sainte Croix Rose was flying his Gladiator, K7987, on a night-training exercise when he crashed one mile north of Bletchingley. He was a twenty-nine-year-old barrister of aristocratic background, who had been at Cambridge and at Lincoln's Inn. *The Times* noted his death 'on active service', and a few days later its announcements carried a message from his mother, Mrs. F.H. Rose, and his sister, Jean, thanking people for their letters of condolence. [22]

On the 24th September, Pilot Officer D.S.H. Bury of 615 Squadron, hit a soldier sentry while making a night landing. The soldier was 'injured' and the aircraft 'slightly damaged'. [14]

But there were lighter moments. A theatre company came to entertain the servicemen: the Jack Buchanan Company, with Elsie Randolph and Fred Emney, which came from London and took over a hut as a makeshift theatre to perform musical comedy items. [5]

Other visitors to Croydon during that first month of the war were Sir Kingsley Wood, Secretary of State for Air, with Sir Edward Campbell his Parliamentary Private Secretary, on the 22nd; and Sir Charles Burnett, Inspector General of the Air Force, on the 28th. [23]

The number of Air Defence Corps cadets at RAF Croydon dwindled as the school term began. Brian Haimes was one of the very last to go. One evening, returning home by bicycle across the darkened field, heading for a gap in the fence which would bring him out in Foresters Drive, close to his home in Carleton Avenue, he rode straight into a new piece of fencing and cut his face. With blood flowing, he stumbled towards the nearest tent, surprising its RAF occupants, but receiving sympathetic treatment and even a proper field dressing for his wound. He made his way home, where anxious parents replaced the dressing with something less dramatic. After that, his trips to Croydon ceased: although travelling up every day to the John Fisher School in Peaks Hill he, along with other local boys, continued to take a lively interest in everything that went on at the aerodrome. Anti-aircraft guns had been set up at the perimeter, with suitably sandbagged protection for the men in charge of them: including "Tug" Wilson and Bill Light, who made friends with Brian Haimes and later invited him to share their Christmas dinner of steak cooked on their open brazier; a memorable way for a teenager to spend his first wartime Christmas.

The Army provided a guard for the aerodrome from the first days of war onwards. In late 1939 this was provided by the Honorable Artillery Company (mentioned by Keith Belcher), 'C' battery arriving on October 20th and being replaced by 'B' battery on November 3rd. [23]

Croydon's second fatal war casualty was another Pilot Officer from 615 Squadron, John Charles Mackenzie Hanbury, who was killed in a flying accident near Dorking while carrying out night flying in his Gladiator, N5582, on October the 1st, having apparently lost his way.

Keith Belcher recalled that, in a desperate attempt to help Hanbury locate Croydon, the massive neon beacon at the end of the old Air France hangar was switched on, and this caused considerable alarm amongst local residents. "In those days if you so much as lit a cigarette in the street, a voice from somewhere would shout out, 'Put that light out', so you can imagine the effect that the light from that beacon had. There were certainly a lot of incoming telephone calls!" [13]

On October 4th, there was an afternoon visit from Air Chief Marshal Sir Hugh Dowding, Air Officer Commanding-in-Chief Fighter Command, who was accompanied by Air Vice Marshal Gossage of No. 11 Group. Dowding wished 615 Squadron luck; they had been told that morning that they would soon be off to France. In fact, they did not go until more than a month later. The Lord Lieutenant of Surrey, Lieutenant Commander Sir Malcolm Fraser, visited the Squadron in October, and on the 29th there was a further visit from Winston Churchill. [14]

No. 3 Squadron finally departed for Manston on the 12th October. Their stay at Manston was perhaps highlighted by an incident on 18th October, when Green Section landed at Boulogne in mistake for Dover, causing air raid warnings to be sounded throughout Northern France. Sergeant Sims, the leader of Green Section, found a very irate Air Commodore awaiting him on his return. [21]

On October 26th, listeners to "Lord Haw Haw" (Nazi propagandist William Joyce), on Hamburg radio, heard him offer a grim warning: "Croydon must beware. She is the second line of defence. We know the aerodrome is camou-flaged but we know just what kind of camouflage it is. We shall bomb it and bomb it to a finish, and would advise people there to evacuate the area this next weekend, as we shall do the job thoroughly. But we shall be merciful and only use incendiary bombs."

No raid however took place. The town of Croydon had, in any case, under-gone a massive evacuation programme following the outbreak of war, not least because of bombing fears due to the proximity of the aerodrome. Large numbers of children, young mothers, and disabled and elderly people, had left for rural areas in the first days of September. Official records note that by October 23rd the town's population had fallen from 242,300 (in July) to 196,000. [24]

On 10th October, No. 145 Squadron, under the command of Squadron Leader J.D. Miller, came to the aerodrome. 145 Squadron had been formed in the First World War, but it had been disbanded in 1919. Now it was re-formed as a day and night fighter squadron, equipped with Bristol Blenheim fighter bombers.

Throughout October, November, and December, the squadron was acquiring machines from Kemble and Aston Down in Gloucestershire, and Ternhill in Shropshire. Pilots from the squadron were sent to Hendon to learn to fly the Blenheim; until January 13th when the Blenheim Conversion Flight there was disbanded, and squadrons started to train their remaining pilots themselves. [25]

Not all the machines being ferried to Croydon arrived successfully. On the night of October 18th a Blenheim crashed in flames on the playing fields to the east of the airfield, between Pampisford Road and Purley Way. It came from 604 Squadron based at North Weald. The pilot and gunner were both killed. They were Flying Officer Edward Nevil Prescott (whom the *Croydon Advertiser* described as being about 27 years of age) and nineteen-years-old Leading Aircraftman Albert Roberts. An inquest reported in the *Advertiser* on October 27th described them as coming from "a Middlesex aerodrome" and recorded a verdict of misadventure (North Weald aerodrome was, in fact, in Essex.)

On November 14th another Blenheim heading for Croydon crashed before it arrived. Two more machines had been collected from Kemble, Gloucester-shire, for 145 Squadron. One, piloted by Flight Lieutenant Wells, landed safely at Croydon; but the other, L 1286, flown by Pilot Officer W.A. Ross (who was the only occupant of the machine), crashed at Harwell. Ross was killed. He was another pilot from 604 Squadron attached to Hendon Conversion Flight. [25]

Flt. Lt. Wells became responsible at Croydon after January 13th for the six pilots still requiring conversion courses to Blenheims. He had arrived from Hanworth on 21st October, appointed to command "A" Flight of 145. Commanding "B" Flight was Flying Officer A.H. Boyd, who had come from 65 Squadron at Northolt. Wells left to take command of 600 Squadron in February.

On 23rd October, the log of 145 Squadron noted the names of nine pilot officers posted from the No. 11 Group Flying Training School which was at Shawbury in Shropshire: P.W. Comely, K.R. Lucas, M.A. Newling, P.H. O'C. Rainier, W.A. Sanders, L.D.M. Scott, R.W. Shrewsbury, J.E. Stonrar and H.J.C. Wakeham. On the same day, Flying Officer Boyd was promoted Flight Lieutenant. Three more pilots arrived on 30th October from No. 11 Group Pool at St. Athan, Glamorganshire: H.J.V. Benson, R.N. Hogg and H.D. Yule. At the end of October the squadron strength was noted as eighteen officers, four airmen pilots, and 136 airmen. In November, another pilot arrived: Flying Officer C. Bowen; but he was posted away again shortly afterwards. As there were other postings the log at the end of 1939 recorded the squadron's strength as: "Officers: pilots 16, administrative 1. Warrant Officer 1; Airmen: pilots 4, observers 2, gunners 10; Airmen [unclassified] 103".

On November 13th, No. 607 Squadron, commanded by Squadron Leader L.E. Smith, came to Croydon; remaining only two days before taking off, with 615 Squadron, for overseas. This was a mass flight, together with impressed civil aircraft; which, because of its size, has been referred to as an 'air armada'.

No. 3 Squadron had been notified on 10th November that they were to return to Croydon; but because of the shortage of accommodation at Croydon due to the preparations for the 'armada' of aircraft leaving for France, they did not make the change until the evening of the 15th.

On the 19th of November, Flight Lieutenant Patrick Gifford took over as C.O. from Squadron Leader Chapman; and ten days later Gifford was awarded the D.F.C. for an action against Heinkels over the Firth of Forth.

During December the squadron established a forward base at Hawkinge, and troopship protection patrols were undertaken. With heavy fog throughout the Christmas period at Croydon, no flying took place until the 28th, when 'B' flight managed to take off in snow but had to 'pancake' at Hawkinge due to more fog at Croydon. [22]

On the 29th December, No. 92 Squadron, commanded by Squadron Leader Roger Bushell - later to achieve posthumous fame as part of the 'Great Escape' team in German prison camp Stalag Luft III - joined No. 3 Squadron at Croydon.

Throughout January, No. 3 Squadron was divided, with 'A' flight at Hawkinge and 'B' flight at Croydon. With fog, ice and snow restricting flying to only 332 hours for the month and all personnel being recalled from leave on the 14th January for an anticipated move to Manston, which was subsequently aborted, it was probably with some relief that the squadron found itself re-united when it moved to Kenley on the 29th January. [22]

No. 3 Squadron had been notified on 10th November that they were to return to Croydon; but because of the shortage of accommodation at Croydon due to the preparations for the 'armada' of aircraft leaving for France, they did not make the change until the evening of the 15th.

CHAPTER TWO

Civil Aviation Goes to War

Croydon had been the hub of Britain's civil aviation activities before war broke out. What, then, happened to civil flying in these early days of the war? The answer is relevant to the history of Croydon Airport: not only because pre-war Croydon airlines, personalities and aircraft were involved, but because war-time 'civil' developments affected Croydon's future when the war ended.

Following the war scare during the summer of 1938, which had illustrated the importance of a civil aviation capability to the Government, and shown just how ill-prepared Britain was in this area, the Director-General of Civil Aviation produced an 'Appreciation of the Employment of Civil Aircraft in War' for consideration by the Committee of Imperial Defence. [1]

This 'appreciation', which was circulated in October 1938, was, in fact, a complete review of the state of British civil aviation. It contained details of nineteen private companies, as well as Imperial Airways and British Airways Ltd.; and listed every aircraft available, giving payload and passenger capacity; together with an analysis of pilots, wireless operators, ground engineers, and administrative staff serving the industry. The conclusion drawn by the Director-General, Sir Francis Shelmerdine, was that there were three possible options should war come.

First, complete militarisation of civil aircraft fleets, crews, and staff. Secondly, State ownership of all aircraft, operated on a civil basis; and, finally, the operation of a National Air Communications organisation, using existing air transport companies under state charter. It was this option which Sir Francis saw as the best one.

In January 1939, the Air Ministry submitted to the Inter-Departmental Committee on International Air Communications a memorandum on 'The Role of the Department of Civil Aviation in the Precautionary Stage and in War'. [1]

This memorandum, in effect, sought permission to go ahead with planning for a National Air Communications organisation as outlined by the Director-General. The main thrust of the Air Ministry argument was that the growth of the civil aviation industry had been so rapid, and reached such dimensions, that careful consideration needed to be given to how best to use such a national asset in time of war. "It is no longer possible, nor does it appear to be in the national interest, to look upon Civil Aviation as a subsidiary of the Royal Air Force which in the event of war would automatically close down and have its resources dissipated", the memorandum concluded.

This view won the day, and the Department of Civil Aviation began planning the N.A.C. system.

Air Britain's *Impressments Log* by Peter W. Moss describes NAC as "an Air Ministry organisation created out of necessity because of the . . . Air Navigation Restriction Order, on August 31st". The Air Navigation (Restriction in Time of War) Order, 1939 prohibited (a) all aircraft from flying over eastern areas of England and Scotland; (b) civil flying anywhere over the United Kingdom without a special permit for each flight; and (c) private and club flying. Peter Moss continues: "N.A.C. were allotted two main tasks: the first being to assist in the transportation of R.A.F. personnel and supplies to France and operate certain Continental and overseas services. The N.A.C.'s second task was to maintain the internal routes that were considered to be useful to the war efort."

Maintaining the domestic services in the United Kingdom involved the co-ordination of the smaller private companies. Those concerned at Croydon were Olley Air Service, Wrightways, North Eastern Airways, Surrey Flying Services, Personal Airways, and Air Despatch. These private companies were contacted and issued with sealed orders, only to be opened on the receipt of a secret code-word.

Mrs Victor Bruce, who ran Air Despatch at Croydon, gives a vivid description of what happened to her fleet, in her autobiography *Nine Lives Plus:* [3]

Soon after the Munich crisis, an official from the Air Ministry called at my office in Croydon. He asked me whether my company would be prepared to sign a dormant contract, one which would become operative only in the event of a national emergency, when our entire fleet of twenty-three aircraft would be subject to any order from the Air Ministry.

As 'Air Despatch' was more or less 'me', I agreed to sign. Before the official left, he told me I would receive sealed orders, to be opened only if a dispatch with a special code word was delivered. He went on to say that there would be three messages in the event of an emergency. The first would be 'Get ready to stand by'. On receiving this, all pilots and wireless operators were to be told to report to the aerodrome every two hours. On receipt of the second dispatch, 'Stand by,' the complete fleet was to be lined up on the tarmac, and engines started up every hour.

If and when the third dispatch arrived, with the code word 'Lascelle', the crews were to remain in the aircraft and await a signal from the control tower ordering them to take off. Only then was I to open the sealed orders, which contained details of the secret bases to which the pilots were to go.

Within a few days I signed the contract, and the sealed orders were delivered and put in the safe.

Life went on as usual for about nine months and we carried on with the army co-operation flying. Then on the morning of 31 August 1939, the first message was delivered by a dispatch-rider from the War Office: 'Get ready to stand by'. All pilots and wireless operators who were operating in the Midlands and Wales were recalled to Croydon. The next day the second message arrived: 'Stand by'. The fleet was at once lined up on the tarmac and engines started up every hour. Lorries were loaded with spares. The aerodrome was blacked out and great bulldozers were digging trenches round the Aerodrome Hotel, tearing up the geraniums. Everyone was tense and resigned for the worst.

The suspense was broken on the evening of 1 September. I had just arrived home and was putting the key in the lock of the front door when I heard the telephone ringing. It was the young traffic clerk. He said he had just received a special message delivered by a dispatch rider from the War Office. He started to spell it out slowly: 'L . . . A . . . S . . . C . . .'. 'Stop', I cried, 'I will come down to the aerodrome immediately'.

I reached my office and opened the sealed orders. It was war. Within an hour ten of our planes left for RAF bases, and the remainder for Cardiff, which was to be our wartime base.

The dispersal of Britain's merchant air fleet was based upon a war scenario - the Western Plan - that assumed France would remain an ally, but that the aggressor - unnamed in the plan - would have the capacity to reach Britain by air.

This resulted in Britain's air space being divided into two, by a line running north to south through the length of the country. To the east of the line would be restricted air space, under the control of Fighter Command. So it was to the west of Britain, to nine aerodromes in England, Scotland, Wales, the Isle of Man and the Channel Islands, that the fleet was to be sent. Aircraft of the eleven private companies from the east of England, including Croydon, were dispersed to Liverpool (Speke), Manchester (Barton), Isle of Man (Ronaldsway), and Glasgow (Renfrew).

On Saturday September 1st, the code word was issued and all the planning was put to the test, as Mrs. Victor Bruce's account describes. The National Air Communications Headquarters was established under the control of the Deputy Director-General of Civil Aviation, W.P. Hildreth, at Stoke Bishop, Bristol.

With regard to Imperial and British Airways Ltd., machinery existed for the requisitioning of these under Clause 44 of the Empire Agreement, and Clause 30 of the Northern Europe and South Atlantic Agreement respectively, and so secret negotiations began with both companies on the practical and financial implications.

Mr. Arthur Quin-Harkin, who in 1939 was Imperial Airways' Chief Accountant, recalls:

The organisation began shortly after the Munich crisis. We hadn't had any decisions before that as to what to do in the event of war. After the Munich crisis the two companies, Imperial Airways and British Airways, got together with the Minister and had a certain programme laid down by which we then knew what we were required to do and from that we were able to plan on the belief that we could run these services - and also we were told that we were going to operate from Whitchurch in Bristol and, as far as possible, from Croydon and anywhere else - Shoreham, too. From that, we decided on which staff we would retain and which staff we would release. So the organisation was a very big joint affair over months as to who would be retained and what jobs they would do, and we had to find out which people would be prepared to go, decide those whom we wanted to go, and choose the right ones. So far as I personally was concerned, I had been put in charge of staff by Sir John Reith when he joined us in 1938, although I remained chief accountant, and so I had to deal with the personnel angle, with all that aspect - with staff and the notices to them. [4]

Staff at Imperial Airways knew of evacuation plans and it was rumoured that the destination was the West Country but they were not told it was Bristol until the last minute. Some were told a month before war broke out that, should hostilities start, their services would not be required, and they would be given a month's salary and a promise of re-employment after the war. Then, as Quin-Harkin remembers:

"I went down with the advance guard myself on 1st September, and I took down with me an accountant, a typist and a comptometer operator. But already we'd been down a month before: I'd been down with Air Commodore Fletcher [Imperial Airways' Ground Servicing Manager] and a lot of people - we'd seen the Lord Mayor. We knew we were going to be billeted there, so we had all the help from the civic authorities and I went down in the knowledge that billets would be available. Although I was put up in a hotel, and people *were* for the first few nights, immediately billeting came into effect and it was enforceable, people were put into houses where families got so-much for billeting our staff . . . we probably had to billet something like four hundred people. [4]

The Secretary of Imperial Airways at this time was Mr. Temple Miller, who was later to take over Quin-Harkin's job as Chief Accountant. The two shared the same lodgings for a while after leaving the hotel where they had all spent the first few nights.

On the day war broke out, all those who had already arrived in Bristol from Croydon assembled in the Grand Spa Hotel to hear the Prime Minister's broadcast.

Imperial Airways had taken over the hotel, and its other guests had had to find alternative accommodation.

Mr. Norman Griffiths, as a fitter with Imperial Airways at Croydon, remembers travelling to Bristol by train from Waddon station on that day:

On arrival war had been declared on Germany. All the Imperial Airways and British Airways coaches were assembled outside, and we boarded these until they were full. The coaches toured the streets of Bedminster, and billeted 2 or 3 staff at various houses, allowance 21/- per week . . .

Pick-up next morning was at 0730 hours by the same coaches at various points around Bristol, and eventually we arrived at Whitchurch Airport. Tents had been erected for canteen use, and beside this there was one small hangar, all the aircraft were picketed around the perimeter of the airport. Pots of green and brown paint and brushes were doled out and we were detailed by our chargehands to a particular aircraft: all aircrew were assigned similar tasks, and I worked on an Ensign alongside a Captain. The equipment and stores were deposited in batches on the grass, and other groups were working on these. We worked all day camouflaging the aircraft with only one break, and I will never forget the paraffin-tainted tea which they dished up from those tents! Nearly half the H.P.42s and Ensigns were completed by the end of the day, and the air was impregnated with the smell of 'dope'. 5

The coming of war had effectively brought about a premature merger of Imperial Airways and British Airways Ltd., pre-dating the actual formation of the British Overseas Airways Corporation. Mr. Quin-Harkin says:

By accident of war, Imperial Airways and British Airways came together in Bristol on the 1st, 2nd and 3rd of September, something that would have happened some months later when the Corporation was formed. We all assumed the positions that we would have with the new Corporation, which had already been agreed. I was to be the Administration Director of the new Corporation, so I became Administration Manager immediately. I'd already recommended that Temple Miller, the Secretary of Imperial Airways, should become the Chief Accountant of the Corporation ... so in that way, although we were still separate, British Airways and Imperial Airways, we were all on war service. 4

It was not until September 5th, however, that the Air Ministry got round to dispatching to Imperial Airways and British Airways a letter confirming the Government's requisitioning of the airlines; and backdating the take-over to midnight of August 31st.

The move to Bristol was to prove fatal for two of Imperial Airways' famous fleet of H.P.42s: G-AAUD *Hanno* and G-AAXC *Heracles*. The story is told graphically by Charles Hartnall in John Pudney's *The Seven Skies:* 6

Life at Whitchurch with anything up to twenty-three degrees of frost became largely a fight to keep from freezing rather than to keep aeroplanes flying. Yet engines had to be started and run regularly: the work of maintenance had to go on. This question of starting engines was a snag of the toughest order.

One day in March 1940 [it was the 19th] we had a gale. It gave little warning, but there was no need to consult 'Met' to realize that this was no ordinary wind. All hands made a rush across the flying field to the dispersed aircraft and hung on grimly. There were DH 86s, Hudsons, Ensigns, DH 91s and HP 42s. The latter, with their huge wing area, were the biggest problem. By the time Foreman Griffiths and F/E Caseley had reached them, the mooring pegs had already been wrenched out and *Heracles* was lifting, first one side, then the other, with the opposite wing tip hitting the ground finally to heave backwards through a barbed wire fence into the next field. She never flew again.

To save *Hanno*, Griffiths climbed into the cockpit and Caseley managed to get the two-stroke going and started the top engines. The idea was to hold her against the wind. Before the lower engines could be started, however, the two-stroke wheezed and cut out with the huge machine rolling over on to its wing tips like a ship in distress, and the wind shrieking through the rigging as if she was in actual flight. It was while Caseley was striving to turn the two-stroke handle in an effort to restart it that *Hanno* came back on an even keel; a heavy gust caught her and she rose in the air flying backwards with the Flight Engineer still hanging on to the handle. This aircraft, too, after nearly ten years of excellent service, finished up in the next field wrecked beyond repair.

Of the remaining four H.P. 42s (G-AAXE *Hengist* had been destroyed by fire in Karachi before the war, in May 1937 and G-AAXD *Horatius* had been wrecked in a forced landing at Tiverton, Devon, on 7th November 1939), none was to survive 1940. G-AAUE *Hadrian* was also destroyed in a gale, this time at Doncaster, on 6th December 1940. G-AAGX *Hannibal* was lost at sea over the Gulf of Oman on 1st March 1940; G-AAXF *Helena* was fatally damaged on landing at Donibristle on 1st August 1940; and G-AAUC *Horsa* was burnt out after a forced landing near Whitehaven, Cumberland, on 7th August 1940.

Meanwhile, even in these very early days of the war, it was clear that National Air Communications was not fulfilling the role envisaged for it in the pre-war plan. Indeed, the war itself was not following the predicted path in two major respects affecting it. Italy had remained neutral; and Britain had not come under the expected immediate air attack.

This meant that it was unnecessary to implement schemes for diverting the trans-Mediterranean section of the Empire route; and, because of the absence of any serious enemy attacks, the anticipated demand for rapid air communications within Britain had not occurred.

It was not the case, however, that National Air Communications found itself idle. During the first month of war its aircraft flew over a quarter of a million miles on 'fetch and carry' work, in addition to the mileage flown by the Empire and Foreign services of Imperial and British Airways. One major operation carried out by NAC aircraft was the 'air armada' to France, as will be described in the next chapter.

NAC was in possession of thirty flying boats and 200 landplanes of some thirty different types; together with all the specialised commercial expertise of operation, management, and maintenance of airlines, gathered over the years. A formidable organisation had been established in just forty-eight hours; and all the planning of 1939 paid-off in the smoothness of transfer from a peacetime to a wartime footing.

NAC had set out to show that a single organisation, composed of a varied fleet, operated and maintained by professionals, could meet the many different demands made upon it, cheaply and with great flexibility. It was soon apparent, however, that the main stumbling block to this aim was the attitude and demands of the RAF, although liaison staff from National Air Communications had joined Fighter Command.

At the outset of war, NAC had split the private companies into two groups, the Railway and non-Railway groups. It was decided that the new policy should be to allow the Railway companies to continue with scheduled services which involved routes that crossed water, and that the non-Railway companies' aircraft should be requisitioned for the RAF (which was more or less what the RAF wanted).

The non-Railway companies had formed themselves into an organisation called the Group of Independent Operators, under the chairmanship of F.C.R. Jacques of North Eastern Airways. Mr. Jacques and Mrs. Victor Bruce led the fight for what they considered adequate financial compensation. Mr. W.P. Hildreth, Deputy Director-General of Civil Aviation, in a memorandum written on 29th October 1939, had made it clear that the policy of NAC was to be 'Not a penny for the Directors', and this hard financial line towards the independent companies gave little hope of success to those operators about to see their companies collapse. [7]

The RAF, having won their point, found themselvs with a considerable number of civil aircraft, and a job to do with them. In March 1940 the decision was taken to form a new Squadron, No. 271 Transport Squadron, and to base it at Doncaster. Among the civil aircraft that found their way to Doncaster were H.P. 42 G-AAUE *Hadrian* and the Ford Tri-Motor, G-ACAE, which had been owned by the Hon. A.E. Guinness.

The Railway Group, which consisted of eight companies, was formed into the Associated Airways Joint Committee, which began to function from May the 5th, 1940. The companies involved were Railway Air Services, Air Commerce, Great Western & Southern Air Lines, Isle of Man Air Services, Olley Air Service, Scottish Airways, Western Isles Airways and the West Coast Air Services.

The need for regular air services across water was mainly due to the unreliability of shipping ferry services as well as the threat to shipping lanes from enemy action.

The central organisation of the AAJC was established at Liverpool (Speke) under the management of Wing Commander A.H. Measures with Gordon Olley as Deputy Manager. Sir Harold Hartley of Railway Air Services was Chairman.

Although operations had commenced on 5th May, the evacuation of the British Expeditionary Force from France and the demands made by the Air Ministry on its aircraft, had made the AAJC unable to commence regular services until the 27th of June, 1940.

The scrapping of NAC and the setting up of the AAJC coincided with another major development in British civil aviation. Four weeks before the outbreak of war the Royal Assent was given to the British Overseas Airways Corporation Act and the formal establishment of the Corporation, under the Chairmanship of Sir John Reith, formerly Chairman of Imperial Airways, had taken place on 24th November 1939.

The road to creating Britain's first wholly publicly-owned airline was proving a difficult one; and the advent of war complicated an already difficult situation. The problem centred around money.

As early as July 10th, 1938, during the second reading of the BOAC Bill, the Labour opposition, who naturally favoured public ownership, nevertheless objected to the Bill on financial grounds. Apparently the Government had informed Imperial Airways shareholders that their 1,500,000 shares would be purchased for 32s. 9d., whilst their quoted price on the Stock Exchange was only 30s. Captain Balfour, the Under-Secretary of State for Air, was quick to refute allegations of share dealing, and stated that only 500 shares had changed hands. [8]

The disputes continued, and reached such a pitch that Whitehall was giving serious consideration to scrapping the whole plan; but, eventually, the financial problems were resolved, and on the 1st April, 1940, the Commissioners for the Reduction of the National Debt purchased £4,250,000-worth of Airways Stock, issued by the Corporation that same day.

Cash payments were made to Imperial and British Airways, and a promise given that, should BOAC shares be publicly listed, their shareholders would receive preference. BOAC was, of course, required by the Secretary of State for Air to place at his disposal the whole undertakings of the Corporation.

And so, Imperial Airways, which had contributed so much to the development of civil aviation across two decades, and whose history was inextricably interwoven with that of Croydon Airport, passed into history; as did British Airways Ltd., its later and brasher rival, which also, for a while, in the late 1930s, had operated from Croydon

5. Military and civil aircraft at Croydon in the last days of peace: two RAF Hawker Audaxes photographed by Miss Lettice Curtis in the last week before war was declared; with, behind, an RAF Miles Magister trainer between *Horatius* (G-AAXD) and another Handley Page H.P.42. There is a third Audax in front of the H.P.42 on the left.

In the last week before war was declared, aircraft, especially those of Imperial Airways, 'piled-up' on the airfield.

6.   *ABOVE:* Three Handley Page H.P.42s are seen beyond the wing-tips of a fourth, including G-AAXD *Horatius*; and, on the left, a jumble of four Armstrong Whitworth Ensigns, including G-ADSW, *Eddystone*. A fifth, G-ADSX, *Ettrick*, lies to the right of *Horatius*.

7.   *BELOW:* The collection of aircraft includes Ensign G-ADSY, *Empyrean* on extreme left, with a de Havilland D.H.86 to its right.

8.   *ABOVE:* 615 Squadron prepare defences, on the Foresters Drive side of the aerodrome, with "old bedsteads, sandbags and a 1914 Lewis gun — the name of the chap with the white scarf and the shovel was Gayner". (Leslie Penfold). The view is looking east across the aerodrome.

9.   *BELOW:* Cadet Brian Haimes sits on sandbags at what seems to be the same post. The tall structure visible in both pictures is a landing beacon, part of the civil equipment.

10. *ABOVE:* Squadron Leader Arthur Vere Harvey (afterwards Lord Harvey of Prestbury) of 615 Squadron on his motorcycle at Croydon.

11. *BELOW:* 615 (County of Surrey) Squadron, Royal Auxiliary Air Force, the 'Saturday afternoon airmen', before the outbreak of war. Many of this group were killed in France or in the Battle of Britain. Second left, standing, is Tony Eyre, later Wing Commander, who won the D.S.O. and D.F.C., with bars, before being shot down and becoming a prisoner of war.

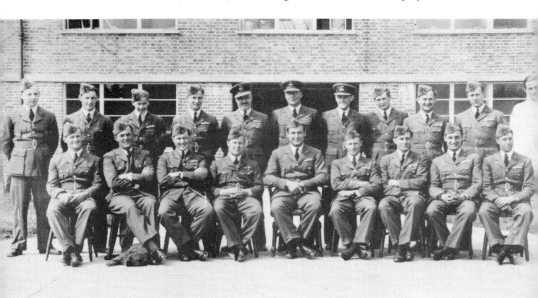

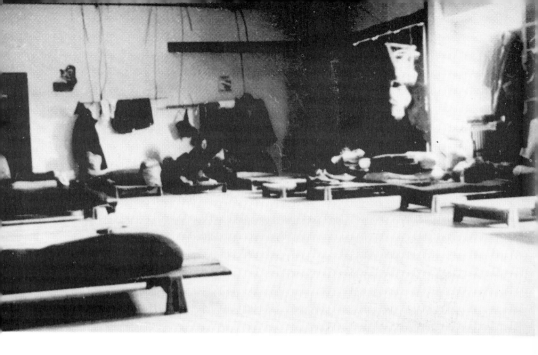

12.   *ABOVE:* 615 Squadron airmen were billeted in Imperial Airways worskhops: ". . . our beds were three planks on trestles, straw palliases, and blankets" (see p. 5)

13.   *BELOW:* 615 Squadron members off duty at Croydon, possibly in the Aerodrome Hotel. Leslie Penfold is second from left.

14. *ABOVE:* 615 Squadron 'digging-in' at Croydon by Gladiator dispersal points near Roundshaw Park (Foresters Drive) on the 2nd or 3rd of September, 1939.

15. *BELOW:* Airmen from 615 Squadron relax around tents on the edge of the airfield, by Foresters Drive, in the early days of the war.

615 Squadron Gladiators at dispersal by Foresters Drive in September/October 1939.

16. *ABOVE:* On the right is the first house at the north end of Foresters Drive.

17. *BELOW:* The position is a little to the north of Roundshaw Park, looking north towards Waterer Rise.

18. & 19.   Airmen of 615 Squadron worked, ate and slept near their aircraft, within a minute's call, in the early days of the war; even *(below)* getting their hair cut almost beneath the wings of a Gladiator. "The 'hairdresser's' name was Lloyd" (Leslie Penfold).

20. An anti-aircraft post in October 1939. 'Tug' Wilson (writing) and, probably, Bill Light, relax in the shelter behind sandbags. On the post at the left is mounted a tannoy; and in front of them is a brazier, probably the one on which, at Christmas 1939, they cooked steak and shared it with Brian Haimes (see p. 11)

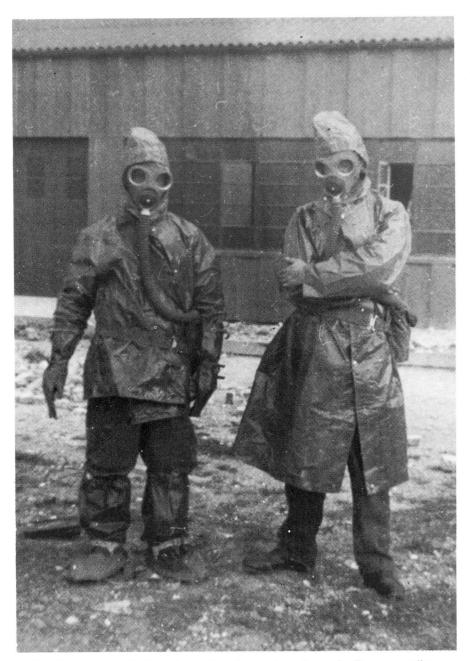

21.   Two members of 615 Squadron at Croydon wearing anti-gas suits. They are standing at the rear of the 'Flight Shed' (Hangar D).

22. Vickers Wellington Mk.I bomber (L.4303) of 148 Squadron photographed at Croydon in November 1939. 148 were at Harwell at this date, and this is not one of the Wellingtons fitted with degaussing rings by Rollasons (see p. 4), so the reason for its presence here is unknown.

Some of the first Hurricanes at Croydon in the autumn of 1939:

23. *ABOVE:* Three aircraft fly over Wallington backgardens.

24. *BELOW:* A Hurricane of No. 3 Squadron parked by Plough Lane, Purley, in October. In the foreground is Tony Parnell of Wallington, who himself entered the RAF, trained in Blenheims, and became a prisoner-of-war.

CHAPTER THREE

Croydon and the 'Phoney War'

The Allied armies in France anticipated action by the end of 1939. Croydon aerodrome became the gathering-point for RAF machines, supplies, and men, who were to be flown to the Continent as part of the air contingent of the British Expeditionary Force. As already reported, 607 Squadron arrived at the airfield on November 13th only to fly off, accompanied by 615 Squadron, on November 15th, bound for Merville in France.

The 'air armada' included several machines from Britain's merchant air fleet. There were the two Short L.17s, G-ACJJ *Scylla* and G-ACJK *Syrinx*, which had been an important part of Imperial Airways' pre-war fleet of large passenger biplanes. The new generation of Imperial Airways monoplane airliners, which had appeared belatedly in 1938, was represented by at least four Ensigns, of which one is known to have been G-ADSV *(Explorer)*. There were four D.H.86s, an Avro 10 and a Fokker F.XII, G-AEOS (the latter, which had been operated by British Airways Ltd., was withdrawn from service in June 1940 by BOAC).

There were also the Gladiators of 607 and 615 Squadrons. The machines now assigned to 615 Squadron had belonged to 605 'County of Warwick' Squadron, which flew them into Croydon on October 4th.

With a total of forty-five aircraft in the air this 'air armada' was one of the largest formations until then seen leaving for France. The Operations Record Book for RAF Croydon for 15th November noted laconically: "'615' and '607' Squadrons left for overseas. Wing Commdr Moore visited Croydon".

It may be worth noting here the disappointing nature of the Operations Record Book (the Station log). It customarily records the trivial and omits the important and dramatic. Daily, it notes the weather but usually only in general rather than meteorological terms; and when it does note a significant event (such as a crash or a court-martial) it often fails to give the essential details.

It is perhaps ironic that in the only period of Croydon aerodrome's history for which a daily record appears to have survived, the record should be so inadequate - a historian many years hence attempting to discover from this source what was happening at this fighter airfield during crucial months of war could be forgiven for assuming that little or nothing was taking place.

In the case of the air armada, however, we are able to discover more details from 615 and 607 Squadrons' Operations Record Books. First, 615's log says:

CROYDON 15th: Pilot Officer Anthony Eyre appointed Officer in charge of Croydon detail of Squadron. Squadron moved to Merville, France in mediocre weather. Sixteen Gladiators were flown by the following officers:- Squadron Leader A.V. Harvey, Flight Lieut. L.T.W. Thornley, Flight Lieut. J. G. Sanders, Flying Officer H.S. Giddings, Flying Officer P.N. Murton-Neale, Flying Officer J.R.H. Gayner, Flying Officer H.N. Fowler, Flying Officer L. Ereminsky, Pilot Officer B.P. Young, Pilot Officer D.J. Looker, Pilot Officer L. Fredman, Pilot Officer T.C. Jackson, Pilot Officer R.D. Pexton, Pilot Officer S.N. Wicknem, Pilot Officer K.T. Lofts, Pilot Officer P. Collard.

Also one Magister aircraft flown by Flying Oficer J.R.T. Bradford and Pilot Officer J.A. Caslaw. Flying Officer W.O. Stern and Pilot Officer J.R. Lloyd with 54 airmen and stores were flown in two 'Ensigns', two 'Scyllas' [i.e. Short L.17s] and one Avro ten. The Squadron took off at 1130 hours and arrived at Merville at 1300 hours. No. 607 Squadron led by Squadron Leader Smith took off immediately afterwards so that the number of aircraft in the air at the same time consisted of 45 aircraft as follows:- 32 Gladiators, 4 Ensigns, 4 D.H. 86s, 2 Scyllas, 1 Magister, 1 Avro ten and one Fokker. The whole move was completed without incident or casualty.[1]

The Squadron log for 607 Squadron - handwritten by fountain pen and thus conveying a personal touch lacking in the typed logs - adds to the picture:

Acklington 13-11-39. At 1415 hrs on 13-11-39 the overseas party of the squadron left Acklington for Croydon. The entire squadron party proceeded by air, the convoy consisting of 16 Gladiators, 2 Ensigns, 4 De Havilland (86) and 1 Fokker. One D.H. aircraft carrying 7 passengers left ½ hour after the others, as did also the Fokker carrying equipment only.

After refuelling at Digby the 16 Gladiators arrived at Croydon at 1720 hours. The civil aircraft (owing to an erroneous order) arrived at Heston airport at 1710 hours - with the exception of one D.H.86 and the Fokker which, having started later, were unable to go beyond York and Digby respectively. The party from Heston proceeded to Croydon by special omnibuses and arrived at Croydon at 2115 hours. The other two civil aircraft arrived at Croydon the following day, the aircraft from Heston flying to Croydon at daybreak on this day [14-11-39].

14-11-39. On Tuesday 14-11-39 weather conditions were unsatisfactory and departure had to be postponed. At Croydon the Squadron came into touch with 615 Squadron AAF who were also equipped with Gladiator aircraft and were under instructions to proceed overseas with 607 Squadron. The overseas party of 607 Squadron consisted of the following personnel: 1 Squadron leader (i/c), 1 Adjutant, 17 pilots (officers), 1 Warrant Officer (Engr.), 8 senior NCOs and 73 other ranks, total strength 101.

15-11-39. The weather improved on the following day, and at 1130 hrs on 15-11-39 the squadron moved by air from Croydon to Merville, 8 miles north of Bethune in France. The whole party flew in convoy together with 615 Squadron aircraft, the total number of aircraft in the convoy being 45. The route followed was Croydon - Shoreham - Le Treport - Merville, and the convoy arrived at Merville Aerodrome at 1300 hrs on 15-11-39.

The following officers piloted Gladiator aircraft of 607 Squadron: S/Ldr L.E. Smith; F/Lt J.R. Kayll; F/Lt J. Sample; F/Os W.E. Gore, W.F. Blackadder, J.M. Bazin, J.R. Hawkes, M.M. Irving, R.E.W. Pumphrey, G.D. Craig, M.H.B. Thompson, J.W.B. Humpherson; P/Os H.P. Dixon, W.H.R. Whitty, A.D. Forster and H.P.J. Radcliffe.

F/Lt White (Adjutant) crossed in one Ensign with a party of 27 and F/Lt J.A. Vick and F/O N.S. Graeme in the other Ensign with a similar party. The second Ensign returned to Croydon to pick up a rear party of 6 men and some further equipment which had travelled by road from Acklington to Croydon and carried over the final party the following morning 16-11-39.[2]

Peter Cooksley, then a schoolboy living in Collyer Avenue, Beddington, recalls the return of some of the machines a few days later:

They flew back in small groups and I remember them flying circuits over the airfield, waiting for their turn to land. The upper parts of the civil aircraft had all been painted in camouflage colours and some also had RAF roundels. Mixed in with the civil machines were RAF Harrows and Bombay bombers.[3]

The departure of the 'air armada' had shown the needs of the allied forces on the Continent (the aircrafts' cargoes included equipment and spares for servicing and repairing aircraft); but back at Croydon, daily life still seemed divorced from the harsh realities of war. The guard at the airfield in the early weeks of 1940 was provided by the Scots Guards. One of the young subalterns was William Whitelaw, later to become an M.P., and then Home Secretary, before going to the House of Lords as Viscount Whitelaw. In a letter to the authors he recalled:

I was a 2nd Lieutenant at the time in the Scots Guards detachment at Croydon Airport, early in 1940 as I remember it. We had a detachment there guarding the airport, of something less than a company, with a Captain and two subalterns. Our Captain was very strict and as a punishment for us if he thought we were not doing well enough, he insisted on us going round every hour at frequent intervals. He eventually told me to go round every hour, which meant I was continuously moving. A guard sergeant and I went in a small car that we had at the time. Unfortunately it got bogged and great efforts had to be made to get it out before the Captain woke in the morning! [4]

At the beginning of January, 92 and 145 Squadrons were busy with night flying: 92 on the nights of the 2nd (on which occasion Pilot Officer Bryson got lost and had to land at Harwell and stay the night) and the 3rd; and 145 on the 3rd.

Squadron Leader Roger Bushell, commanding 92 Squadron, was by profession a barrister, and had appeared in one or two sensational criminal cases before the war. Paul Brickhill in *The Great Escape* gives a vivid description of him:

"He was a big, tempestuous man, with broad shoulders and the most chilling pale-blue eyes I ever saw. In his early twenties he had been British ski champion, and once in an international race in Canada he had come swooping downhill like a bat out of hell and taken a bad spill over a boulder. The tip of one ski caught him in the inner corner of his right eye and gashed it wickedly. After it had been sewn up the corner of his eye drooped permanently and the effect on his look was strangely sinister and brooding.
. . . Though he was a squadron leader in the RAF Roger Bushell had been born near Johannesburg and at the age of six he could swear fluently in English, Afrikaans and Kaffir and spit an incredible distance. Later he acquired public-school polish by being educated in England at Wellington. [5]

Larry Forrester in *Fly for Your Life* completes the picture:

Often he [Bushell] had a single tear coursing down his left cheek, the result of [the] eye injury. No one had ever seen him wipe the tear away - he simply ignored it, even when the eye streamed for hours on end. His sight was unimpaired and this inconvenient ailment had only one result: he always held his head slightly tilted to the right.
It was hard to tell how old he was, though he must have been about thirty. Of medium height, dark and indelibly tanned, he was wonderfully compact and fit. At practice 'scrambles', when the pilots sprinted across the grass, vaulted into the cockpits and strained every fibre to get into the air in a matter of seconds, the 'old man' nearly always won the race.
Bushell's voice was strong and cultured, and his diction was like an actor's, yet there was no false, courtroom pomp about him and he could bellow cheerful vulgarities and roar the bawdiest choruses with the rest of them. He was never one to stand on ceremony, but a candid and open character, ready to joke or play the fool with all. Yet when there was serious talk, the affability and the humour fell away and he became direct, shrewd, commanding. He engendered a fine squadron spirit with his overwhelming, enveloping aura of personality and strength. [6]

It was a very harsh winter at the beginning of 1940, and flying was constantly interrupted by fog, or snow, or both. On January 1st and 4th, night flying had to be abandoned. On January 5th, a low, shallow belt of fog over Croydon prevented any flying until noon. Four Blenheims of 92 Squadron left at 12.30 for a gun and interception exercise round the sector. When they returned over Croydon, at about 2.00 p.m., visibility was too bad for landing, and they were instructed to proceed to Tangmere, where they landed at about 3.30 p.m. Again, no night flying was possible.

It took four days to get these aircraft back to Croydon, in two separate batches. On January 6th and 7th the weather prevented any movement by air, although the men travelled back by train on the latter day. On January 8th, although there was still bad weather with fog and low cloud, it cleared after lunch sufficiently to enable Flight Lieutenant Byrne and four pilots (the same four?) to fly to Tangmere to collect the machines. The log tells us: "Only two of them got back, so that there are three pilots at Tangmere." These managed to return the following day; thus ending a five-day saga. It was not the Squadron's only experience of this type; as on January 15th, after two more days on which flying had been impossible, Flight Lieutenant Green and Pilot Officer Edwards took off to take part in anti-aircraft exercises and were unable to land at Croydon as the weather had deteriorated drastically, and once again took refuge at Tangmere. The next day a sudden snow storm, with five aircraft in the air from Croydon, produced another guest for Tangmere and also one for Gatwick. Meanwhile, Squadron Leader Bushell was on leave in Cornwall, and Flight Lieutenant Green was diverted to collect him on the 16th, bringing him to Tangmere on the 17th; from where he returned to Croydon in an aircraft of 601 Squadron, because Green's Blenheim had developed trouble in one engine. [7]

Engine trouble seems to have been a general feature of 92's life at this time; since on January 11th the squadron log reported that, although the weather permitted flying, only a limited amount was possible as there were few machines serviceable. 'Few' in fact seems to have meant two; as Sergeant Haigh, returning from night flying at 3 a.m., damaged his aircraft; and the next day the log reports that the damaged Blenheim was brought into the hangar and: "only one sector reconnaissance was possible as only one aircraft was serviceable." [7]

Amidst the bad weather, and problems with aircraft, there were relaxations: on January 22nd the entire squadron went to the Grand Theatre at Croydon. The snow also offered its own possibilities of entertainment; and after a four-inch fall on the night of January 27th, a party of officers set out for Box Hill, ten miles distant, with a toboggan. However, surprisingly, Box Hill that day was not ideal for winter sports, but the group made the best of a bad job. The log notes: "In the afternoon a party of officers tobogganed on Box Hill regardless of the fact that there was no snow there". It must have been irritating, because back at Croydon the next three days were spent in snow-clearing operations involving 100 men (some borrowed from the Army) and two snow ploughs. [7] Not until February 5th had the snow gone completely, although the thaw set in on January 31st.

The log book of 145 Squadron summed up this difficult month:

Weather conditions during most of the month were exceptional, lower temperatures than the average prevailing for this period of the year.

From the 1st to the 26th of the month the aerodrome at Croydon was icebound and from the 27th to the end there were heavy falls of snow. The frosty conditions were accompanied by typical specimens of low lying mist apparently peculiar to Croydon.

The effect on the Blenheim Mark 1 type of aircraft with which the Squadron is equipped, was considerable; landings on the ice-bound uneven surface of the aerodrome resulted in damage to the stern frames of 7 aircraft. Difficulty was experienced in starting up engines from cold after aircraft had been dispersed and in removing the accumulation of ice and frost from the Perspex.

Despite the limitations imposed by the weather conditions and unserviceable aircraft however, programmes both of day and night non-operational flying were undertaken with results, in terms of flying times, as follows:

By day	172 Hrs. 40 Mins.
By night	29 Hrs. 50 Mins.
	202 Hrs. 30 Mins. [8]

Presumably some of these flying hours were accounted for by an unexplained exchange of Blenheim aircraft between 145 and 222 Squadrons. This took place on 9th and 10th January when 145 flew six aircraft to Duxford, Cambridgeshire, and received five in return. Being one down in strength was compensated for on the 25th, when a Blenheim which had earlier been transferred to Hendon was received back. [8]

For 92 Squadron, anti-aircraft exercises formed the routine work throughout January whenever flying was possible. On January 24th, Pilot Officer Williams had a narrow escape whilst on sector reconnaissance: he was flying over Brighton when part of his port engine and the airscrew flew off. Making an emergency landing at Gatwick, on his remaining engine, he was later brought back to Croydon by Squadron Leader Bushell.

On January 25th training exercises included a mock raid at Tangmere led by Squadron Leader Bushell which, the log notes, was "highly successful". [7]

There is an interesting entry in the Squadron's log for the same day: "P/O Bartley mistook Ascot Concentration Camp lights for Lingfield and Benson for Croydon, and landed there, and spent the night". The 'Ascot Concentration Camp' was in fact Bertram Mills' Circus winter quarters, which were at that time being used as a transit camp for those deemed to be enemy aliens, and interned as such. One notes that in early 1940 the term 'concentration camp' was still a neutral term, and had not yet acquired the connotations of death and torture which the horrors of Dachau, Auschwitz, Belsen and their like were later to give it.

Problems with aircraft, and with the weather, continued for 92 Squadron throughout February. There is a cry from the heart in the squadron log for February 16th: "serviceable aircraft which were so plentiful at the beginning of the month are fast becoming a rare luxury". The entry continues: "L.1361 has a cracked stern frame and there is nothing right with L.1236 . . . Night flying with three machines was carried out between 1730 and 2200 hours in spite of an adverse weather report and gale warning. The last pilot landed ¼ hour before a young blizzard descended on the aerodrome".

On February 10th, two Blenheims from 145 Squadron were involved in what the log book of 92 described as "a very curious and lucky mid-air collision." The log for 145 tells us that the accident involved a collision between K7114, flown by Pilot Officer Hogg, and K7091, flown by Pilot Officer Comely, and took place west of Gatwick. On board K7114 were Leading Aircraftman A. Tideler, Aircraftman First Class L. Hayes and Aircraftman First Class C. Crowe; whilst in K7091 were Leading Aircraftman J. Sutton and Aircraftman First Class A. Jarman. No one was injured, and Tideler jumped out, landing safely by parachute at Colgate, Sussex. The rest stayed in both aircraft until they were safely landed at Croydon. K7114 had suffered the worst damage - its rudder had been torn off and its fin and stern frame damaged. The other machine had damage to its nose. This incident was to earn a commendation for Aircraftman Hayes at a parade in April.

On February 23rd, a pilot and crew from 145 Squadron had a narrow escape when they successfully landed a damaged machine in Wallington. Pilot Officer A. Elson flying K7165 noticed that one engine was not running properly and decided to turn back to the aerodrome. The trouble got worse, until one cylinder and the cowling of the starboard engine fell away; and as the other engine was also failing he had to make an emergency landing on a spot described by the squadron log as "near a densely populated area"; not further specified, but which we know now, from a photograph taken by Brian Haimes at the time, to have been on what was then a piece of wasteland north of The Drive, Wallington (see photograph on page 89).

The very next day saw a far more serious accident in Wallington. It involved a young pilot from 92 Squadron and was to lead to a change in official policy at Croydon. The *Daily Mirror* under the headline, "Mother, Child, Die in Hit House" reported:

> Jack and Jill were almost the only children in their road who were not evacuated. In fact, in their section of Foresters Drive, Wallington, Surrey, theirs was the only house occupied. Their father, Mr. Montagu Bridge, a builder, had recently added to his house a wing in which Jill, aged five, occupied a room.
>
> They were a happy family and had plenty of friends. In fact, on Saturday afternoon, Jack was having tea at the home of a schoolmate. Mr. Bridge, his wife Doris and Jill were at home when a twin-engined plane was taking off at nearby Croydon. The plane failed to gain height and the underpart of the machine hit the Bridge's house and the house next door. [9]

The pilot, Pilot Officer Reginald Jervelund Whitmarsh, was a twenty-year-old man from Devon. He had been under instruction from Flight Lieutenant Vincent Byrne, and had completed three circuits and landings on the airfield before being told he could go solo. The squadron log noted:

> A night flying programme was started at dusk. The weather was clear beneath high cloud, nearly 10/10. At night 1900 P/O Whitmarsh who had just completed about one hour's night dual took off on his first night solo. For some reason - not yet determined - he crashed from a low altitude into houses on the west boundary of the aerodrome . . . P/O Whitmarsh was the sole occupant of the aircraft Blenheim L.6724. Night flying ceased. [7]

A very recently-researched account of the incident *(Night Solo to Eternity)* describes the tragedy on the ground:

> Scots Guardsmen John Lyall and William Mackenzie were outside the west guardroom of the aerodrome when the Blenheim crashed. Running towards the scene of the disaster, they saw a house enveloped in flames; as they climbed the boundary fence a man and a woman with two children ran out of the burning house into the back garden. The woman and one child, a girl, were on fire. Guardsman Lyall tore the clothes off the child and carried her to the guardroom accompanied by the boy. Meanwhile, another soldier, Guardsman Ronald Burpitt had arrived in time to help Mrs. Bridge into the next-door garden and carry her into the house. Wrapped in an overcoat, her hair singed and her face charred, the unfortunate woman was naked, her clothes having been burnt off. Strangely, Mrs. Bridge seems to have been allowed to wander away alone wrapped only in the overcoat, before meeting Dr. William S. Moore. Dr. Moore helped her to his surgery at 50 Foresters Drive and laid her on a couch where, upon examination, he found she was extensively burnt on her lower limbs. Leaving his daughter to apply tannic acid jelly to her poor flame-scorched body he went in search of an ambulance. He found an RAF ambulance driven by AC1 William Watterston, and Mrs. Bridge was carried out on a stretcher and taken to Carshalton War Memorial Hospital. With her was her husband and badly injured daughter. Little Jill Bridge had been taken to 37 Foresters Drive after leaving her burning home. At the hospital she was found to be suffering from second and third degree burns . . . Sadly, mother and daughter died in the early hours of Sunday, February 25. [10]

At Croydon Police Station, Police Constable J. Herner was working in the telegraph room and received the official report of the crash. As the *Daily Mirror* said:

> It was not really his duty. He was deputising for a sick colleague. As he began to transcribe the report sent by the officer at the scene of the tragedy, Police-Constable Herner said to a comrade "Foresters Drive! That is getting mighty near to my aunt's house". His aunt was Mrs. Bridge.
>
> Then he learned the names of the victims and knew that his aunt and a cousin were dead. He was allowed to leave duty and he went at once to Wallington.

Eight people were hurt in the crash. Besides Mr. Bridge, they were: Reginald Balmer [i.e. Palmer] and his wife, Jane, both aged forty-five; Robert McWilton and his wife, Gladys, both aged fifty; Frederick Whiting [sic - actually Whiteing], aged forty and his wife Emily, forty-five, and their niece Eileen Whiting, twenty-two. [9]

Eileen Whiteing was in fact the daughter-in-law of Mr. and Mrs. Frederick Whiteing and not their niece. Her wartime memories have been published. In these she writes:

Saturday, February 24th began as a lovely day and we went into Sutton in the afternoon for shopping and afternoon tea at the Plaza cinema, together with Dennis's [her husband's] parents. We all returned to the Foresters Drive house to spend the evening and have supper, little dreaming of the tragic event that was to take place there at 6.45 p.m. when an RAF Blenheim bomber plane took off on a night training flight from Croydon Aerodrome (which adjoined our back garden), failed to gain height and crashed on to the house next door. The wing of the plane demolished the corner of our own house, the actual wing-tip finishing up on the spare-room bed. [11]

The *Daily Mail*, getting the maximum out of the gruesome story under the headline "They Drew the Curtains in Foresters Drive", quoted Mr. Frederick Whiteing as saying that he used to be very proud of his house and garden but now never wanted to live there again and was taking his wife right out of the district. Eileen Whiteing notes, however, that the house had been requisitioned, and the family was already looking for alternative accommodation, at the time of the crash.

The inquest was held three days later in the Carshalton Council Chamber, and then, on February 28th, came the RAF's Court of Inquiry. Its members included Wing Commander Patrick Tweedie of the Air Ministry's Accident Investigation Branch. Croydon was familiar territory for him: only a few months before, in civilian life, he had been a pilot with Imperial Airways and had been one of those who flew the H.P. 42 'Silver Wing' service from the aerodrome.

The Court noted that there had been a lack of proper lighting arrangements on the night in question, and recommended that procedures for night flying at Croydon should be reorganised. It was also suggested that an error of judgement had been made in allowing Whitmarsh, who was inexperienced, to fly under the prevailing weather conditions.

Sir Hugh Dowding, at Headquarters of Fighter Command, in forwarding the Court proceedings to the Air Ministry, noted that he felt that both Flight Lieutenant Byrne, and the officer in charge of night flying on February 24th, Squadron Leader John Miller, commanding 145, had been dealt with leniently. He went on to say that the completion of runways at other aerodromes had rendered the occupation of Croydon unnecessary and it would be evacuated "as soon as possible (except as a satellite)". The squadrons stationed there would be moved to Biggin Hill and Kenley. [10] However, the coming of the Battle of Britain later in the year meant that any such idea was abandoned: in time of crisis Croydon was still needed.

Reginald Whitmarsh was buried at Plymouth on February 28th and on the same day Mrs. Bridge and her daughter were cremated at Norwood. Flight Lieutenant Byrne and two other officers of 92 Squadron attended the latter funeral.

Squadron Leader Bushell had to hurry back from Catterick, by train, for the Court of Inquiry. It is not clear what had taken him to Yorkshire, but five days previously, on 23rd February, the squadron log noted:

Flt. Lt. Green and crew left on special mission to St. Athan [South Glamorganshire] at 1440 and arrived 1545 in spite of low cloud. Sqn. Leader Bushell and crew left at 1530 and had to put down at Cardiff due to thick weather conditions. [7]

On 27th, Bushell is described as weather-bound at Catterick. Flt. Lt. Green (and Pilot Officer Bartley, who was apparently with him) did not return from there until 2nd March when, the log notes, they had "completed their special duty". It is something of a mystery what Bushell and the others were doing at Catterick, or why they went there via South Wales.

March saw the momentous change, for 92 Squadron, from Blenheims to Spitfires. After several more days of bemoaning the limited number of serviceable Blenheims available, the squadron log on March 5th noted: "F/Lt. Byrne took some pilots to Northolt to examine a Spitfire, as this day our allotment for 21 Spitfires was received. Eight from No. 9 Maintenance Unit Cosford and 13 from No. 27 Maintenance Unit Shawbury. One Master aircraft was also allotted us this day from Reading." The next day saw Pilot Officer Bartley collect the Miles Master (L7534), whilst Squadron Leader Bushell took the commanding officers of 145 and 3 Squadrons (Flight Lieutenant Boyd and Squadron Leader Gifford respectively) to collect the Spitfires with the help of Flight Lieutenant Byrne and three pilots borrowed from Northolt. They returned with two formations, a total of seven Spitfires; the eighth aircraft being not yet serviceable.

It was on 3rd March that 145 Squadron learned that it was to acquire Hurricanes; and on 6th March it collected its first eight (equipped for flying practice only) from Aston Down. These were numbered N2598 to N2605. There were two accidents in the first few days: on 13th March Pilot Officer K. R. Lucas force-landed N2599 at Loughton near Lewes, Sussex; and, on the 22nd, Pilot Officer W. E. Hunt badly damaged N2604 when he stalled it during a landing approach at Croydon. [8]

On April 21st Pilot Officer C.D. Gordon-Wilson was killed during practice attacks - his aircraft N2600 crashed at Warninglid near Cowfold in West Sussex. An inquest was held at Horsham on the 23rd; and, on the 25th, Squadron Leader Miller (himself soon to lose his life in France), seven officers, and forty airmen, attended a service at Kenley. [8] Gordon-Wilson's grave is at Whyteleafe.

For 92 Squadron the second week of March 1940 was devoted to intensive training in Spitfires, starting with a lecture on the 8th by Flight Lieutenant Boyd of 145 Squadron. On the same day, Mr. Rose of Vickers Supermarine (the company which produced the machine) visited the Squadron, as did Flight Lieutenant Healey from 11 Group. Four pilots went solo straight away: Flight Lieutenant Green, Pilot Officer Learmond, Sergeant Fokes and Pilot Officer Blomeley. The following day, three more pilots went solo on Spitfires; whilst a fourth, Sergeant Eyles, "went on his nose taxi-ing a Blenheim on a bad patch on the aerodrome".[7] Probably few tears were shed when the order came through from Kenley on the 11th that no further flying was to be done on Blenheims. On the same day Pilot Officer John Bryson and Flight Sergeant Payne fetched the eighth Spitfire from Cosford. On the 15th we find a Blenheim being used as a target in mock attacks from Spitfire formations: whether this was one of 92's old Blenheims we do not know.

Damage was caused to three more aircraft on March 19th, even though there was no flying: first, in high winds at midday, a recently-landed Spitfire was tipped up on its nose in the middle of the airfield; and then, during the night, an air-raid warning caused the hasty dispersal of the aircraft around the aerodrome, during which two were pushed into each other, causing damage to the wing tips.

On March 20th, 92 Squadron was ordered to Gatwick. Pilots had gone to Shawbury to collect nine more Spitfires when suddenly an order came through from Fighter Command to take all available aircraft to Gatwick, and "disperse them there". No reason is given in the log, but it seems likely that it was the result of intelligence reports of an expected German air attack on Croydon, which did not, in fact, materialise at this stage. Only the Adjutant and two officers were left at Croydon. The bulk of the squadron stayed at Gatwick until the 27th of March. Routine flying seems to have been carried out during this period. On 25th, Flight Lieutenant Byrne had a narrow escape: "During an interception exercise, Flt. Lt. Byrne's engine was observed to be pouring out black smoke and oil; and he prepared to force-land on a racecourse near Edenbridge, Kent. Unfortunately, at the last minute, the unexpected appearance of horses and riders in the field he had selected caused him to make a quick 90 degree turn into a small field alongside; the result being that the Spitfire was written off. Flt. Lt. Byrne escaped with a bruised head and a little concussion. A leaking oil-pipe is suspected, or the absence of the requisite amount of engine." [7] Byrne's Spitfire was N3291.

The day after the return to Croydon should have seen the arrival of more Spitfires; but the attempt to fetch them was, as the squadron's log says, "frustrated by the only remaining serviceable Blenheim going U.S. [unserviceable]." The new machines were eventually collected from Shawbury two days later.

The Spitfires of 92 Squadron, although not yet used in action, were continuing to suffer damage. In a rather unusual incident, on March 31st, an airman was standing on the tail of a machine, running petrol out, when the pilot, Sergeant Havercroft, started to taxi behind two other machines. Leaping off hurriedly, the airman was uninjured; but the sudden change in weight at the rear of the Spitfire, coupled with the effect of the slipstream of those ahead, forced the machine to turn on its nose, and its airscrew was badly damaged. [7]

The harsh weather was slowly giving way to spring; but the hot summer days that would accompany the Battle of Britain were yet to come. The station record at Croydon notes only the weather; the changes of Army Guard (and then inconsistently and with many omissions); and the visits of senior officers, both Army and RAF. A Captain Wolf of the Scots Guards (was this the Captain who was to reprimand a future Home Secretary?) came on January 30th; and, on April 17th, Colonel Pearson and his ADCs from the 12th Queen's Regiment visited to make preparations for a change of Army detachment. On April 25th, Colonel Laurie of the Essex Yeomanry appeared; on May 10th "E" Company, 2nd Battalion London Rifle Brigade were attached for duty; and, on the same day, a detachment of the 12th Queen's Royal Regiment arrived. [12]

The Home Secretary, Sir John Anderson - memorable for the type of air-raid shelter which bore his name - visited RAF Croydon on April 6th and watched air-raid and fire-fighting exercises. Three days later came another official visit: this time from Air Vice Marshal Welsh, who, notes the station record [12] "addressed personnel and complimented A/C Hayes of 145 Squadron". The reason for this distinction being accorded to A/C Hayes is not given in the station record, but relates to his bravery in the Blenheim collision of February 10th.

The squadron log for 145 notes, on April 10th, that the Air Officer Commanding "congratulated 641354 AC1 Hayes L.J. on his gallant action for supporting AC1 Crowe C. 646428 in Blenheim K7114 after that machine had collided with Blenheim K7019 [sic - actually 7091] on 10th February 1940". [8]

The log of 92 Squadron reports:

A Station Parade was held at 1015 hours to enable the AOC - who arrived by air - to address 145 Squadron and congratulate A/C Hayes on the subject of his gallantry on the occasions of two Blenheims being in collision in mid-air on February 10.

Irritatingly, none of these three official RAF records says *exactly* what Aircraftman Hayes did - or what sort of support he afforded Aircraftman Crowe. In fact, Leslie Joseph Hayes was "commended for gallantry in rescuing a comrade who was caught by his parachute pack whilst the aircraft was out of control" [13] - although this still leaves some questions unanswered.

Air Vice Marshal (later Sir) William Lawrie Welsh was Air Officer Commanding, Technical Training Command. He was later to be responsible for RAF operations in north west Africa, and died in 1962.

92 Squadron was still having problems with Spitfires: on April 14th Pilot Officer Bryson tipped another machine onto its nose, an accident attributed at the time to a too-slow landing speed and over-use of brakes.

A much more serious incident took place on April 27th, one which gave prolonged anxiety to the pilot. The squadron log tells the tale:

P.O. Mottram who had taken off at 1430 in a Spitfire aircraft noticed that his starboard wheel would not come up nor would his port wheel go down. After getting in R/T contact with RUNICK [presumably Croydon Control], and through them with the C.O., who made various suggestions to P.O. Mottram, and after considerable time had elapsed, it was found possible to retract the starboard wheel, and hold it up by constant pumping. At 1700 hours, the starboard wheel down about 45°, P.O. Mottram made a perfect 'veutre-a-tesse'* landing before a large and enthusiastic audience doing the minimum amount of damage under the circumstances, and with only 10 gallons of petrol left.

On May 4th Flight Lieutenant Byrne was posted to 74 Squadron (he was later to be shot down over France and made a prisoner of war); and command of his flight was taken over by someone who was to become a famous Battle of Britain 'ace' - Flight Lieutenant, later Wing Commander, Robert Stanford-Tuck. He had come from 65 Squadron and was perhaps dubious about joining an auxiliary squadron of "weekend fliers" - many of them well-to-do people who had regarded flying as a sport and not a profession. As his biographer, Larry Forrester, puts it:

Tuck had expected to find them very different from the 'professional' pilots of 65, and was astounded and delighted to discover the atmosphere of the Croydon mess even wilder and woollier than Hornchurch. Moreover, in some mysterious way, these war-time chaps had managed to learn the entire range of Raff slang and idiom, all the rude songs, all the traditional nick-names ('Chippie' Wood, 'Shady' Lane, 'Dickie' Bird, etc.) and, most surprisingly of all, they had the same cynical approach to anything that savoured even faintly of militarism, rhetoric or red tape. Even the youngest of them had acquired the languid arrogance of experienced pilots.

Because the Spit was new to most of them, and because each one realised the 'phoney war' was over and that very soon - perhaps within days, or hours - the squadron would go into battle, they had practised combat drill with a quiet ardour. Between flights they had squatted in a circle on the grass and listened to Tuck, wide-eyed and attentive as children listening to a bedtime story.

* (In the margin of the log someone with better French has corrected 'veutre-a-tesse' to 'ventre-à-terre').

They were a cosmopolitan bunch, and the range of Commonwealth accents gave the mess a vocal tapestry of rare richness. There were two Canadians, 'Eddie' Edwards and John Bryson, a former member of the 'Mounties'; Howard Hill, from New Zealand; Pat Learmond from Ireland, and Paddy Green from South Africa. For administrative purposes the squadron at this time was sub-divided into two flights of six or seven, but in the air they flew in three sub-units of four. Tuck's flying section were all English - Bob Holland, Allan Wright and Sergeant 'Tich' Havercroft - so short that he had to have two rubber cushions under his parachute before he could see over the instrument panel. John Gillies (son of the distinguished plastic surgeon), Peter Cazenove, Roy Mottram, Hargreaves, Bill Williams and Tony Bartley completed the 'native' contingent. Green led the second flying section, and the C.O. headed the third. The two or three remaining aircraft, with their pilots, were held as reserve. 6

On May 8th the squadron moved to Northolt. Bob Stanford-Tuck went on to win the DSO and DFC (two bars). He became possibly the top British fighter 'ace' of the Second World War: credited with up to thirty confirmed victories, eight 'probables' and six enemy aircraft damaged. He himself writes, in a letter to the authors, in March 1984:

I think my official credited score should be 29 confirmed, although they dug up another one of mine a few years ago in the Dymchurch Marshes, which I had only claimed as a probable, and was later credited with it. The pilot of this ME 109 was Lieut. Werner Knittel, who was Adjutant of the Richthofen Squadron, and sadly what was left of him was still in the cockpit, but, of course, he was given a full military funeral at Cannock Chase, and I was presented with the mounted and polished oxygen bottle, which I later gave to the existing Richthofen Squadron in Germany, many of whom I meet now-a-days at various air gatherings in Germany.

Wing Commander Stanford-Tuck was wounded twice and baled out four times. Shot down over France in 1942, he was captured and made a prisoner of war, but eventually escaped. He now lives in Kent, and is a Vice-President of the Croydon Airport Society.

It may be of interest to give the listing from the squadron's log of the transfer flight of 92 Squadron from Croydon:

aircraft type & no.	crew	time up	time down
P.9316	Sgt. Klipsch	1445	1540
P.9368	P/O Bryson	1445	1540
P.9374	Sgt Fokes	1445	1540
P.9373	S/Ldr Bushell	1445	1540
P.9367	F/Lt Green	1125	1145
P.9370	P/O Bartley	1125	1145
N.3194	F/O Casenove	1445	1540
N.3290	Sgt Havercroft	1125	1145
N.3192	Sgt Barraclough	1445	1540
P.9371	F/O Hargreaves	1445	1540
N.3285	F/Lt Tuck	1125	1145
N.3193	P/O Holland	1125	1145
N.3249	P/O Learmond	1125	1145
N.3248	Sgt Eyles	1445	1540

The war was now quickening, and events in Europe were soon to move swiftly. The station record at Croydon notes, apart from the weather, a number of changes in Army guard detachments. On May 11th a mysterious entry says: "The 413rd Battn. 147th (EY) Regt. Royal Horse Artillery left Croydon" -

there is clearly some mistyping here. The 13th saw a visit from Sir Charles McGrigor of the London Rifle Brigade; and on 15th the "457th Troop, 148th Lt AA Battery Royal Artillery proceeded to another destrination [more typing problems!] their place being taken at RAF Croydon by a detachment of 83rd Battery". [12]

On 23rd May Colonel Cobb RASC visited; on 27th "G" Company, 2nd Battn. of the London Rifle Brigade were attached to the station, replacing "E" Company, and the next day 217th Troop 83rd Light Anti-Aircraft Battery were attached in place of the other detachment from 83rd Battery, who left.

What relevance, if any, these changes had to the worsening situation on the Continent is not certain; but the 'phoney war' was about to end and the real war begin. RAF Croydon would soon be in the front line.

CHAPTER FOUR

Croydon and the Fall of France

Following a major Parliamentary debate on the war's progress on May 7th and 8th, 1940, Neville Chamberlain had resigned as Britain's Prime Minister. He was succeeded by Winston Churchill, who, on 14th May, following fierce fighting and defeats in France, told Britain, in an historic radio broadcast, that he had "nothing to offer but blood, toil, tears and sweat". On the same day it was announced that a new force - the Local Defence Volunteers - was to be created to defend Britain in the event of an invasion. It was soon to change its name to the Home Guard and to become a large force with sections in every town; but at first having few weapons or defences, and with a personnel, mostly, of those men too old, or young, to be in the 'real' forces.

On the 10th of May the phoney war ended abruptly, with the beginning of the German attack on the Western defences. A pincer movement; through the Ardennes on the one hand, and Belgium and Holland on the other, was the start of a high-speed offensive, the force of which was soon to be reflected in events at Croydon.

Only a few days after leaving Croydon, 92 Squadron escorted Winston Churchill to France and back again. He himself had an aquaintanceship with Croydon aerodrome which had dated from 1917 and was to reach through to the 1950s. This journey to France was from Hendon, and the escort was three Spitfires led by Bob Stanford-Tuck. They flew to Le Bourget on the 16th, when Churchill had been Prime Minister for just over one week. 92 was called on to perform the same duty again on the 22nd May.[1]

In France the fighting was severe, and took a heavy toll of lives. The squadrons (607 and 615) which had flown out from Croydon in the 'air armada' of November 15th, were joined by 145, which left the aerodrome on May 10th, travelling first to Filton aerodrome near Bristol, from whence they ferried Hurricanes to the Continent and threw themselves into the battle.

These large events, however, do not disturb the style of Croydon's Operations Record Book. An entry for May 19th tells of an incident in which the camouflage netting on the terminal building caught fire, and the Beddington and Wallington Fire Brigade, plus that of Croydon, hurried to the scene.

At 1800 hours the outbreak was extinguished and the fire brigades left the Camp. Damage to Air Ministry property was the destruction by fire of a quantity of camouflage netting. There was [sic] no personal injuries. The station booster pump was started at 1745 and run for eight minutes.[2]

Nevertheless, the reality of war was roaring home to the aerodrome with the arrival back from France of broken machines and weary pilots. The entry for 20th May reads:

The following aircraft arrived at Croydon from the B.E.F. and were taken in by Messrs. Rollasons for repair and overhaul: P2566, P2565, P2627, of No. 607 Squadron; L1945, L1952, of No. 504 Squadron L2003, L2871, of No. 615 Squadron. [L2871 is a mistake; this serial number belonged to a Blackburn Skua which had crashed in January 1939. It must have been Hurricane P2871]

On the same day there arrived a detachment of Canadians - a sergeant and twenty-seven airmen from No. 110 Squadron, Royal Canadian Air Force. They had come from the School of Army Co-operation at Old Sarum, to service aircraft of No. 2 Squadron which were due to arrive from the British Expeditionary Force.

No. 2 Squadron's retreat through Belgium and France was, perhaps, typical of that of many Squadrons. On the 19th May the major part of the Squadron was at Bethune, under orders to retreat to Boulogne. The Squadron's Lysander aircraft were to be flown to Lympne, together with a Belgian Leopard Moth salvaged from a hangar at Wevelghem. 'C' Flight unfortunately ran out of daylight, and spent the night at Berck-sur-Mer. The main party managed to cross the Channel safely and touched down at Lympne at 9.30 p.m.

On the ground, Aircraftman Patterson, who had been left behind at Douai Aerodrome with Lysander KO-N, had to set fire to the aircraft to prevent it from falling into enemy hands. The Squadron's HQ and operational staff were travelling throughout the night to Boulogne, which they reached at 7 a.m. on the morning of the 20th, by which time "C" Flight had already reached Lympne; and, with the rest of the Squadron, apart from four aircraft left behind to operate with No. 16 Squadron, were on their way to Bekesbourne.

At Bekesbourne they received fresh instructions to fly to Hawkinge, refuel and continue on to Croydon, where they eventually arrived at 9.30 p.m.

The groundstaff spent May 20th crossing the Channel and travelling by train to Tidworth camp, where they spent the night. [3]

The aircrew at Croydon had hardly digested breakfast on the 21st when they were put on standby for a move back to Lympne, subsequently cancelled in favour of a move to Bekesbourne which was completed by 1.10 p.m., the aircrew being followed by the maintenance party from No. 110 Squadron RCAF.

With the Lysanders gone, Croydon now welcomed the ground party from Tidworth. The Squadron log records: "The men were given baths, food and accommodation. The officers were accommodated at the Aerodrome Hotel."

The next day No. 2 Squadron was once again in action over France, flying tactical reconnaissance flights. [3]

But, meanwhile, more machines from 615 and 607 Squadrons arrived from France for repairs by Rollasons, as well as one from 601 Squadron (all these Squadrons were flying Hurricane Is at the time). These were P2801, L1789, N2328, L1998, N2310 and N2337 of 615; P2092, P2874 and P2586 of 607; and N2434 from 601. The next day (22nd May) came the men: 219 airmen and two officers from 615 Squadron, plus the whole of 607 Squadron, thirty-nine NCOs and airmen of No. 242 Squadron, and a further five airmen from No. 2 Squadron. [2]

607 Squadron had been in action since the German invasion of the Netherlands on May 10th, and had sustained heavy losses. By May 20th they were at a deserted

village near Audry au Bois, their airfields having been over-run. The Squadron log, apparently written up (probably at Croydon) for this whole period some while later, describes events thus:

On the 20th May all personnel were instructed to abandon all kit, equipment, etc., and board transport which was supposedly forming up just beyond the Aerodrome boundary on the North side. Such a convoy, however, did not exist and having received instructions to proceed to Le Havre via Desures and Boulogne, transport proceeded independently in small groups. At Boulogne congestion was so acute that instructions were given to return to the 'rest camp'. The greater part of the Squadron arrived at Boulogne on that evening. During the night 20/21 May several raids were made upon the town at intervals until approximately 0500 hours. Squadron personnel were reassembled and 4 officers, 227 NCOs and airmen embarked at midday on the steamer 'Biarritz'. Personnel arrived at Dover the same afternoon, and proceeded by train to Luggershall [Ludgershall], Tidworth, arriving in the evening.

On the afternoon of 22nd May, the Squadron was instructed to entrain and arrived at Croydon at approximately 2200 Hours.

. . . During the period 10th to 20th May the following casualties occurred:-

> S/L Smith Missing
> F/O Weatherill Missing
> A/S/Ldr Fidler Missing now believed prisoner of war
> S/Pt Townsend Missing now believed prisoner of war
> F/O Le Brulle Killed
> F/O M.H.B. Thompson Killed
> F/O Pumphrey Missing now believed prisoner of war
> F/O J.B. Russell Reported missing on 15.5.40
> F/O G.I. Cuthbert Reported missing on 15.5.40
> F/O (A/F/Lt) J.L. Sullivan Reported missing on 14.5.40 now believed killed

During the period 10th May to 20.5.40 the Squadron destroyed 72 E/A confirmed, and a further 56 probably damaged, unconfirmed.

Of the Squadron airmen personnel, only one casualty occurred - No. 646783 AC2 Clark A. Wireless Operator being reported missing on or about 25.6.40 whilst on attachment from this unit to No. 63 FWSU Merville.

[The following is handwritten in the original]: During the last few days of May officers, NCOs and men of the Squadron arrived at Croydon Airport by various routes for re-forming after evacuation from France. Virtually all records and most of the Squadron's equipment were lost or destroyed in France. [4]

Croydon's Station Record however merely notes on May 23rd:

The following aircraft arrived at Croydon on 22nd and 23rd May and were dispersed to Hendon and to Heston as shown:

DISPERSED TO HENDON: 23.5.40. D.H.89s ACTT, W6455, V4725, AEPE, ACPP, AFEO; D.H.86s - AEWR, ADVK, ...246 [this must be N6246, previously G-ADYG of British Airways Ltd.], ADYI; Bombays [L]5851, [L]5853, [L]5855, [L]5857; Ford Tri-motor - GACAE.

DISPERSED TO HESTON: 23.5.40. D.H.84 - ACIT; D.H.89 OAFF [sic], AFOIL [sic], AERN, AFRK, ADAJ, AEAL, AEBW, ADDI [sic - actually a D.H. 84 Dragon], and GAEWL. [2]

The Bristol Bombays were from No. 271 Squadron. The D.H.89 Dragon Rapide W6455, had, as G-AENN, been part of the Olley Air Service fleet at Croydon in pre-war days.

Beyond the bare list of aircraft registration letters was the reality of exhausted and wounded men and battered machines.

An eye-witness account comes from Mr. Ken Steel, then working at Rollasons:

They came in low over the Surrey hills. Flying slowly, so slowly and smoothly, to slip down to a most gentle landing. They did not make the customary circuit of the airfield, but came straight in to touch-down as closely after one another as they could with safety . . . All day they came in to land, touching down very gently for, temporarily, they were air ambulances ferrying the wounded from France.

Croydon had never handled so many arrivals in twenty-four hours but everything appeared to be very well organised. The car parks around the Administration Buildings were filled with all kinds of ambulances. They came from the armed forces, St. John's, ambulance units all over the south of England and the municipalities for miles around. All day they were loaded and despatched to hospitals around London. [5]

Amid all this, supplies were still being ferried out to France: Bristol Bombays of No. 271 Transport Squadron (then based at Doncaster) were flying tinned food to the troops. The squadron log for May 22nd notes that a Bombay, L5852, flew from Doncaster to Croydon, took on board 4,000 lbs of tinned food and then flew to Merville via Hawkinge. Another, L5853, flew from Le Bourget to Hendon and thence to Croydon, also stocking-up on food before taking the same route and returning with its mission completed. Similar trips were made by L5854 and L5855. [6]

Wing Commander G. Harvey arrived at Croydon to take charge of the ferrying of food, ammunition and equipment to the BEF. This was a massive operation noted in the Station Record as follows:

There were 33 aircraft available, and delay was due to Army transports and also to difficulty in connection with Fighter escorts. The operation was ended by collaboration between Air Ministry and War Office and was due to enemy action. One Ensign was destroyed on the ground at Jenkin (Merville) and two Savoirs [sic - i.e. Savoia-Marchettis] and one Douglas missing (at 1900 hours on 23.5.40) the destruction of the Ensign was witnessed by Captain Buxton of Imperial Airways. The Savoir aircraft were presumed destroyed over the Channel while returning to Croydon from Merville, and one Ensign which was badly damaged over the Channel by enemy action eventually force-landed and crashed at Lympne. There were no injuries to personnel in this aircraft. [2]

The Ensign damaged at Lympne was G-ADTA *Euryalus* of BOAC, formerly of Imperial Airways. The BOAC Annual Report for 1941 says of this aircraft that it "was finally written off and reduced to produce on 17th November 1941."

The Ensign mentioned as being destroyed on the ground at Jenkin was G-ADSZ *Elysian* which was shot-up by Messerschmitt Me 109s and burned out. A viewpoint from the other side of the Channel at this time is presented by Mr. Lloyd C. ('Digger') Ifould who was BOAC's manager at Le Bourget airport, Paris.

In his book *Immortal Era*, describing his work in aviation, he wrote:

On May 10th, Germany invaded Belgium and Holland, followed not long afterwards by the break-through at Sedan, which came as a frightful and most unexpected blow to the people of Paris, who had never doubted for a moment that the advance of the enemy would be very promptly halted. We lost our first aircraft in France to enemy action, a few days later, on May 23rd when five of our aircraft on the ground were attacked by Me 109s, at Merville, near Lille. One of the machines caught fire and was burned up. Others were damaged, but managed to leave. Some of them were attacked again over the French coast, but succeeded in getting back to England. One, badly shot up, just struggled into Lympne, where it was, fortunately, able to put down. [7]

A dramatic story of events on May 23rd is given by Paul Brickhill in his account of Squadron Leader Roger Bushell's experiences. Bushell, leading 92 Squadron, flew from Hornchurch, where the Squadron was now based, and:

. . . led the twelve Spitfires of his squadron in over the coast between Dunkirk and Boulogne. Down below men in sweaty battledress were digging in on the beaches and spilling blood on the sand from the bombs. There weren't many RAF fighters about because there weren't many RAF fighters, and most of them were over on the rim of the battle trying to stop the dive-bombers getting through.

Forty Messerschmitt 110s had slid down towards the Spitfires and five of them picked on Bushell. He steep-turned and they overshot and pulled up. As he saw the last one sliding above, Bushell straightened out, pulled up and was almost hanging on his propeller when his stream of bullets hit the German. Smoke poured out of the Messerschmitt's port engine andd it turned on its back and went straight down.

Another Messerschmitt was coming at Bushell head-on. They were both firing; everything was red flashes, and then Bushell shot inches above the German and saw the German behind shoot steeply up, flick into a stall and spin down, smoking. Bushell was on fire, too, smoke pouring into his cockpit. His engine seized and the smoke cleared away.

Gliding down, he picked a field, and as he slid the Spitfire into it on its belly, flame spurted under the engine cowlings. He had cracked his nose on the gun-sight and scrambled out with blood pouring down his face. Watching the plane burn while he fished for a cigarette, he judged he was in British-held territory and with any luck would be back in his squadron in a couple of days.

A motorbike came pelting down a lane and turned in at the far end of the field. Bushell waited placidly for it and then he saw that it wasn't a crash helmet that the rider was wearing but a coal-scuttle helmet and a moment later he saw a gun pointing at him. (If the Germans had realised what a troublesome man they had caught, they would possibly have shot him then. It would have paid them.) [8]

Bushell was imprisoned in Stalag Luft III where he became "Big X" of the escape committee and masterminded the tunnels that enabled seventy-five officers to escape from the camp, in the biggest single such attempt of the war. A very great number of Germans were involved in the extensive searches across German-occupied Europe and fifty of the recaptured prisoners, Bushell amongst them, were shot by the Gestapo. At the War Crimes Court in Hamburg in July 1947, the details of Bushell's death were revealed: with another officer he had been captured by security police at a railway station in Saarbrücken, taken to the local prison and interrogated, and then taken, their hands handcuffed behind their backs, by car along the road towards the town of Kaiserslautern. It had been decided by the top Gestapo authorities that all the escapees from Stalag Luft III were to be shot, and Dr. Spann, the local Gestapo chief in Saarbrücken, had received a message that this was to be the fate of Bushell and his colleague. Along the road to Kaiserslautern the car was stopped and they were ordered out and shot by Dr. Spann and another Gestapo officer, Emil Schulz. Spann was later killed in an air-raid but Schulz lived to be tried and was hanged for murder in February 1948.

May 23rd saw also the death of Pilot Officer Pat Learmond, shot down over France when flying with Bushell and Bob Tuck earlier in the day.

As May 1940 ended, Croydon, with an atmosphere obviously dramatically different from that of the snow-less tobogganing days of a few months previously, was ready to play its own part in some unique months of British history.

The speed with which France fell took everyone by surprise. Le Bourget airport, Croydon's "opposite number" in Paris, quickly came under attack. Lloyd C. Ifould describes in *Immortal Era* what happened:

On the morning of June 3rd, I awoke with a song in my heart that surged its way buoyantly to my lips and set them a-whistling as I shaved and dressed. "War or no war, to be alive and well and in Paris in the Spring is certainly something to be happy about", I thought, as I drove my little Peugeot from Montmartre to Le Bourget, revelling all the way in the bright sunshine and the sensuous warmth of a perfect spring day - a perfection that, alas, was destined to be short-lived.

During the course of the day, one of our four-engine Ensigns arrived from London, G-ADSX. Buxton, the Captain, reported to me that it was impossible to run No. 3 engine at more than 1,000 R.P.M., owing to popping in the carburettor and high cylinder-head temperature. [7]

G-ADSX was *Ettrick;* and it was Captain Buxton who had, as noted in the Croydon station log eleven days earlier, witnessed the destruction on the ground at Merville of *Ettrick's* sister, *Elysian.* Mr. Ifould goes on:

We had decided to investigate the trouble; when the air-raid warning sounded. We had had other warnings, but had not taken much notice of them. My brother, Bill and Eric Morgan, the Australian, who were working with me, thought something was going to happen this time, and suggested that we allow No. 3 engine to wait a little while, to which I had no sooner agreed than we saw the roof of a factory go up in the air. This was in Dugny, which is on the other side of the Le Bourget aerodrome.

We stood spellbound looking towards the terrific explosion which hurled bits and pieces up into the air. For a moment, we did not realise that it was the result of bombs, as the warning had just sounded that very instant, and, as a rule, in all raids, we were warned of enemy aircraft approaching long before they were in our particular vicinity. Usually, one had plenty of time to go and lie down under his favourite tree, or to find himself a ditch or cellar. There was no sign of any aircraft in the air, or of the usual white traces in the sky, left by aircraft when flying at high altitudes. No anti-aircraft guns had gone into action, and we thought an explosion had taken place at a factory. When more thuds, followed by explosions, occurred, all in the same vicinity, and within a few seconds of each other, "Boys, this is it!" someone shouted, and we decided to make for cover, or at least protection of some kind from the flying fragments. [Ifould and his companions sheltered in a cellar while the airport was virtually destroyed around them]: The air was foul, and we were half choked with smoke, but we hung on. There was nothing else to do, with the shower of bombs that were dropping around us. The worst thing about this raid was the knowledge that the very building we were in was the objective the Luftwaffe was trying to destroy. It is a pretty awful experience to be the immediate target, and aware of the fact, with no defence but a few machine guns.

At the end of the air-raid, Lloyd Ifould was delighted to find that, although the aerodrome car park had been destroyed, and most cars with it, his own, which he had parked at the back of a hangar instead of in its usual place, was safe. Captain Buxton had a bomb splinter in his leg. There was much concern about the number of unexploded bombs which remained on the severely damaged aerodrome. Despite these, he and his companions went back to inspect the Ensign:

Great holes had been torn through the wings and fuselage, and while we stood inspecting the damage, an enormous piece of cement was sent flying through No. 3 engine cowling and into the engine when a delayed action bomb suddenly exploded. The damage, however, proved to be all repairable. Our first job would be to change the wheels on which tyres had burst, and get the machine off the tarmac. The Military Authorities advised us to give the airport a wide berth for the next few days, as a great deal of concern was being caused by two 500lb bombs which had fallen together between the Ensign and the airport building. A French Captain told us, 'If those two go off, they will destroy you, the Ensign, and the best part of the main airport building . . .' As we all felt considerably the worse for the day's experiences, we decided to drown our feelings in the bar of the Ensign, which the Luftwaffe had very kindly opened up for us. We helped ourselves generously, and handed out drinks to any of the boys who happened to come around. Needless to say we did a roaring trade. We were determined that if the Germans should capture the Ensign, they were not going to get any free drinks. We were going to take care of that ourselves. [7]

The machine was, indeed, captured by the Germans when Le Bourget was over-run a few days later. They fitted it with Daimler-Benz engines and used it themselves, with another captured Ensign - G-AFZV, *Enterprise* - to transport V.I.Ps. It would be interesting to know what happened to these finally; but their end does not seem to be on record.

'Digger' Ifould was the last of B.O.A.C.'s engineering staff to leave France; collecting his wife and small son and arriving in England three days later. He writes:

"The next ship near us was sunk with over two thousand on board. We landed in the south of England, near Penzance". [9] Mr. Ifould, in 1984, is living in California.

On June 4th and 5th, 607 Squadron, which had been resting at Croydon on its return from France, left for Usworth. At the end of the month decorations were announced arising from the Squadron's actions in France and the log noted them:-

> D.S.O. awarded to Flight Lieutenant W.F. Blackadder
> D.F.C. awarded to Flying Officer W.E. Gore
> D.F.C. awarded to Flight Lieutenant (now Squadron Leader) J. Sample [4]

As 607 Squadron left, No. 111 Squadron, commanded by Squadron Leader John H. 'Tommy' Thompson arrived at Croydon from North Weald; with thirteen Hurricane Is flying in on June 4th, and 82 airmen coming on the 5th. 607 had left on June 4th, some in the Armstrong Whitworth Ensign G-ADTC *Endymion,* the main body by train.

It was on June the 4th that Churchill delivered his rallying call: "We shall fight on the beaches . . . we shall never surrender". On the 17th of June he told the nation: "The battle of France is over. I suspect that the Battle of Britain is about to begin . . . let us so conduct ourselves that, if the British Empire and Commonwealth last for a thousand years, men will still say, 'This was their finest hour'".

On June 21st, 501 Squadron, commanded by Wing Commander M.V.M. Clube, and flying Hurricanes, arrived at Croydon. They had been in the thick of the fighting in France, culminating with a hectic time operating from St. Helier, Jersey, covering the evacuation of the British Expeditionary Force from Cherbourg. Their log for 20th June reports:

Squadron left St. Helier for England per Train Ferry No. 1 arriving at Southampton at 0900. Road party proceeded to Yatesbury where they were supplied with a hot meal and accommodated for the night. The air party left St. Helier at 1900 hours and arrived at Tangmere at 2100 hours.

The Squadron reassembled at Croydon. The airmen were re-kitted and were granted four days Special Leave. [10]

On the 22nd of June an armistice was signed between France and Germany; and on the 30th of June the Germans occupied the Channel Islands.

On June 29th, 501 Squadron had a change of command: Wing Commander Clube was posted to Headquarters No. 10 Group and Squadron Leader H.A.V. Hogan took over. The squadron did not become operational from Croydon until 3rd July when it carried out several patrols; the next day it left for Middle Wallop, Hampshire.

June had been chiefly a period of waiting: although attack and even invasion by Germany was confidently predicted, there seemed to be a lull in the war. Twenty years later, Edward Bishop in *The Battle of Britain* was to describe it thus:

The British people, their confidence built up by Mr. Churchill's inspiring oratory and cherubic example of that native resilience which is the national bedrock, had recovered from the shock of seeing the British Expeditionary Force bundled off the Continent in early June.

During the bonus weeks of respite that followed, Germany like cat with mouse had been pawing playfully at Britain with very small numbers of aircraft from the three Air Fleets now assembled at their stations in the west.

25. *ABOVE:* The new hangar (build in the late 1930s), Hangar D, known as 'The Flight Shed', is seen here camouflaged in autumn 1939. Stafford Road is in the background.

26. *BELOW:* The Hurricane of Flt. Lt. Blake of No. 17 Squadron, upside-down in a trench in the grounds of Purley War Memorial Hospital after a crash-landing (see p. 10).

27. Hurricanes of No. 3 Squadron at dispersal alongside Plough Lane, Purley, in September or October 1939. Note the tents, chalk thrown-up in digging trenches, and the Austin 7 parked inside the fence. In the distance can be seen the cooling towers of the Croydon Power Station along Beddington Lane.

28. The RAF in the Control Tower at Croydon. The newspaper in the background has been identified as *The Daily Mail* for Wednesday 24th January, 1940. Headlines read: (left) "20 m.p.h. limit in the blackout"; and, (right) "Second disaster in four days —Destroyer sunk with all hands". This was the loss of H.M.S. *Exmouth*, which is the subject of the photograph on the centre of the page. The air of inactivity, the greatcoats, and the white appearance outside suggest the presence outside of the snow of early 1940. (Thanks to Peter Cooksley for research.)

Imperial Airways and British Airways aircraft evacuated to Whitchurch, Bristol, in September 1939. Camouflage painting is in progress.

29. *ABOVE:* On the left is A.W. Ensign G-ADSY, *Empyrean;* to the right, facing, is another Ensign, with, in front, a Junkers Ju52/3m. To the right is the Ensign G-ADSS, *Egeria.*

30. *BELOW:* Far left: Junkers Ju52/3m; a D.H. Albatross is to its right. To the right of that are two Ensigns (probably the same as above). In the centre is a Lockheed Electra; and there are two Lockheed Hudsons, one facing forwards to the right of the Electra and one in the foreground.

Two H.P.42s in RAF markings after impressment.

31. *ABOVE: Hadrian,* ex-G-AAUE at Odiham in 1940.

32. *BELOW: Helena,* ex-G-AAXF, probably at RNAS Donibristle in 1941.

The end of *Helena:*

33.   *ABOVE:* Being dismantled by RAF and RNAS personnel at Donibristle in August 1941.

34.   *BELOW:* Her fuselage was kept for a while and used as a squadron office at Donibristle. The photograph was taken in September 1941.

35.   A defensive gun emplacement (RAF 2) on the Purley Way playing fields to the east of Croydon Airport. In the background is the chimney of the pumping station on the north side of Waddon Way and the buildings of the old open-air swimming pool, now a garden centre, to the south of Waddon Way.

36. *ABOVE:* Another gun emplacement (RAF 5).

37. *BELOW:* The view shows the location of RAF 5 as being near Stafford Road, to the north-west of the Bourjois scent factory and the British N.S.F. factory. The pumping-station chimney by Waddon Way is visible on the right. The photograph dates from before the big air-raid of 15th August 1940.

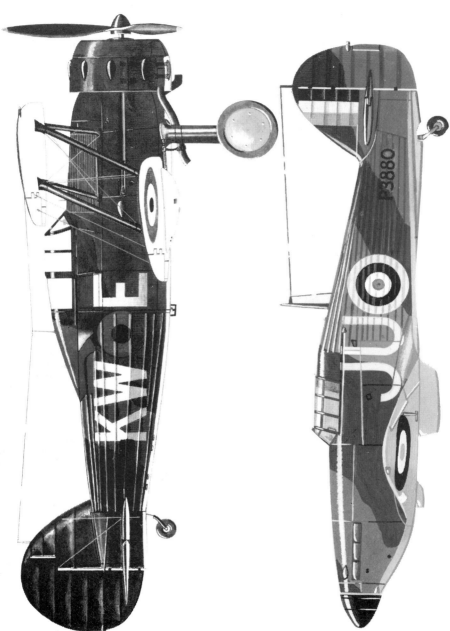

Profiles by Peter G. Cooksley of examples from two generations of fighter aircraft flying from Croydon in 1939 and 1940.

38. *ABOVE:* Gloster Gladiator Mk.II of No. 615 (County of Surrey) Squadron, September—November. 1939.

Some of Croydon's pre-war airliners returned, on November 13th, 1939, to fly ground staff
and equipment of 607 and 615 Squadrons to France, accompanied by the Squadrons' aircraft
— the so-called 'Air Armada'.

40.   *ABOVE:* Prominent are a Short L.17 *(Scylla* or *Syrinx)* and two A.W. Ensigns.

41.   *BELOW:* One of the Ensigns is refuelled for the trip.

42.   615 Squadron airmen pose, with jocular 'Heil Hitler' salutes, beneath the wings of an Ensign before their departure for France on November 13th 1939.

More of the 'Air Armada'.

43. *ABOVE:* Two Ensigns (one behind the Red Cross vehicle) and the twin L.17s, *Scylla* and *Syrinx*.

44. *BELOW:* (left to right) Fokker F XII, G-AEOS; *Scylla* and *Syrinx*; two Ensigns; and Gladiators (the two nearest are of 607 Squadron). Engines are being run-up for departure. Behind can be seen the camouflaged control tower.

The departure of the 'Air Armada'.

45. *ABOVE:* The Fokker XII (G-AEOS) and an L.17 run up their engines, as do, on the left, two Gladiators of 607 Squadron. An Ensign is already in the air.

46. *BELOW:* Gladiators of 615 Squadron in their take-off run.

47. The original photograph reads, on the back: "615 Squadron records Croydon Nov. 1939". The Squadron records appear to be being loaded to leave Croydon by road after the Squadron's departure by air on the 13th. However, there is snow on the ground, not present in the photographs of the departure by air; and we have no record of snow at Croydon in the winter of 1939/40 until the 21st of January. The photograph is certainly of Croydon, however; and the view of the front of the building behind the lorry is the only photograph we have seen which indicates that there was camouflage netting over the main hall as well as the control tower.

Unaware that they owed this immediate immunity to German grace (Hitler still hoped for a negotiated peace), the British people momentarily indulged in a dangerous mood of self-congratulation upon the many and varied measures they had taken towards survival and retaliation. [11]

But the Battle of Britain was looming. On July the 2nd the German High Command issued an order entitled 'The War against England', which began: "The Führer and Supreme Commander has decided that a landing in England is possible . . . "

As Drew Middleton wrote in *The Sky Suspended* [11]

Unlike the fighting in France, the Battle of Britain did not open with a sudden, massive attack. All through June the Luftwaffe had launched small, widely-scattered attacks, mostly by night, against British targets. Most daylight attacks had been confined to the ports. Gradually in the early days of July the attacks extended inland. They were heavier in scale, more bombers, more fighters. The sirens sounded in Wales and on the east coast. Then the Luftwaffe revisited the ports Dover, Weymouth, Portland, Plymouth and again the attacks were heavier. The convoys moving through the Channel were heavily attacked. [12]

111 Squadron was kept busy flying from Croydon, as its squadron history notes:

Every day saw 'Treble One' on patrol over the Channel with 615, 601 and 141 Squadrons as company. Little was seen of the Luftwaffe but A.A. fire was accurate from behind the German lines.

It was soon obvious that heavy bursts of fire on the fuselages of Do 215s and Ju 88s had no effect. Very heavy armour plating was fitted, but the engines and wings were very susceptible to attack.

Midway through June 1940, the squadron score was 47 enemy aircraft destroyed and 14 probables. News came through that Sgt. Brown was safe in Stanmore hospital with an injured thigh after baling out. He was attacked by 14 He 113s and his engine caught fire.

On the 21st, 111 acted as escort to No. 801's Skuas and some Rocs [both Blackburn-built Fleet Air Arm machines] who dive-bombed gun emplacements S.W. of Calais. 801 Squadron later phoned through to say how pleased they were with the support.

Early in July, two Hurricanes were scrambled to intercept unidentified aircraft. These turned out to be Spitfires of No. 54 Squadron, one of which fired on P/O Fisher's Hurricane, holing the petrol tank and ripping the tailplane. Later in the month, help was given to 141's [Boulton and Paul] Defiants who were being attacked over the Channel by Me 109s. Six Me 109s and four Defiants were shot down. At the end of the month our losses were four pilots, ten aircraft, one pilot wounded in the leg and one injured baling out. Aircraft were now painted the new light blue underneath the wings and fuselage [13]

Invasion now seemed more likely than ever. Barrage balloons hung over London, designed to prevent low-level attacks from the air. People began to say "He's coming" - meaning Hitler - and comparisons were made with another Continental would-be invader, Napoleon, a century and a half earlier. There was a noticeable sense of national confidence and unity, marked by a good deal of humour. The weather was good, with bright sunshine and blue skies. Tea was rationed (two ounces per person, per week) and the tennis courts at Wimbledon were given over to pig-farming; but people felt more acutely English than ever. It was still a very correct and old-fashioned nation: wing-collars for Members of Parliament; parlourmaids still busy at work in many middle-class homes. People found it easy to laugh at German propaganda: reports that press gangs were recruiting youths at cinemas to dig trenches; that a general sense of panic was pervading England; and alcoholism increasing every day; were reproduced in *The Times* and other newspapers with great glee and treated as a joke. It was in this spirit that people read Hitler's "Last appeal to reason" - his speech to the Reichstag on July 19th calling for peace with Britain, which was distributed by the Luftwaffe over Southern England. Copies became collectors' items and were raffled in aid of the Red Cross.

But Hitler was serious: his plans for the invasion of Britain - code-named *Seelöwe* or 'Operation Sealion' - included details on how the pound (£) would be valued in terms of German marks and pfennigs, and how British youths of military age would be deported to the Continent.

When did the Battle of Britain start? The official qualification for award of the 'Battle of Britain Star' - a gilt rose emblem worn centrally on the medal ribbon of the 1939-45 Star - is to have been an aircrew member of stipulated squadrons in Fighter Command, and to have flown at least one operational sortie between 00.01 hours on 10 July 1940 and 23.59 hours on 31 October 1940.

The 10th of July saw a German attack on Channel shipping and a raid on docks in South Wales. Peter Cooksley, in *1940 - The Story of No. 11 Group . . . .* , describes the fate of a Croydon pilot over the Channel on that day:

Flying Officer T.P.K. Higgs [took off] with others of No. 111 Squadron from Croydon to intercept an attack by Dornier 17Z bombers on another convoy off Folkestone. The Hurricanes had encountered a huge formation of attackers and had passed this in order to commence stern attacks. After some exchange of fire with the aircraft of 3/KG2 which accounted for one of the enemy, Higgs was seen to collide with another of the Dorniers, although there were those who believed that he had deliberately rammed the bomber. This seems doubtful but what is certain is that a moment later the wing of the fighter was seen to fall away, while the greater part of the Hurricane with the pilot still aboard dropped away like a stone. From this, Higgs was seen to escape by parachute only to plummet into the ocean. 'A rescue launch was despatched immediately' records the Squadron diary, but the crew failed to discover any sign of the fate of either the British pilot or those aboard the Dornier which had likewise dropped into the Channel. [14]

Later, Higgs' body was washed ashore and is now buried in Noordwijk cemetery in the Netherlands. Two of the Dornier crew were captured, but two remained missing. [15]

The local press during July prepared the people of Wallington for the worst: a sample notice in the *Wallington and Carshalton Times* read:

What do I do . . . if I hear news that the Germans are trying to land, or have landed? I remember that this is the moment to act like a soldier. I do *not* get panicky. I *stay put*. I say to myself: Our chaps will deal with them. I do *not* say: 'I must get out of here'. I remember that fighting men must have clear roads. I do *not* go on to the road on bicycle, in car or on foot. Whether I am at work or at home, I just *stay put*.

Cut this out - and keep it! [16]

The notice bears the imprint of the Ministry of Information; above this it says: "Space donated to the Nation by the Brewers Society".

June had seen further changes in the Army guard at the aerodrome. This spate of energetic movements possibly reflected a greater sense of the importance of the task of guarding the site in the light of the imminently expected invasion.

Regiments involved at this time included the 2nd London Rifles, the 12th Queen's Royal Regiment, the Middlesex Regiment, the Tower Hamlets Rifles - 114 of them - and the 148th Light A.A. Battery, Royal Artillery. In the middle of these changes an inspection of the Army defence arrangements was carried out by Brigadier-General Speed and Colonel Sherbrook-Walker. On 27th June, this time with Major-General Anderson, Brigadier Speed visited again. There was also a visit from the General Officer Commanding, Inspector of Army Defences, General Sir B.S. Brooke, on 3rd July. [2]

The end of June and beginning of July saw a rash of visits from high-ranking RAF personnel: Air Marshal Sir William Gore Sutherland Mitchell, Inspector General of the RAF, came on June 26th; on the 29th Air Vice Marshal Keith Park arrived in a Hurricane, N2520, from Northolt and flew out again two hours later. On 2nd July Air Vice Marshal P.H.L. Playfair came, again from Northolt, in a D.H. 89, W6456 and left for Andover in a Percival Vega Gull P1754. Less than three hours later, the Under-Secretary of State for Air, Captain H.H. Balfour arrived in the same Vega Gull from Biggin Hill and left in it two hours later for Hendon. He visited Croydon again on the 6th. [2]

As July progressed, it seemed as if everyone of importance within the RAF structure wanted to check on developments at Croydon: from 11 Group at Henley, from Fighter Command Headquarters, and from the Air Ministry; they came almost daily.

Meanwhile, more squadrons were coming and going: on the 19th to 21st of June, No. 501 Squadron had arrived from France for a refit, leaving on July 4th for Middle Wallop, from whence they were to play a major part in the fighting.

On July the 4th, at 7 p.m., No. 1 Squadron, Royal Canadian Air Force (also known as No. 401 Squadron - the designation they themselves used in their log at this time), under the command of Squadron Leader Ernest McNabb, brought their Hurricanes into Croydon. [17] This was the renewal of an old link between Croydon and Canada - back in the First World War volunteers from Canada had joined the Royal Flying Corps at the then Beddington Aerodrome. Indeed, it is believed that in 1919 the former 81 Squadron RAF, redesignated No. 1 RCAF, was present at Croydon. The squadron which flew in on 4th July 1940, however, was not the same No. 1 Squadron. That had been disbanded on 1st February 1920. This was a newly-formed squadron equipped with Canadian Hurricanes. As these were not up to British standards, the squadron had been moved to Croydon to effect modifications, including camouflage and squadron markings. Their aircraft were easily recognisable by the 'YO' squadron code on the fuselage.

Throughout their stay at Croydon, the writer of their log, at least, believed Croydon to be in Middlesex, since this was how he datelined his entries.

Their time at Croydon was spent in flying and firing training, relieved by an ENSA concert on the 21st of July, and a 'smoker' in the airmen's mess on the 31st.

They do not appear to have been operational as a squadron whilst at the station; and left for Northolt on 17th August, still apparently believing themselves to have been in Middlesex all along. During their last days at Croydon they received visits from the Hon. Vincent Massey, High Commissioner for Canada; Air Commodore Walsh and Group Captain Heakes; Wing Commander Van Vleit, RCAF; Brigadier Arthur Potts of the Canadian 2nd Infantry Brigade; and Wing Commander Campbell and Major Drewey, RCAF.

Just before the Canadians left, however, Croydon experienced, on August the 15th, the most traumatic day in its history.

CHAPTER FIVE

Black Thursday

Thursday August the 15th, 1940, was a delightful sunny day, like so many of that summer. The local residents around the aerodrome went about their business and pleasure; unaware that, before the day was done, there was to be for them a bitter foretaste of the devastation that Londoners would know as "The Blitz".

From Norway to France, that day, the Luftwaffe sent out raid after raid. They flew across the North Sea to attack as far north as Newcastle; across the Channel to attack as far west as Weymouth. The day was to see the largest number of raids by the Luftwaffe of any day during the Battle of Britain: the main targets being the airfields of the RAF, and radar installations.

During the afternoon, the Germans concentrated their attacks against No. 11 Group in the south-east; and No. 111 Squadron at Croydon began what their Squadron log calls: "a period of intense activity". At 3 p.m. the Squadron commenced its first action of the day, over Dover. Attacking an enemy formation of Dornier 215s head-on, Sergeant W.L. Dymond sent down one Dornier, whilst Flight Lieutenant H.M. Ferriss and Sergeant J.T. Craig both later claimed 'probables'. Green Section turned their attention to the fighter escort, but the Me 109s refused to come down and engage the Hurricanes; so the section leader, Flight Lieutenant S.D.P. Connors, was able to attack an isolated Dornier, into which he emptied his guns with damaging effect. Blue Section, led by Squadron Leader Thompson, with Squadron Leader E.A. McNabb and Sergeant H.S. Newton, met two Dornier 215s at 16,000 feet over the Thames estuary.

This was the first time that McNabb, the C.O. of RCAF No. 1 Squadron, had been in action, and he immediately demonstrated his skills by sending one of the Dorniers crashing down into the marshes off Westgate. Thompson accounted for the other Dornier, though this aircraft managed to inflict some damage to Harry Newton's Hurricane before crashing into the Thames.

Two other pilots from 111 Squadron sustained damage to their aircraft during this engagement: Sergeant Dymond had to land at West Malling, and Flight Lieutenant Ferriss landed at Hawkinge.

The Squadron had no sooner refuelled and re-armed than they were scrambled again. This time they had been reduced to nine aircraft, and were soon without their C.O., Squadron Leader Thompson, who had to return to Croydon with engine trouble.

Directed to Thorney Island, the Squadron was to intercept an incoming enemy formation of Ju 88s with Me 110 escorts. At 15,000 feet the enemy were engaged, and what must have been an intense few minutes of fighting began. The Squadron log records the following claims:

One Ju 88 destroyed and one damaged by Flt. Lt. Connors. Three Ju 88s destroyed 'probable' by Sgt. Craig. One Ju 88 damaged by F/O B. Fisher and P/O A. Fisher and one Me 110 destroyed by Sgt. Wallace. Squadron landed Croydon 17.45/18.25 hours except P.O. McKintyre [sic: this was Pilot Officer McIntyre, a New Zealander] slightly wounded who landed at Hawkinge and F/O Fisher [in P3944] shot down in flames over Selsea [sic]. Enemy losses one Ju 88 destroyed, one Me 110 destroyed. Three Ju 88s destroyed probable. Two Ju 88s damaged. Our losses one killed and one wounded. [1]

What drama lay behind such a brief entry can only be imagined; but what is clear, is that the 'intense activity' was taking its toll of 111 Squadron, and the day was not yet over.

At 6.15 p.m. another seventy-plus aircraft were plotted coming in from France, and by 6.30 p.m. were over the English coastline and heading inland for their targets. With most of 11 Group's squadrons on the ground refuelling, only two squadrons intercepted the raiders as they crossed the coast; but this was enough to break up the enemy formation into smaller units.

One of the units was Erprobungsgruppe [Test Group] 210, a specially trained strike group led by Swiss-born Hauptmann Walter Rubensdorffer, flying two-engined Me 110 fighter bombers with an escort of Me 109s. There is some discrepancy in the reports of the number of aircraft now searching for their targets, generally believed to have been Biggin Hill and Kenley; but there were probably not less than twenty.

An air-raid warning was sent to the aerodrome at Croydon, and 111 Squadron prepared themselves for battle for the third time that day. However, no public alarm was sounded; and, as the nine Hurricanes roared across the airfield, to the west, at 6.50 p.m., the local residents would not have been unduly alarmed.

Approaching Croydon from the east, Test Group 210 - it is usually considered - mistook it for Kenley. It is difficult to imagine how such an error of identification could have occurred; but, error or not, Rubensdorffer put down the nose of his Me 110, his group moved into attack formation, and the raid on Croydon had begun.

Memories of that raid are still, as we write, extremely vivid to many people; and the event has become, over the last forty years, part of local folklore.

Mrs. Margaret Cunningham was then a teenager living in Pine Ridge, Carshalton, and remembers:

I was mowing the front lawn for my father in order to earn some extra pocket money. My mother, who was the Road Leader of the W.V.S. was standing in the front doorway of a house on the opposite side of the road, where she was discussing urgent business with another member of her organisation.

The planes had already taken off from Croydon aerodrome some while before then and were busy at their usual practice - or so we thought. Suddenly there were bursts of machine-gun fire and, on looking upwards, I saw what appeared to be one of the usual mock battles. However, on this occasion, there was a new type of plane taking part and this one had black crosses on its wings! A few empty machine gun clips started to clatter down around me, and one dropped at my feet. My first thoughts were that they were really practising in earnest this time.

For a few moments I stood in the garden enjoying the scene and completely oblivious of the danger. Suddenly I became aware that my mother was shouting instructions at me from across the road and trying to tell me to go indoors. My father opened the front door and pulled me to safety. He then tried to persuade me to get under the large mattress which stood in the corner of the front room, and was our only shelter at that time until the one in the garden had been completed. Determined not to miss the excitement I made the excuse that I needed to pay an 'urgent call' upstairs and was thus able to gain my usual favourite view-point of the back bedroom window from whence one could look across to Croydon as well as London and the Thames estuary.

As I approached the bedroom windows, I heard, for the first time, the uncanny whine of the Stuka dive-bombers, saw minute objects drop and disappear behind the distant trees in the direction of Croydon Aerodrome. Then came the 'crump' as each bomb exploded and palls of rubble and smoke rose into the sky. The curtains at the open windows jerked upwards as if unseen hands had pulled at them and released them quickly, as the blasts from the bombs came across from Purley Way. I stood fascinated and without fear - the excitement was too great! [2]

Brian Haimes, then living in Hamilton Way, had a view from his home which was just west of the airfield:

I had this very small sister who was about three, and my mother was giving her a bath and had laid out some tea for me and my brother - ham and salad - so we settled down to this while she was up in the bathroom . . . And - I'll always remember this with tremendous clarity - it would be about quarter to seven in the evening, when all of a sudden there was a terrific roar from the airfield and it was the fighters taking off. I always dashed to see this spectacle, it really was rather like some ancient cavalry charge - knights in armour - as these fellows went thundering up and away. There'd been quite a lot of this kind of thing, obviously, because of the earlier battles further south. People had been scrambled from Croydon but we knew nothing about what they were doing except that you always knew if they'd been fighting because of the black holes in the fabric in front of the gun muzzles. They were normally covered with undoped fabric which was a bright terracotta colour. This time, the aeroplanes took off to the west, and that was it as far as I was concerned - show over . . . Perhaps five or six minutes went by while we were stuffing away the ham and cos lettuce, and suddenly I heard another extraordinary noise like an aeroplane coming down out of control . . . it even motivated my mother to fling the bathroom window open and she was looking out . . . I shouted to my mother 'Look out - it's a Messerschmitt 110' - and she said, 'What's a Messerschmitt 110?', and at that moment there was the most God-awful crash. I have never heard anything like it in my life. It was as if the whole sky had split open - not just a bang but . . . very, very difficult to describe, it wasn't so much a noise as a sort of physical phenomenon, and a great gout of earth and stuff rose into the air from the gas company sports ground. This character had presumably been aiming at the hangars on the north side and the factories, and he'd missed. (I went round later to have a look and there was this great hole in the sports ground and he'd totally wasted his bomb. I think it was a 1100 kilo bomb, which was a pretty big bomb for those days, especially if you'd never heard one before.) Next thing, of course, my mother was coming down the stairs four at a time with this small child wrapped in a towel and she scrambled under the stairs . . . I hustled my small brother in there, and there was a tremendous to-do going on outside. There'd been no air-raid warning, you see. No sirens, nothing. One realises now that the fighter squadron had advance warning through their own network and they had gone off to the north-west to climb and gain height for the attack. But at the time it seemed as though local people had been deserted and given no warning - everybody thought it was outrageous. What happened in the few minutes after this first bang, I'm not too clear about, because there were these two kids to be thought of, and I felt I had to be brave and calm . . .

Anyway, as soon as I'd got these kids tucked away at the back I went to the french windows. I didn't want to miss the battle. There was another Messerschmitt 110 climbing away in the general direction of Peaks Hill and Hillcrest Road and two Hurricanes, one coming up and one going down, and I thought to myself, 'Well, there's one that's had it - he won't get very far'. I remember that there was a tremendous tinkling and clattering of spent cartridge cases. I knew very well that Tug Wilson and Bill Light, the two RAF friends of mine who were anti-aircraft gunners, had 20 millimetre Oerlikon cannons in this big emplacement where Plough Lane jutted out into the aerodrome, and I heard their cannon open up. It fired about twenty rounds and stopped and I thought, someone must have hit them; and yet there was nothing happening over there - the attack was on the north and east. [3]

Leslie Penfold, who had moved into Croydon with 615 Squadron on the very first morning of the war, was by this time at Kenley; but had returned to Croydon to make use of the sports facilities at the gas company's sports ground:

August 15th was a lovely summer day, although very hazy, and I had made arrangements with my friend, Frankie Grievson, to have an early tea and go over to Croydon on my old motorbike, for a game of tennis at the Gas Company Sports Club. We left the court at somewhere around 6.30pm and as we walked over to the clubhouse we watched a squadron take off in a very loose and ragged formation. We saw a patrolling guard and asked him what the panic was about. 'Oh', he replied, 'there's a "purple" up'. Purple was the colour code for enemy aircraft in the vicinity, but no sirens had sounded, so we ignored it. We were chatting away merrily and washing our hands when quite suddenly there was an almighty explosion. 'Christ! That was a bomb!'

As we stared at each other, we heard an aircraft in its dive and then the screaming whistle of the next bomb. We rushed into a little adjoining room, not much bigger than a cubby hole, really, and stayed there. Whether we thought it was safer there, or whether we were too scared to move, I can't remember - probably a bit of both.

Now, there was a clockwork regularity about the dive, whistle and crash procedure. The noise was incredible. Holes appeared in our roof; the window was smashed to pieces and the door hung in a drunken fashion from a split doorframe. As the whistle got closer, we crouched lower and lower, and then after the crash we would stand up, take a cigarette, then start crouching as the whistle started. After that crash we stood up and just had time to light the cigarettes before starting to crouch again. I've wondered since - 'what was the point of the crouching business?' [in fact, the danger from flying window glass, etc. was a good reason for crouching]. After what seemed an eternity, there was silence. In a dazed state we looked around to see if there were any injured in the clubhouse, which was shattered. The few people that were about seemed dazed. Then the sirens went! We went to a shelter but soon realised that the sirens were for the raid that we'd already had! There was a crocodile of ambulances and make-shift ambulances coming away from the Bourjois scent factory and Rollason's where I believe there were many casualties. We went to my motorbike, which was covered in red shale from the tennis court, skirted round a complete window frame blown out of the head groundsman's house, and left the Clubhouse. I have never been back there since.

Unfortunately, Frankie Grievson cannot give his impressions of the raid, as he was killed later in the war, when his plane crashed in Canada. [4]

In the air over Croydon, on that evening in August 1940, 111 Squadron, warned of enemy aircraft in their area, spotted them making their approach to Croydon. Squadron Leader Thompson formed his Hurricanes into line astern, and they were amongst the Me 110s before the latter reached the perimeter of the airfield. No. 32 Squadron from Biggin Hill now arrived on the scene, making some forty aircraft dog-fighting, bombing and machine gunning, over and around Croydon. All was confusion; and one Squadron Leader is reported to have said of the scene: "It was like watching the moving stairway at Piccadilly Underground Station". [5]

Squadron Leader Thompson caught an Me 110 climbing away after delivering its bombs. Bullets from his guns hit the starboard engine on the enemy aircraft, and it exploded. Thompson's next victim was an Me 109 which was chased along the Purley Way at almost zero feet. Sergeant Dymond and Sergeant Craig both shot down Me 110s, and Flight Lieutenant Connors and Sergeant T.J. Wallace claimed an Me 110 between them.

No. 32 Squadron was also having its successes. Flight Lieutenant M.N. Crossley recalled his participation in the fight:

. . . when we approached I saw a large party in progress. Masses of Me 110s were dive bombing the place. As they did not appear to notice our approach, I steered straight past them, with the object of getting between them and the sun. This was successful and we charged at them. I put a long burst into the first one I saw and he promptly caught fire and went down in flames. Then I saw another detach itself and make off, so I made after it and gave it a long burst, at which the starboard engine caught fire. I broke away and the Mandarin [a nickname for another 32 Squadron pilot] gave it a long burst and it altered course inland as if looking for somewhere to land. I nipped in and gave it another bang, and as I broke off I saw the starboard airscrew revolving slowly and then stop. Another burst from the Mandarin and one of the crew baled out and the aircraft crashed into flames in a wood near Sevenoaks. [6]

On the ground there was as much confusion as in the air. The aerodrome's defences, unlike the civilian population, had been forewarned. The Vickers machine guns and Oerlikons were quickly in action. This was the first taste of warfare, and, despite all the practice and training, must have been disorientating to many. With enemy aircraft so closely mingled with British fighters, selecting targets with accuracy was difficult; and, once the bombs started to fall and the Me 109s added the noise of their machine guns to the cacophony, the next few minutes were to embed themselves into the memories of all who witnessed them.

The extent of the damage and death inflicted by Test Group 210 on Croydon was greater than that suffered in any other raid on Britain that day. Within the airfield, the Terminal Building was hit by armour-piercing and incendiary bombs. The Armoury took a direct hit and was completely burnt out. The Control Tower was machine-gunned, and 'A' and 'D' hangars suffered minor blast damage. 'C' hangar, previously used by Rollason's, took a direct hit, which destroyed many training aircraft that it was housing.

Six airmen were killed, five of them from 111 Squadron and one from the Station HQ. Two civilian telephone operators and an airman from No. 1 Squadron RCAF were taken to hospital badly wounded.

But it was outside the airfield perimeter that the greatest havoc and destruction were caused. At the Bourjois scent and cosmetics factory, just over the northern boundary in Waddon Way, it was five minutes to seven as seventeen-year-old apprentice Bill Whitehead said 'Goodnight' to Georgie Beard, the night foreman of the soap department. Having clocked out, he stood for a few seconds on the steps of the side entrance to the factory and exchanged a few words with the relief commissionaire. In the distance he could see and hear the approaching German aircraft. "I don't like the look of those", said Bill. "Neither do I", replied the Commissionaire, "you'd better get off home son".

Bill began walking towards Stafford Road when the sound of the aircraft turned to a high-pitched scream, and they seemed to be diving straight at him. Instinct rather than reason made him run to the side of the road and crouch down beside a wall.

The first bomb made a direct hit on the soap department, instantly killing three of the four soap millers, including Georgie Beard. The only survivor was Johnny Putts, who suffered a broken neck when a milling machine fell on him, and permanent deafness from the blast.

As the aircraft came in over the industrial estate they began machine-gunning. "They came in really low," recalls Bill, "just getting their wings above the rubber company buildings. It [his survival] must have been an act of God, for the bullets were hitting the other side of the road from me, just like rain."

The relief commissionaire was not so lucky, however, for when his body was discovered after the raid, it was clear that he had died from the machine gun bullets.

When the first aircraft had passed, Bill decided to make a run for it; but such was his panic that he stumbled, cutting his knees. Uncaring, he was soon running again.

Then a bomb fell outside the Hatcham Rubber Company, and this one blew me flat on my face. I managed to get back on my feet, and ran into what used to be the Day and Night Café. It never had any doors on it; it had big canvas sheets, all in blue with black letters saying 'Day and Night Café'. There was nobody else there, they must have run over the road to Bert's café, and I dived under the counter. Then another big bomb went off, I don't know where, and the counter came down on top of me. I remember being smothered in pound notes, cream cakes and Player's cigarettes . . . shortly after, a couple of burly firemen came along and pulled me out, and, seeing me covered in blood, one of them said: 'Cor, look at his legs, he'll have to go to the hospital'. But I saw a trolley bus coming along the Stafford Road, broke free, and jumped on the bus and went home. [7]

On the opposite side of the road to the Bourjois factory was the Central Electricity Generating Board's stores; and at five minutes to seven there were five men inside, including the charge-hand, Ernest Jones (who, as a boy had delivered papers to the Royal Flying Corps on Beddington Aerodrome - see *The First Croydon Airport*). The only warning they had of the raid, he said, was the sudden shrill of the engines of the diving Me 110s. From the Stores, to Purley Way, there ran an underground cable tunnel, which was to have been used as a shelter; however, there was no time to raise the grille that covered the entrance.

We were always taught to get up against a wall, or lie down in front of a wall, so that's what we did, [recalls Ernest:] The blast from the bomb that fell outside the Bourjois factory blew in all the doors, including a heavy iron door. Eight-foot panes of glass from the roof came crashing down, scattering glass everywhere, but somehow the walls remained intact.

When it was all over I got up from the floor and realised that I had been sheltering under a great big mirror. It that had come down from the wall, it would have cut us to pieces. [8]

The factory that suffered most from the onslaught in both deaths and damage, was British N.S.F. Ltd. There were many who believed that the raid - far from being a mistake on the part of the German pilots - was, in fact, a deliberate attack upon N.S.F. The company's own history makes the following claim:

It is clear from the official records that British N.S.F. Ltd., making the small electrical components essential to aircraft production, was a selected target for this savage attack on Waddon Way. [9]

These essential components were a range of multi-pin plug and socket connectors, developed by the Royal Aircraft Establishment at Farnborough, and used for aircraft electrical harnesses.

British N.S.F. Ltd. had come to Waddon in 1932, being the off-shoot of a German company. What N.S.F. stood for seemed doubtful to us at first; nowhere did the name appear in full. Local people remembered the letters being accounted for in various ways, ranging from Nuremburg Screw Factory to National Sunday Flying ! The former is nearly correct: the German firm (which still exists) was the Nuremburg Schraube Fabrik, making screws, nuts, bolts, etc.

74

The British company still exists too, under totally different ownership as part of the Lucas Group, at Keighley in Yorkshire, as N.S.F. Switches and Controls.

At Waddon, British N.S.F. had been incorporated as a private company by two German Jewish brothers, Hans and Justin Saemann. Hans, who was the Managing Director, became a naturalised British subject. A number of German men and women were recruited from Nuremburg, including Herr Hans Lipperer, Works Manager; Herr Bitter, Chief Engineer; and Herr Graf, Electrical Engineer.

Victor Wood, who joined the company in 1934, recalls those pre-war days at N.S.F.:

> In those days the firm was making components for the radio trade: wave changers, on-off switches, tone and volume controls, wirebound and carbon resistors, tubular and electrolytic condensers. Our busy time was during the summer, with the industry building-up stocks ready for the 'Radio Show' at Olympia in the autumn and the Christmas trade.
>
> Our workforce would build-up to some 400 for this, and then cut back to about 200 during the winter. An average female wage rate would be about 4d an hour. Instrument makers about 1s 4d per hour. I started at 7d. [10]

Just before the outbreak of war, the last of the German employees, including Herr Bitter and Herr Lipperer, returned to Germany. Before departing, Hans Lipperer gave his micrometer to Vic Wood, with the comment: "I am going away for a few days, Wood. This is my micrometer and I want you to look after it for me until I return." [10]

Two German girls did not return to Germany on the outbreak of war, for they had both married local men, one of them the brother of Joss Spiller.

Joss Spiller had worked at N.S.F. since 1934, knew Hans Lipperer very well, and was surprised that when he left not a word was spoken: "I thought he would at least have said goodbye, because you can't work with someone for so long without having some respect for each other."

Whether or not the Germans who left had any idea that British N.S.F. was to undertake work for the RAF on the outbreak of war is a matter for speculation; but there is no doubt that they would have had considerable knowledge about Croydon Airport and the industrial estate which bordered on it. August the 15th, 1940, came at a time when German policy was to destroy the RAF both in the air and on the ground, to clear the way for the projected invasion of England. Although Hitler had apparently commanded that Metropolitan London was not to be attacked, Croydon Airport was an RAF Fighter Squadron base, and the nearby industrial estate was producing vital RAF radio equipment; and these facts may lead to the conclusion that the raid was deliberate rather than accidental.

Vic Wood was in the drawing office at N.S.F., and so engrossed in his work that he was taken completely by surprise by the falling bombs:

> I remember rather hazily that the building was falling down about me. Then people began running from the works past my office door and I was urging them to hurry. The next thing I remember was being outside the main entrance among several parked cars when another bomb was on its way. I dived under the nearest car, when there was an almighty explosion, and rubble began to rain down on the car, which began to squash me. I said to myself, 'Hold out, hold out, there won't be much more', then I blacked out.

The next thing I remember was sitting on a bench in the factory air raid shelter with a crowd of my workmates, and playing hell with them because they would not join me in singing 'It's a lovely day tomorrow . . .'

I was delirious from a blow on the head and I have a depression in my skull to this day! I finished up in Croydon Hospital where I spent a week before being moved to a hospital at Epsom. I had a fractured shoulder and my arm in a sling. [10]

It was two days after the raid when Vic Wood's wife - they had been married for less than a month - found him in the hospital.

Joss Spiller was in the toolroom making precision instruments when the first bomb struck.

As we had steam and impregnating boilers, my first reasoning was that they had exploded, but almost immediately I realised the terrible truth, for I heard the screaming of a bomb, if not bombs.

Mr. Parker of the machine shop was shouting 'Bloody Nazis' and everything was so black. Then there was a gush of fire and I realised that the gas main had been struck. After the second explosion I must have blacked out for I came-to under the bed of a lathe - covered with debris - which was at least 12 yards from where I had been working. I have no idea how I got there, I wasn't hurt, just a little shrapnel in my arm - I was very lucky in that respect.

You can imagine the scenes were pretty horrific to behold. Whilst doing what one could for the injured, I remember going to the aid of Jack Lake. I thought then that the poor chap was beyond help, so it was a very pleasant surprise when he eventually turned up at Keighley some months later. [11]

Amongst the many killed at N.S.F. (and Vic Woods believes the number to have been near to 35) were Hans Saemann, Bob Hutchings (Works Manager) and Miss Magraten (Secretary), who were holding a meeting in the Board Room. Ken Phillips was killed in the test room and two clerks were killed in the wages office.

British N.S.F. had been taken over on the outbreak of war by the Government; and with the destruction of its factory, the Ministry of Aircraft Production found the new premises for it - perhaps an indication of its importance - at Keighley. Twenty-two of the Croydon workers, together with families, were taken there by coach to get the new factory started, and Vic Woods recalls that "those refugees from the London bombs were not very popular with the Keighley people".

Another Croydon Airport factory which received a direct hit was that of Redwing in the most easterly hangar of 'C' block, the hangars which had been part of National Aircraft Factory No. 1, and then of the Aircraft Disposal Company. In *The Great Days* we told of the move by Redwing Aircraft Ltd. from Croydon to Blue Barns Aerodrome, Colchester, in 1932. The company also, shortly afterwards, acquired Gatwick Airport; but did not establish a factory there, using it as a flying school. After eighteen months, however, Redwing sold Gatwick, abandoned Blue Barns, and returned, in January 1934, to Croydon. They did not continue to manufacture aircraft (only twelve Redwings were ever built) but concentrated on repair and overhaul of aircraft. John K. Lane, at the outbreak of war, was Assistant General Manager, and had been with the firm since its inception; and at Croydon, with the Aircraft Disposal Company, since 1923. He died in 1981. His widow, Mrs. Phyllis Lane, writes:

During the War in its first raid by the Luftwaffe on Croydon on August 15th 1940 a 500lb bomb burst through the roof of Redwing's main hangar at the Airport causing a fire which was quickly extinguished. The seven [strong] first-aid team of the firm who were at practice when the raid began

76

were first on the scene and were able to render good service to the many injured in the raid. Employees went back into the hangar to help dismantle the Vickers aileron assembly jigs. Care had to be taken not to make too much noise like dropping tools or bits of the jigs in case the vibrations brought down more of the reinforced glass from the shattered roof.

The factory was then transferred to Bensham Lane, Thornton Heath and many other premises were used in Croydon until the end of the hostilities.

At Willet Road, Croydon, and Major Motors, Purley Way, Redwing built details, also tube bending and sand filters, for the Hawker Typhoon. The Palais de Dance, Croydon, was Production Headquarters, Planning and Tool Drawing. Three houses in Bensham Lane, Thornton Heath were used for personnel, A I D [Aircraft Inspection Department] and transport. In Brigstock Road there were four houses for hostel, Home Guard HQ, buying, accounts and Head Office. The Home Guard HQ was demolished by a direct hit from a flying bomb, killing the NCO on duty. Woolworth premises, Church Street, Croydon; the Tizer Drinks Factory; Stewart & Arden's Garage, Bensham Lane; and two houses in Coulsdon were used for storage of parts and materials. Carr's Autos was headquarters for all transport.

20 Factory [different premises, in Progress Way] on Croydon Aerodrome was used for C R O [Civilian Repair Organisation], tank repairs, and, in a nearby building said to have been a Tithe Barn [opposite The Propeller Inn], petrol tanks for Mosquitos, and Boulton and Paul Defiant ailerons. At Derwent Works, also adjoining the aerodrome, they built parts of Wellington bombers and Fairey Battle components. They also built tubular mountings for Lancasters. Some Rolls Royce Merlin engines were removed by Rolls Royce as soon as the flying bombs started . . . After the war the toolroom returned to 20 Factory at Croydon until the early 1950s when it was closed and the toolroom and tool design department returned to Bensham Lane. 12

Back on the Croydon Airport industrial estate, however, in the evening of August 15th, Ernest Jones had picked himself up from the floor of the C.E.G.B. store, where he had weathered the bombing attack.

We went outside . . . Black smoke and fire were coming up from the N.S.F. factory. I don't know how many men were in there, but I'm sure they never found many of the bodies; they couldn't have done with such a direct hit. We went back inside our Stores to make it as safe as we could, and it wasn't long before the Superintendent, Mr. A.F. Warr, who lived in Stafford Road, arrived. One of the men gave him the keys. 'What use are these?' he said, 'there isn't a door left standing in the place!'

I'm sure we were all a bit shocked, and Mr. Warr sent us home early. It was then that we saw the crowds of sightseers. There must have been hundreds and hundreds of them, the fire brigade had a blinking job to get up the road and that's the truth. They had to call in the police to shove them back. I got bloody wild and remember pushing this woman and telling her to go home. 8

The crowds were, indeed, so dense that they were said to hamper the rescue work. Brian Haimes recalls:

We went . . . along Stafford Road where the Government Training Centre and the shops are, and there were thousands of people. They had come out of their houses, great crowds, and I remember thinking: 'If the Germans come back they're really going to cause some slaughter'; and I remember seeing a lad I knew called Bernard Epps . . . and we swapped stories . . . It was while we were round there with all these thousands of people in the street that the air-raid sirens went off and I thought 'My God - are they coming back again?'. But no, it was the warning for the air-raid we'd had . . .3

After the raid, Test Group 210, having delivered their blow on Croydon, were now faced with the prospect of having to fight their way home. Turning south they went flat out for the Channel and safety. With the German aircraft from the raid at West Malling also turning for home at this time, the sky south of London was full of dogfights.

82 Squadron, led by Squadron Leader J. 'Baron' Worrall, turned their attention to the bombers, and were surprised to find the Me 109s not coming to the support of their slower compatriots. "They were not helpful to their bombers," Worrall said later. "You just waded in and did what you liked; they were killed off like frogs. It was the most murderous thing I'd taken part in." [13]

Between Test Group 210 and safety lay the Spitfires of 66 Squadron who were informed by Kenley control of the attack on Croydon and given an interception course:

Oxspring [Pilot Officer Robert Wardlow Oxspring] turned on to the course he was given, pushed the stick forward, and led the Spitfires into a screaming dive down to the ground near Redhill. Then he sighted the 110s against the skyline ahead, going flat-out for the coast, with their throttles through the 'gate' and black smoke trailing from their over-revving engines. Slowly, much too slowly, the Spitfires began to close the distance. Oxspring gave the 'Tally Ho!' call, and the course of the escaping raiders. This new procedure was designed to off-set the time-lag between a radar or Observer Corps sighting and the instruction being given to Squadrons already airborne. The lag was only a matter of minutes, but those minutes were vital at speeds like these. A controller picked up the 'Tally Ho!' and Oxspring could hear him vectoring Hurricanes into the path of the escaping Germans.

Halfway to the coast the Hurricanes intercepted, the Messerschmitts broke away to try to avoid them - and the Spitfires came screaming into the fight with throttles fully open. At about 2,000 ft a mass of aircraft unravelled across the sky, the Germans outnumbered nearly two to one. Oxspring and another pilot fastened onto a 110 until it came down - afterwards they thought they had got them all. This was not so, but nevertheless the 110s were roughly handled. [13]

It was probably in this engagement that the leader of Test Group 210, Walter Rubensdorffer, and his gunner (previously thought to have been Feldwebel Richard Ehekercher, but now established as Obergefreiter Kretzer) were killed, when their Me 110 crashed in flames near Rotherfield. A list supplied to the authors gives the names of the other German pilot casualties as Oberleutnant Fiedeler, Leutnant Koch, Leutnant Beudel and Oberleutnant Habisch; all shot down by pilots of 111 Squadron. [14]

Other aircraft which raided Croydon that day fell at Nutfield aerodrome, Hooe, Horley, Ightham, Hawkhurst and Frant.

Despite wartime censorship, the raid made headlines all over Britain the next day. *The Times,* with "Whistling Bombs on Croydon - Raiders Chased by RAF Fighters - Buildings Damaged", had a report "from our correspondent" with a Croydon dateline:

Whistling bombs were used by German raiders this evening in an attack on Croydon aerodrome. Flying at a height of more than 2,000 ft, a twin-engined bomber, escorted by a formation of six Messerschmitts, dropped a salvo of bombs in the region of Croydon Airport . . .

The Times, in common with the rest of the press, was claiming that in the raids on various parts of Britain, a total of 144 German machines had been shot down. This figure has been drastically revised by historians, as has the claim that only twenty-seven RAF fighters were lost on that day. The *Daily Mirror* (16 August 1940) set the Croydon story in the context of its front-page coverage of a peak day in the Battle of Britain:

For hour after hour through the day, and then into the night, our fighters swept against the huge raiding squadrons.

The German Air Force used more than a thousand bombers and fighters in the attacks . . .

Although the name of Croydon and many details of the raid had been widely publicised, the official communique quoted at the end of this news report still insisted on anonymity and said merely that: "At an R.A.F. aerodrome some damage was done to buildings causing a number of casualties."

On the day after the raid, sightseers were evidently still out in large numbers, and the *News Chronicle* reported, under the heading "Scarred but Cheerful Croydon":

The streets of Croydon - which got London's first taste of the Nazi bombs - were, from early morning yesterday, crowded with people who came to see the extent of the damage.

They came from little council houses which had rocked in the blast of explosions, and from nearby districts, until the green near the aerodrome looked like a Bank Holiday scene. The car park was packed . . .

I found no sign of fear, writes a *News Chronicle* reporter, only stimulation and alertness, as if people had experienced the worst and found it not as bad as they had expected . . . .

One family of four - their roof open to the sky, every window broken and their furniture buried in dust and plaster - were cheerfully singing and whistling as they cleared up the mess . . . .

Another account of the raid came from Geoffrey Dorman, a journalist who lived in South Croydon and wrote for *The Aeroplane* and for the *Croydon Advertiser*, and who was also a Flight Lieutenant in Brian Haimes' Air Cadet Squadron. Geoffrey Dorman kept a diary at the time; and these extracts were published in the *Croydon Advertiser* in 1945. It will be noticed that his account does not always agree with others as to the facts of the matter:

Thursday, August 15, 1940.

. . . The bombers came over without hindrance, a few half-hearted flak bursts greeted them but without effect. We were, evidently, taken completely off our guard. Fighters, mainly Hurricanes, engaged them on their way out but without visible effect.

I got on my bike and rode to the airfield. So far as I could see the main booking-hall building was on fire, all the glass was out of the windows, there and from the hotel, and Rollason's shed was burning furiously. A biggish bomb had fallen in the public enclosure, and Purley Way was several inches deep in rubble and chalk, and there was a chalk-dust haze hanging in the air.

It was a perfect evening without a cloud in the sky. The fire at Rollason's was burning for a long time after the raid and seemed to be spreading.

I notice that everyone has done their black-out very carefully tonight and there are not the usual chinks of light to be seen. No one at the airfield can have had any time to get to shelter as the raid was so very sudden. Bad show on our part!

Friday, August 16, 1940.

Everyone seems to have different ideas as to what happened during the raid . . . The B.B.C. said there was no military damage. If setting fire to Rollasons, burning about 100 aircraft under repair and killing about 100 people and hitting the main building where all the R.A.F. offices and armoury were, was not military damage, then what is? The armoury was burning and 'ammo' was popping all over the place when I was there.

Saturday, August 17, 1940.

B.B.C. and papers announce that 'It is learned that all bombers which raided Croydon aerodrome were destroyed'. No source of this is given. It is an 'Air Ministry News Service' item which I do not believe, not an 'Air Ministry Communique' which latter are usually substantially correct.

. . . There is little sign of damage to the administrative building from the outside, but it got an incendiary through it which did it no good. The papers make great play out of the fact that a scent factory was hit. It was, but that was only a small part of what was done. The shed, 400 yards long, housing Rollason's repair factory was gutted and several other factories were damaged severely. Surrey Flying Services' old engine shop got an incendiary through the roof. There are several craters in the playing fields which are now being turned into machine-gun posts, and a shelter at the corner of the swimming pool was demolished . . .

After an account of the raid on Kenley Aerodrome on Sunday August 18th, Mr. Dorman's diary entry for that day (as published) reads:

As at Croydon it is officially given out there is 'no damage'. If Kenley and Croydon are samples of what happens when there is 'no damage' I fear that other targets where there has also been said to have been 'no damage' must have been pretty badly hit. I feel that we are not being told the truth, as also do many other people.

There were indeed many different accounts of the casualties suffered. There was a tendency to under-estimate or exaggerate casualties according to the writer's predilections and purpose. On 15th August the BBC's nine o' clock news announced that there had been only one death, which was wildly untrue and known as such by all living locally. Similarly, as Dorman indicates, there was scepticism over the next day's newspaper claims that not a single German raider had returned home safely. In fact, the truth seems to be that seven were shot down, as we have said.

In Croydon Council's *Croydon and the Second World War*, Mr. W. C. Berwick Sayers writes:

The human results of the raid were the deaths of sixty-two persons, serious injury to thirty-seven, and lighter injuries to 137. It was the immediate policy of the Air Ministry and the Ministry of Home Security that the name of places attacked should not be published nor the number of casualties divulged. As for the place, Croydon was indeed mentioned in the wireless reports but that, it was assumed, was because no plane that took part in the raid returned to Germany to tell the story; according to report all were brought down. As for the casualties, the number was not made public and rumour multiplied them wildly as she usually does, 'a thousand deaths' being on the lips of people. Another fiction, which had brief local currency, emanating from the excitable imaginations of some people, was to the effect that passers-by the wreckage of the 'Scent Factory' a fortnight after the raid could still hear the moans of injured girls trapped beneath it. [15]

Much controversy remains over the facts of the raid. Is the final offficial figure of sixty-two civilians killed the correct one? The differing contemporarily published reports were due to the circumstances in which the raid took place, and the security and propaganda needs of the time. And, as this was the first air-raid on Metropolitan London, perhaps the procedure for recording civilian casualties was not yet fully established.

Miss Rosalind Prest who, as a Red Cross VAD nurse helped with the injured at Croydon General Hospital on the day after the raid, remembers that she was asked "to rinse out their shirts and clothes. The screws, bits of metal, etc., amongst them were horrifying and sickening . . . we were absolutely sure the numbers of killed and wounded were never officially let out." [16]

One piece of irrefutable evidence, not to the numbers killed, but to the full horror of the raid, is contained in the burial register for Saturday 24th August at Mitcham Road cemetery, Croydon. It reads: "27 portions of unidentified bodies from Croydon Airport incident."

This mass grave for the victims eventually became a memorial on which the following inscription is written: "To the memory of the men, women and children who lost their lives as the result of enemy action during the Second World War 1939-45."

The other disputes include those over the intended target for the raid, and the number and nature of the aircraft involved. On the German side, it is probable that only Messerschmitts made the attack, despite the claim for Dorniers.

Then, too, there is the question of whether or not dive-bombing, as opposed to flat trajectory bombing, was involved. The term 'Stuka' is used. This was simply the German term for 'dive-bomber', but was usually applied to the Ju 87, specially developed for this purpose.

It is unlikely that this aircraft was used, but that low-level attacks by the Messerschmitts did take place. A statement by Mr. Arthur Bridger, who at the time was an Aircraft Recognition Instructor and Roof-spotter at Clifford and Snell, electrical engineers, in Carshalton Road West, Sutton, agrees with this:

I actually witnessed the attack through my binoculars. Contrary to general opinion, the Airport was not dive-bombed, but subjected to a low-level attack carried out by Messerschmitt 110s. [17]

Over Croydon, the British squadrons fighting were equipped with Hurricanes, not Spitfires as reported by some observers. A fortnight after the raid, the *Croydon Advertiser* was moved to publish a leading article on the subject of censorship under the headline "The Truth, The Whole Truth And Nothing But The Truth." After assuring its readers that "we know, for instance, and we know for an absolute certainty, that the statements as to the punishment we have inflicted on the raiders, and the losses our gallant Air Force has suffered, attain the highest standard of accuracy since they are understatements of fact"; the article went on:

The numbers of killed and injured that are to be heard bandied about in conversation in the districts around Croydon . . . are really fantastic. There is only one way in which to silence these rumours, and that is by publishing the full casualty list. The public would certainly be agreeably surprised. People can stand up to the truth, even though it hits them hard and square between the eyes. But they will not - they cannot - willingly stand up to half the truth.

The casualty list was never published.

The local newspapers have returned to the bombing raid again and again over the years; full-length features appearing on many anniversaries - one year, twenty years, twenty-five years, etc.

References to the raid, and personal accounts, still continue to appear in the local press from time to time. In a page of general war-time reminiscences published in the *Wallington Times*, October 16th, 1980, Mrs. D. Elcombe of Pond Hill Gardens, Cheam, recalled that workers at the Philips factory were just about to go home and were changing their shoes when the raid took place. They thought the aeroplanes were British ones and were going to look at them when the foreman realised what was happening and rushed them inside:

We managed to get to the air raid shelter. It was such a terrible sight to see so many people injured, I will never forget it. My friend and I lost our shoes, and our cycles were smashed, so we had to walk all the way to Carshalton. No one would give us a lift, they were too interested to see the sight. But if they had been there they would, like us, have been longing to get away from it and get home.

After the raid many local people were left wondering why the air-raid sirens had not sounded until after the raid was over. Sir John Anderson, the Minister of Home Security, visited Croydon the next day (Friday) and was made aware of the many complaints which had been directed at Croydon Council, when he attended an A.R.P. Committee meeting at Croydon Town Hall. Mr. Ernest Taberner, the Town Clerk, was quick to point out to local people that it was the responsibility of the military authorities to control the sounding of the air-raid warnings, and: "a matter over which local authorities had no control at all."

Sir John assured the Committee that an investigation would be made, and on the following Tuesday, in response to a Question, made the following statement to the House of Commons:

It is the policy of the Government that the public air raid warnings shall be sounded only in areas where an actual attack is likely to be delivered; and it is the duty of those responsible for giving the warnings to endeavour to forecast, on the basis of their information regarding the movements of hostile aircraft and in the light of their knowledge of the enemy's probable objectives, where each particular formation of enemy aircraft may be going to drop its bombs. During the afternoon of August 15th successive waves of raiders had crossed the coast and headed towards London, but had turned away before reaching the Metropolitan area.

Shortly before 7 in the evening another raid was reported to be approaching London from the same direction. A few moments later it was reported to have turned away as the earlier raids had done. In the light of what had happened earlier in the afternoon, it appeared that the threatened attack on the London area would not materialise, and Fighter Command decided to withhold the order for the sounding of the public warning. Subsequently however a portion of the enemy formation broke away from the others, changed their direction suddenly and delivered their attack on Croydon. Some minutes later the public warning was given in London, not as the result of the bombs having fallen in Croydon, but because this enemy formation had changed its direction and was flying on a course which suggested that it might after all deliver an attack on the Metropolitan area.

The officers operating the warning system have a heavy responsibility - (cheers) - and an unenviable task in exercising the discretion which has been entrusted to them. They cannot be infallible; and on this occasion their judgement of the probable course of the raid, which they formed on the best information available, was proved by the event to have been mistaken. I deeply regret the loss of life and the injuries sustained in this raid, and I am sure the House would wish to join me in extending our heartfelt sympathy to the relatives of those who were killed, and in wishing a speedy recovery to the injured. (Hear, hear.) [18]

Perhaps this statement by Sir John was the origin of the belief that the raid on Croydon was a mistake, and that Erprobungsgruppe 210, who pressed home their attack with such severe ferocity, despite coming under attack by air and land, should never have been at Croydon at all.

Despite exaggerations, the losses of the Luftwaffe on the day of the major attack on Croydon were heavy. For them, the 13th of August was to have been *Adler Tag* - Eagle Day - the day when Britain's air strength was finally crushed. Instead, two days later, the 15th of August, it was to the Luftwaffe that the day Croydon was raided became known as *Schwarzer Donnerstag* - Black Thursday.

CHAPTER SIX

The Battle Rages

Despite the traumatic experiences of Thursday evening, there could be no respite at Croydon from the battle on the next day. While searches continued through the rubble that had been the Bourjois and British NSF factories, the Canadian Squadron, No. 1, flew its Hurricanes to Northolt, where they became operational for the first time. One had been lost on the ground in the bombing of the day before.

Just before midday, 111 Squadron took off for Hawkinge, but were ordered to Dungeness, where they met a formation of some 200 Dorniers and their Me 109 fighter escorts.

Red and Blue sections went into the attack head-on, and Flight Lieutenant Henry M. Ferriss, DFC, appeared to fail to throttle-back enough, surged forward ahead of the Squadron, and collided with one of the leading Dorniers. There was a huge explosion followed by hundreds of small pieces of aircraft falling through the enemy formation to the ground, thousands of feet below. Hurricane R4193, or what was left of it, crashed on Sheephurst Farm near Marden in Kent. What remained of the Dornier, 7/KG 76, fell at Brenchley near Paddock Wood. Henry Ferriss is buried at St. Mary's Church, Chislehurst. The farmer at Sheephurst Farm planted a young tree in the crater left by Ferriss's Hurricane, and it is still growing there today. [1]

Also shot down during this engagement was Sergeant R. Carnall. Although he managed to bale out successfully, he was burnt by the fire from his Hurricane.

Squadron Leader Thompson brought down a Dornier south of the Tonbridge-Ashford railway line, and Sergeant J. T. Craig also destroyed a Dornier, which crashed near Tunbridge Wells. Pilot Officer J. A. Walker claimed an Me 109, and Sergeant T. J. Wallace, who unsuccessfully chased a Dornier back to the French coast, was jumped by six Me 109s on his way home. However, he not only avoided being shot down, but managed to bring down one of his attackers before escaping. [2]

Sunday August 18th was the day when the Luftwaffe made attacks on the primary bases of No. 11 Group, including those at Kenley and Biggin Hill, both of which housed the all-important Sector operations rooms. The raid on Kenley was to be a two-pronged attack, a high-level attack by Junkers 88s and a low-level attack by Dornier 17s with Me 109s giving fighter cover.

In command at Kenley was Wing Commander Thomas Prickman, and, as he studied the plot shortly before one o'clock that Sunday afternoon, it seemed clear that a co-ordinated attack upon his airfield was under way. He ordered all the fighters still on the ground at Kenley, and 111 Squadron at Croydon, into the air in a 'survival scramble'. [3]

At five minutes past one (as the Station air-raid warning sounded) the twelve Hurricanes of 111 Squadron were in the air and climbing to 3,000 feet. With the two Kenley squadrons, 64 and 615, preparing to meet the incoming high-level attack, it was left to 111 Squadron to meet the Dorniers.

Twenty minutes later, with Kenley in their sights, the Dorniers fanned out into attack formation but the Hurricanes were on their tails and closing fast. Flight Lieutenant Stanley Connors led the attack, and with his number two, Pilot Officer Peter Simpson, was seen to fly between three Dorniers and to head away safely. The ground defences at Kenley, Bofors 3-inch and Lewis guns, began firing as the attack swept in, and it is unclear whether it was the Dorniers or the ground defences which hit Flight Lieutenant Connors' aircraft. But hit he was, and in attempting to get back to Croydon he crashed and was killed.

With the Dorniers flying so low, eighteen-years-old Peter Simpson found that having passed the enemy he had no alternative but to break away sideways, presenting to the German gunners a clear view of the belly of his Hurricane, an opportunity of which they took full advantage. The damage to the Hurricane was such that Simpson decided to make a forced landing, which he managed successfully on the practice fairway of the Royal Automobile Club golf course at Woodcote Park (Epsom).

Sergeant Harry Newton, flying Hurricane P3943, was another young pilot of 111 Squadron doing battle over Kenley. Alfred J. Price in his book *The Battle of Britain: The Hardest Day*, recounts Harry Newton's experience:

Sergeant Harry Newton had become separated from the rest of the aircraft of No. 111 Squadron, and was orbiting to the east of Kenley at 3,000 feet. Suddenly his attention was caught by the sight of a stick of bombs exploding across a row of houses. 'For the first time in my young life - I was 19 years old - I realised what war really meant. Then I caught sight of a Dornier, low down. I remember thinking: "Here's one that won't get back!"'. In fact the Dornier was that flown by Guenther Ungar. Limping away from Kenley with one engine shot out, Ungar had released his bombs on the airfield during the low altitude attack; those Newton had seen exploding had come from the high-altitude raiding force. Newton slid back his cockpit hood, so that it could not jam shut and trap him inside if it was hit, then pushed down his aircraft's nose and swooped down to attack.

Ungar's rear gunner, Unteroffizier Franz Bergman, had seen the Hurricane curving after him and swung his machine gun to engage. Newton saw the tracer rounds coming towards him but thought, 'You've got one gun, I've got eight - you don't stand a chance!' He fired one burst at the Dornier but the tracer seemed to go over its starboard wing tip. Newton continued, 'I thought, "Just a slight correction and I've got him!" But just at that moment he got me, because my cockpit seemed to burst into flames.' With his hood open, the slipstream drew the flames backwards and upwards, right over the unfortunate pilot. Then the oxygen in his mask caught fire, burning it on to his face. 'Strangely, I do not remember feeling any heat though I suppose I must have since my face was pretty badly burnt. I closed my eyes tightly - I wasn't going blind for anyone. But I was so annoyed at the thought of that Dornier getting away that I put my hand back into the flames, groped for the stick, made my correction and then loosed off a long burst in the direction of where I thought the Dornier was.'

Then Newton pulled his Hurricane into a climb, to gain height so that he could bale out. On the way up he could feel the flames all around him. They burnt through the three pairs of gloves he was wearing, through his flying suit and his trousers. As he felt the Hurricane going up he undid his seat straps and stood on his seat, braced against the canopy rather like a jockey, still with his eyes tightly shut. The Hurricane got slower and slower then, suddenly, the engine cut. Newton kicked the stick forwards, at the same time throwing himself to the left and pulling the ripcord. 'At that moment I opened my eyes, in time to see the tail of my Hurricane flash past my right ear, about a foot away. The next thing I knew the parachute had opened and the ground was coming up to meet me.' Newton looked down, to see a reception committee waiting for him: about fifteen soldiers, their bayonets fixed and rifles pointing straight at him. He shouted at them, 'Put those bloody things down! I'm on your side!' The soldiers did. During the descent one of his boots fell off, the laces burnt away. He made a perfect landing near Tatsfield Beacon in Surrey, knocked his release box, and the parachute came away cleanly and sailed off into a nearby hedge. About 50 yards away lay a burning heap of wreckage which, less than a minute earlier, had been a perfectly serviceable Hurricane.

. . . Harry Newton was picked up by the soldiers and helped to a nearby pillobx to await an ambulance. He was a ghastly apparition, with one boot missing and the whole of his face, hands and clothing burnt or charred. As he shuffled along the road he passed a young couple who had been out for a Sunday ride on their tandem bicycle. On seeing Newton, the girl collapsed in a faint. Newton asked the soldier helping him what was wrong with the girl. The man replied, as gently as he could, that the reason for the young lady's distress was the pilot's terrible appearance. [3]

The final casualty that day to 111 Squadron was Sergeant Harry Deacon in his Hurricane N2340, who unfortunately was brought down by the ground defences at Kenley.

The Squadron log claims that a Dornier fell victim to Deacon's guns, and he was certainly in the thick of the fighting because he sustained serious leg injuries during the battle. Attempting to fly back to Croydon he flew low over Kenley, when suddenly part of his right wing was shot away by the Kenley gunners, and Deacon was fortunate to survive parachuting from his Hurricane at such a low altitude.

The Hurricanes of No. 32 Squadron from Biggin Hill met the Dorniers of Bomber Geschwader 76 on their approach to Kenley. Squadron Leader Mike Crossley led his pilots into a head-on attack, and forced several of the aircraft to abandon their attack on Kenley and select other targets, one of which was Croydon. [3]

According to the station log, one large high explosive bomb and ten medium-explosive ones, together with indendiary bombs and eight delayed-action bombs fell on Croydon. There was one fatal casualty - a soldier.

Croydon's log records the damage of August 18th at the station as:

'A' hangar damaged by medium-sized bomb and incendiary bomb penetrating roof and exploding inside. Two craters on edge of tarmac close by main building. One bomb in middle of main building. One bomb on roadway between guard-room and airmen's cookhouse, adjacent to Purley Way. Two bombs beyond aerodrome boundary, Purley Way side, on playing fields.

One Hurricane of 111 Squadron was destroyed in 'A' hangar, and one damaged.

Croydon's ground defences were obviously at a high state of alert. With a major battle being fought just over the hill at Kenley, and at Biggin Hill to the south-east, and themselves being bombed by Dorniers, fingers were no doubt very firmly around triggers. For Pilot Officer David Looker of 615 Squadron, Croydon appeared a very welcome place to put down his severely-damaged Hurricane. This was not his usual machine but a reserve Hurricane, now obsolete, from the first production batch of fifty. Looker, unable to make it back to his home base at

Kenley, had in fact been on the point of baling out when he spotted Croydon (where he had been stationed with 615 at the beginning of the war); but, seeing it, he put down his undercarriage, and approached by flying over Purley Way between the control tower and the Aerodrome Hotel. At this point the fingers squeezed the triggers, and Looker's Hurricane was bombarded mercilessly; and he crashed onto the airfield. David Looker remembers that he had not stopped to refasten his safety harness when he changed his mind about baling out. So severe was the concussion suffered by him that he spent the next month in hospital and was unable to remember exactly what happened after his crash. A sequel is told by Philip Burden in the *RAF Flying Review:*

Looker was resigned to regarding the events which followed his crash as a mystery, but enlightenment came in an unexpected manner. He rejoined his squadron which by that time was operating from Prestwick and, in December, 1940, was posted to Canada as a staff pilot in the Empire Training Scheme. There he met an officer who had been Camp Commandant at Croydon. 'Over a drink, this chap began to tell me about some fool who had crash-landed at Croydon', Looker recalls today. 'Obviously this chap didn't realise it was me and he went on to say how he had later put in a strong complaint because he had not been told that Croydon was to be used as an emergency landing field. Apparently this complaint so upset Fighter Command that, according to this officer, he was transferred to Iceland!'

Looker explained that he was the chap who had messed up Croydon Aerodrome and was able to convince the ex-commandant that his landing had been more than urgent.

After the Croydon crash-landing, Looker's Hurricane went to No. 13 Maintenance Unit on August 25th 1940, and was later stored by Maintenance Command on behalf of the Air Ministry Air Historical Branch. It was transferred from the AHB to the Science Museum in 1954 and remained in storage until two years ago when it was reconditioned by Hawkers.[4] [It is now on view in the Science Museum.]

At Croydon, on August the 19th, the Station log says: "Personnel of Station Headquarters and Sections removed from Main Buildings on the aerodrome to neighbouring houses at points dispersed around the airfield." These were houses that had been requisitioned by the RAF.

According to correspondence relating to this requisitioning, now in the Public Record Office, houses in Foresters Drive, Plough Lane, Link Lane, Redford Avenue, Church Hill, Foxley Lane, Silver Lane, Waterer Rise, Carleton Avenue, The Newlands, Great Woodcote Park and Waddon Way were used. Cumnor House School was also requisitioned. A note in the file relating to this correspondence states that number 93 Link Lane was requisitioned on July 17th 1940 but never used due to bomb damage - presumably this damage was inflicted in the raid of August 15th. [5]

Local families had, of course, moved out prior to the requisitioning and were not able to regain their homes until 1945; and sometimes then only as a result of much tussling with RAF officials.

It is perhaps worth noting here that the accommodation in these houses must have varied considerably: Waddon Way, for instance, forms part of a Council estate whilst Silver Lane is one of the most expensive residential areas of Purley.

August 19th must have been a busy day. In addition to the movement of airmen to their new homes in Wallington, Waddon and Purley, a new squadron arrived at the Aerodrome. This was No. 85 under the command of Squadron Leader Peter Townsend, who was later to become equerry to King George VI and to have a much-publicised romance with Princess Margaret. He records in his autobiography:

> My squadron was now moved up to Croyddon, in the forefront of the battle. Of the twenty pilots I led to Croydon on the 19 August, fourteen, including me, were shot down within the next two weeks, two of them twice. The number in itself looks insignificant; never, in fact, did the RAF lose more than a few dozen fighter-pilots in a day. Yet, during these crucial weeks such losses, especially in experienced pilots, began to spell defeat. As reinforcements came pilots from other commands, from the Navy, too, and the flying schools - the latter, boys hardly past their teens, brave as lions but tenderfeet. Our battle was a small one but on its outcome depended the fate of the western world. 6

By this time the aerodromes of Southern England were known by everyone to be the front-line of the battle. A legend was being born - that of the tiny group of British pilots battling against overwhelming odds. On August 20th Churchill had declared: "Never in the field of human conflict was so much owed by so many to so few". But, as Peter Townsend recalls:

> No such thoughts ever bothered us. Obviously we knew we had to win; but, more than that, we were somehow certain that we could not lose. I think it had something to do with England. Miles up in the sky, we fighter pilots could see more of England than any other of England's defenders had ever seen before. Beneath us stretched our beloved country, with its green hills and valleys, lush pastures and villages clustering round an ancient church. Yes, it was a help to have England there below.
>
> She was behind us, too. When, at the end of the day, we touched down and slipped out for a beer at the local, people were warm and wonderfully encouraging. They were for us, the fighter boys, who had once been the bad boys, who supposedly drank too much and drove too fast. Now people realised that, on the job, we were professionals. They rooted for us as if we were the home team, and we knew we had to win, if only for them. 6

85 Squadron had replaced 111 Squadron at Croydon. Having been in the thick of the fighting since May, Treble One were to be given a chance to recuperate at Debden, though only briefly, for they returned to Croydon on September 3rd.

Two days after the arrival of 85 Squadron, Croydon had a royal visit when the Duke of Kent, younger brother of the King, toured the station. He was himself in the RAF, and was tragically to lose his life later in the war. It is presumably of this Royal visit that Wilf Nicoll writes:

> On August 25 [sic] the squadron returned from a scramble to discover that His Royal Highness the Duke of Kent had chosen this particular day for a visit to the old airport but had missed the take-off. On their return the pilots were introduced to the Duke by Peter Townsend - complete with toothbrush sticking out of his top pocket, such had been the rapidity of the scramble. 7

The bright and sunny weather faltered on August 22nd and 23rd, bringing a brief lull to the fighting.

Colin Perry, then a teenager living in Tooting, visited Croydon Aerodrome on the afternoon of August 22nd, and wrote in his diary (since published as *Boy in the Blitz*):

> On to Foresters Drive; here a superb panorama is obtainable, and I wandered down to the barbed-wire fencing, just a few feet from rows and rows of fighters. One, camouflaged with a greenish-brown net, had evidently recently been in action, for the rudder and part of the fuselage were shot away. The pilots and ground staff were lounging around their respective charges, some muffled in raincoats, others with just their ordinary uniform carelessly worn over a navy blue polo. It was a very grey, dull, typical Autumn day, and hardly weather to suit the Luftwaffe. 8

Croydon snowed-in in January 1940.

48. *ABOVE:* A Blenheim, probably of 92 Squadron, parked south of the new hangars: D Hangar block to the left, and the little hangar known as 'The Glove Hangar' to the right.

49. *BELOW:* The location is immediately south of that in the first picture, as shown by the curved railings visible in both.

50. Blenheim K 7165, flown by Pilot Officer A. Elson, of 145 Squadron, which made a forced landing on some waste ground north of The Drive, Wallington, on 23rd February, 1940 (see p. 38). Houses in The Drive are seen in the background.

51. & 52.   Two photographs showing the aftermath of the crash onto No. 45 Foresters Drive by the Bristol Blenheim flown by Pilot Officer Whitmarsh of 145 Squadron on 24th February, 1940.

53. Seven Spitfires lined up at Croydon. The nose and port wing of a Blenheim are seen on the left. The Spitfires bear no squadron identification but may well be the eight which 92 Squadron collected from Cosford on March 5th 1940 (see p. 40) to replace their Blenheims.

54. *ABOVE:* A Hurricane Mk.I of 145 Squadron (N.246) 'pegged-out' on the aerodrome in March 1940, with a drape covering its cockpit. This was the month in which 145 Squadron converted to Hurricanes from Blenheims.

55. *BELOW:* A Hurricane Mk.II at Croydon in March 1940. It bears no squadron identification.

56. Squadron Leader R. R. (Bob) Stanford-Tuck, DSO, DFC and Bar, who, as a Flight Lieutenant, was with 92 Squadron at Croydon in May 1940. Here he is seen at North Weald in November 1940, commanding No. 257 Squadron which was 'adopted' by Burma.

93

57. *LEFT*: Blenheim bomber in the snow at Croydon in January 1940, rumoured to be the aircraft of Squadron Leader Roger Bushell of 92 Squadron; despite the maple leaf on the nose, which suggests a Canadian pilot. A close inspection shows a winged sword, repeated three times, on the maple leaf. A winged sword was the badge of 601 Squadron, who were flying Blenheims at this time and were stationed at Biggin Hill before 29th December 1939, and Tangmere after that; and this is probably a visitor from that squadron. (see p. 36).

58. *RIGHT*: Lloyd C. ('Digger') Ifould, Imperial Airways/BOAC Manager in Paris until the fall of France. He witnessed the raid on Le Bourget in which the A. W. Ensign *Ettrick* was caught (see p. 50). Here he looks at a plaque commemorating the occasion in 1926 when he was Flight Engineer on the first royal flight operated by any British airline.

On the 24th the clouds cleared and the Germans renewed their attack. Now there was to be bombing at night in addition to 'dog-fights' during the day. The air-raid warning was sounded twice at Croydon on the night of August 25th though no bombs fell on the aerodrome; the next night, however, a bomb fell at 85 Squadron's dispersal point, destroying a Hurricane. Two other Hurricanes were damaged. [9] 85 Squadron's log book, however, lists what appears to be the same incident, involving a 'B' Flight aircraft, as happening "during the night" of 23rd August.[10] Other bombs fell near the public air-raid shelter in Foresters Drive, and at other points including the vicinity of the hapless Bourjois factory. There had not been time to sound the siren.

The official report (in the station record) said that the aircraft was, "from bomb fragments known not to be Heinkel". The type of attack was: "gliding attack. Bombs dropped from approximately 6,000 to 8,000 feet in series of three." [9]

Wilf Nicoll describes the raid thus:

On Monday, August 26, at 1.32 a.m. a solitary aircraft throbbed its way around the station for about three minutes at a great height. Eventually it made three gliding attacks, dropping a number of small bombs each time. On the first, three bombs fell: one west of Foresters Drive, one to the east of Foresters Drive close to a public shelter and the third on the west side of the aerodrome near Round Shaw [this, of course, was Round Shaw Park, not the post-war Roundshaw Estate]. During the second attack a number of bombs fell between Nos. 1 and 7 gun posts, while the third group of bombs fell in the vicinity of Waddon. There were no casualties but one Hurricane was destroyed by fire resulting from a bomb splinter in the petrol tank. Two more Hurricanes were damaged but repairable. The raider left on a sweet note, however, as for days afterwards the air of Croydon was redolent with the scent of 'Evening in Paris'. The bombs dropped at Waddon had hit the Bourjois scent factory! It was reported afterwards that the door of a lighted room had been seen opening and shutting at erratic intervals, although whether or not as a signal was never established despite extensive enquiries by the Special Investigation Branch and the local CID. [7]

Later that day Peter Townsend led the Hurricanes of 85 Squadron into action over Maidstone. A formation of Dornier 215s with their usual escort of Me 109s were attacked head-on which resulted in the enemy formation being broken up and the subsequent loss of three of their aircraft.

A three-second burst from the guns of Pilot Officer 'Sammy' Allard's Hurricane was sufficient to bring down one Dornier, which managed to make a successful landing on the aerodrome at Rochford. A second Dornier attempted to escape to sea, but with one engine dead and pieces falling off the aircraft it returned to land and made a pancake landing east of Eastchurch. A third Dornier was not so lucky and crashed into the sea off Foulness.

Pilot Officer Geoffrey 'Sammy' Allard, DFC, DFM and bar, was undoubtedly the most successful pilot of 85 Squadron during the period of the Battle of Britain.

Allard was born in York in 1912 and joined the RAF on September 3rd 1929 - exactly ten years before the Second World War began. He entered Halton as an apprentice, under the scheme started by Hugh Trenchard for boys of 'good education and physical health'; thereby becoming a 'Trenchard Brat' as the older regulars termed airmen commencing in this way. He trained and qualified as a rigger; but his real ambition was to fly, and in 1936 he succeeded in gaining acceptance at the Bristol Flying School at Filton, graduating as a Sergeant Pilot in 1937. He was posted to 85 Squadron at Debden, flying Gladiators. In 1940 he flew Hurricanes in France with 85, and came with them to Croydon in August.

During a nine day period starting on August 24th Allard was credited with the destruction of ten enemy aircraft and three probables. The citation for his DFC credits Allard with a total of seventeen aircraft, though his own combat reports add up to twenty-one destroyed and a share in the destruction of two others.

Allard was tragically killed in an accident at Kirton-in-Lindsay in March 1941 when, shortly after take-off, his Havoc stalled and spun into the ground.

On August 28th Prime Minister Winston Churchill was on a tour of inspection of the south-east coastal defences and was to witness one of 85 Squadron's most successful engagements.

Attacking an incoming raid of about twenty Me 109s over Dungeness the Squadron claimed six enemy fighters destroyed, of which Sammy Allard claimed two. The first plunged into the sea just outside Folkestone Harbour and the second crashed five miles north of St. Ingelvert.

The success of the 28th was quickly followed by a day on which the squadron was to see action twice, resulting in the death of Flight Lieutenant H. R. Hamilton and the loss of three Hurricanes.

The first contact came about 4 p.m. over the Hastings-Beachy Head area. The enemy aircraft, estimated at between two and three hundred, appeared to the pilots of 85 Squadron to be unwilling to engage in combat. One or two would leave the main formation and dive on 85 Squadron in an attempt to trap an unwary pilot. The squadron log records that "one or two Hurricanes accepted the bait and in spite of warnings were promptly set on."

Two of the pilots to be "set on" were Sergeant F.R. Walker Smith, who managed to bale out successfully despite being hit in the foot, and Sergeant J.H.M. Ellis who had to bale out at 1,000 feet and landed safely near Battle.

Some revenge was inflicted on the enemy, however. Squadron Leader Townsend brought down an Me 109 as did Flight Lieutenant H.R. Hamilton, claiming his last victim. At 6.15 p.m. the Squadron was airborne again and, climbing through 24,000 feet, north of Dungeness, they were joined by a Spitfire and Hurricane "weaving behind flank sections". [10] Warned of enemy aircraft to their north the squadron wheeled to attempt an interception and were followed by the two strangers. What happened next is perhaps best told in the words of the squadron log:

> While circling Red 3 (Pilot Officer W.T. Hodgson) suddenly shouted a warning that enemy aircraft were behind. These turned out to be 3 Me 109s, the leader of which was not identified until he was within range on account of the previous presence of the Spitfire and the strong resemblance at a certain distance of a Spitfire to a Me 109 from front view.

With reference to the Spitfire mentioned, a memorandum based on Squadron Leader Townsend's report of this combat was forwarded with a request that it should be circulated to all interested parties without delay. [10]

The consequences of this confusion of identity was that Flight Lieutenant Hamilton's Hurricane had most of its tail unit blown off and part of the starboard wing tip. The crippled Hurricane flipped over and spiralled down to the ground. The body of Flight Lieutenant Hamilton was subsequently found near Winchelsea.

Whether or not the mysterious Spitfire and Hurricane were in fact Me 109s all the time cannot of course be ascertained; but the perils of not keeping a close watch on one's tail were certainly brought home with devastating consequences to 85 Squadron.

The 30th of August showed no respite, and by 11 o'clock that morning 85 Squadron were preparing themselves for a head-on attack out of the sun on a formation of Heinkels. The initial attack had the desired effect of dispersing the enemy, and a general dog-fight ensued, with some Me 109s joining in. Sammy Allard once again did the 'double', sending two Heinkels crashing to the ground, and the Squadron claimed a total of six Me 110s destroyed, as well as Allard's two Heinkels, for the loss of only one Hurricane. "Pilot Officer Marshall was badly shot up and obliged to bale out." [10]

The final day of August was to be for the RAF the day when it was to suffer its highest losses: 39 fighters shot down with the loss of 14 pilots.

Just after midday, over 100 German aircraft crossed the coast at Dungeness and split into two attack forces, one of which had as its targets Croydon and Biggin Hill.

The pilots of 85 Squadron were in the middle of their lunch when the 'scramble' order was given. The twelve Hurricanes were all but airborne when the first bombs exploded on the airfield.

Another hit was made on the Redwing Aircraft hangar (now vacated) as well as the Redwing shelters which fortunately were unoccupied. One bomb exploded in the middle of Purley Way, directly opposite the main gates and a further thirteen bombs fell harmlessly on the open land across the other side of Purley Way. A soldier in the Royal Artillery was injured, and a new Dennis 30cwt lorry was destroyed; but on the whole, damage from the attack was relatively light. [9]

For Squadron Leader Peter Townsend, however, this attack upon his home station was something of a last straw.

> I never felt any particular hatred for the German airmen, only anger. This time, though, I was so blind with fury that I felt things must end badly for me. But I was too weary and too strung-up to care. For a few thrilling moments, I fenced with a crowd of Messerschmitts. Then, inevitably, one of them got me. My poor Hurricane staggered under the volley, my foot was hit. [6]

The squadron leader, with his engine dead, and over a densely wooded area, had no alternative but to bale out. He was quickly picked up by the police at Hawkhurst, taken to the cottage hospital, and subsequently transferred to Croydon Hospital where, as 85's log notes, the nose cap of the cannon shell was extracted from his left foot and his big toe was amputated.

The Hawkhurst police put Squadron Leader Townsend's parachute on display and raised £3 for the Spitfire Fund, a gesture perhaps not appreciated by the Hurricane pilots of 85 Squadron.

Croydon Hospital also received another casualty from the squadron, Pilot Officer Worrall. He, too, was wounded in the leg when his Hurricane had its rudder bar and elevator controls blown away by cannon shells. Despite his injury he managed to bale out and landed safely at Benenden.

In exchange for their two lost Hurricanes, the squadron claimed two Me 109s and one Me 110 destroyed.

85 Squadron's ten remaining Hurricanes were ordered into the air again at 5.10 p.m. and thirty minutes later were engaging thirty Do 215s over the Thames estuary at Purfleet. Diving into the enemy formation in sections in line astern they separated the Dorniers from their fighter escort. Pilot Officer Hodgson attacked a Dornier head-on and saw pieces falling off the nose and starboard wing and then immediately managed to get a long burst of fire into an Me 109 which went down with its engine aflame, crashing near the Thameshaven oil storage tanks. This attack on the Me 109 brought instant retribution, however, and Hodgson's Hurricane was hit by cannon fire, blowing away his oil lines and glycol tank and setting fire to the engine. Struggling to get out of his cockpit he realised that not only was he over a densely populated area but very near to the oil storage tanks, so instead of baling out he struggled to regain control of the Hurricane and by skilful sideslipping he succeeded in preventing the fire from reaching the cockpit and finally made a crash landing in a field near Shotgate, Essex, narrowly missing wires and other obstacles erected to prevent enemy aircraft from landing.

Sergeant Booth, attacking an Me 110, saw the enemy dive away and followed it down. The pursuit continued down for some 5,000 feet until, noticing the fabric seams on his wings were coming apart and his air-speed indicator was registering 400 m.p.h., Booth wisely broke off the engagement. [10]

The squadron had had its successes, and the log records three Me 109s destroyed, three Dorniers 'probable' and two damaged.

Back at Croydon, 85's remaining Hurricanes, now reduced to nine, were refuelled and re-armed, and at 7.15 p.m. were ordered to intercept the raiding force coded 18 C. The squadron spotted anti-aircraft fire coming from Dover, so they circled out to sea and were able to launch a surprise rear attack upon nine Me 109s. Four of the Me 109s fell to the guns of 85 Squadron, and on returning to Croydon the final entry in the squadron's log could read, "Our losses: NIL."

After a day such as this, it is not surprising that Peter Townsend was later to recall:

By the end of August the Luftwaffe, by sheer weight of numbers - four to one in their favour - was wearing us down; we were weary beyond caring, our nerves tautened to breaking point. [6]

CHAPTER SEVEN

The Battle is Won

As September 1st dawned, Dowding's squadrons were suffering from mounting losses, and the surviving pilots from severe fatigue. The Luftwaffe was concentrating its efforts on the destruction of Fighter Command's bases, which meant that even on the ground there was little respite from the battle. Raiders were arriving with depressing regularity, and the question arose as to just how long the squadrons of No. 11 Group could continue to operate under such a bombardment.

Just before 8 a.m., as the pilots and ground crews gathered at their dispersal points to ready themselves for another day's fighting, the Spitfires of 72 Squadron touched down at what was to be their new 'home'. Their arrival was perhaps greeted with some surprise by 85 Squadron, for it was not part of a planned rotation of squadrons, but a result of the incessant raids on the sector headquarters at Biggin Hill. Five attacks in two days had meant that it was impossible for all three squadrons based at Biggin Hill to continue to operate; the final raid on the 31st of August had destroyed the operations block.

No. 72 Squadron's commanding officer, Squadron Leader A.R. Collins, had little time to familiarise himself with his base; by 11 o'clock his squadron of fifteen Spitfires was intercepting a formation of Heinkels at 30,000 feet over Tunbridge Wells. Although the squadron claimed a Heinkel and an Me 109, Pilot Officer R.A. 'Happy' Thomson was injured, and Pilot Officer Oswald Pigg was killed. [1]

No. 85 Squadron, led by Sammy Allard, was also in action before midday, attacking nine Me 109s off Dover. Allard and Sergeant Goodman both claimed an Me 109 destroyed, though Goodman's Hurricane was so badly damaged that it was declared unserviceable on landing. [2]

Only ten Spitfires were available to 72 Squadron for their second mission at 12.50 p.m., and again they lost another pilot, Sergeant Pocock, who was badly wounded during an attack on a formation of Me 110s. [1]

In the afternoon, 85 Squadron's eleven serviceable Hurricanes took off again, this time to intercept enemy aircraft reported approaching, and sighted an estimated 150 to 200 aircraft near Biggin Hill.

In this engagement, Allard forced down a Dornier 17 near Lydd; then his oil pressure dropped and he had to land at Lympne with a dead engine. Whilst this was being repaired, the aerodrome was bombed and the machine damaged, one of the mechanics working on it being killed. Pilot Officer C.E. English (who was later to transfer to 605 Squadron - soon to arrive at Croydon - and to die whilst serving with them) put the starboard engine of a Dornier 215 out of action and watched the machine 'pancake' into a field on Romney Marsh.

Another pilot, Sergeant Evans, saw an enemy aircraft dive down, with smoke pouring from it after he had attacked it: "actual point of crash not seen as Sgt. Evans was attacked by more Me 109s immediately afterwards" as the squadron log reported. [2] Sergeant Evans was then to claim another kill; he attacked an Me 110 and saw that both engines were on fire and the aircraft staggering out of control when he was again attacked himself and so was not able to see where his victim crashed.

The squadron log then records an attack on a Dornier 215 which went down "with black and white smoke coming out. Shortly afterwards two parachutes were seen descending in the same area and a large column of black smoke seen coming from the ground where E/A crashed - position a little south of Tunbridge Wells." The British pilot this time was Sergeant Howes. The aircraft of a fifth pilot, Flying Officer Gower, was raked by cannon shell and he was forced to bale out, his Hurricane crashing near Oxted. He landed by parachute, his hands severely burned and with other wounds, in the grounds of a hospital at Caterham. [2]

Particularly tragic was the fate of Sergeant Pilot Glendon Booth, whose aircraft was also damaged by cannon shell. Glendon Bulmer Booth's family lived at Sydenham. He attended Brockley County School and later worked for the County of London Electricity Company. He joined the Royal Air Force Volunteer Reserve in 1938, was called-up at the beginning of 1939, and posted to 85 Squadron in July 1940. The squadron was then at Debden.

During the combat of September the 1st, Glendon Booth was forced to bale out of his aircraft, and fell heavily, owing to a damaged parachute. His Hurricane crashed at Sanderstead, and he fell into a rose-arch in the garden of a house in Littleheath Road, Selsdon. He was taken to Purley Hospital with burns, a badly-injured spine, and leg wounds. Glendon Booth lingered in agony for five months, before dying on the 7th of February 1941. He was twenty years old. His funeral took place on the 13th February and he was buried in Elmers End cemetery. [3]

Flying Officer Patrick Woods-Scawen met his death on this same patrol. He was listed as 'missing' when he failed to return with the others at the end of the patrol. Four days later his body was found in the grounds of 'The Ivies', Kenley Lane, Kenley. Tragically, his younger brother Tony was killed on September 2nd, flying with No. 43 Squadron. They were the only pair of brothers who flew in the Battle of Britain, and they died within hours of one another.

Scawen is an unusal name, but one well-known in the history of this locality. One wonders if Patrick and Tony Woods-Scawen were descendants of the Scawens who were once Lords of the Manor of Carshalton.

Another casualty of 85 Squadron on 1st September was Sergeant Ellis. The log notes: "Up to date no trace of him or his machine has been found. He is therefore believed killed." [2] (Last-minute news suggests he crashed at Hawley's Corner, near Biggin Hill.)

100

September the 1st was probably Croydon's blackest day in terms of men and machines lost. Three pilots were dead, and one was to die of his wounds later; three other pilots were seriously wounded, and a total of nine British aircraft were destroyed. This rate of attrition could not be sustained by the RAF for many more weeks; but a new factor was about to be brought to bear on the situation: the German Air Ministry was shortly to begin a new phase in the battle, the bombing of London.

The German schedule for Operation Sealion was not being met. The RAF had resisted more stubbornly and effectively than expected, and the Luftwaffe had not gained the air superiority thought to be a necessary preliminary to invasion. There had always been a lobby in the Luftwaffe Command in favour of heavy bombing attacks on London to crack British morale, a lobby which now believed that a change of target to the civilian population would work where attempted destruction of fighter bases had failed (it seems that German intelligence may well have underestimated the results they had actually achieved in this latter respect). The Luftwaffe Command probably also believed that attacking London would force Air Vice Marshal Dowding to throw any remaining reserves into the battle.

Hitler is said personally to have forbidden attacks on London up to this time, believing that the British would sue for peace without the necessity for such measures. However, an attack on central London had been made on the night of August 25th, when, apparently, poor navigation caused aircrews detailed to bomb military targets near London, such as the oil tanks at Thameshaven, to drop bombs instead on the City, and also in the suburbs. Believing this to be deliberate, the RAF the next night bombed Berlin; and the Germans replied by attacks on Liverpool and Birkenhead three nights later. Thus, an accident led to an escalation which made Hitler change his mind and authorise a new phase of bombing, which opened on September the 7th with an afternoon raid by over 300 aircraft on London and its outskirts.

Meanwhile, at Croydon, on the morning of 2nd September, only nine Spitfires of 72 Squadron were available, and by 8 o'clock they were in action over Maidstone and, according to the Squadron log, accounted for three Dorniers and an Me 110. At midday the nine were again in action over Herne Bay, and claimed three Me 110s and one Dornier; but this time the Squadron did not escape unscathed, and, on landing at the forward base at Hawkinge, four of the Spitfires were considered 'Category 3', which denoted unusable aircraft.

Their final engagement of the day took place over Chatham in the early evening and, although the Squadron claimed an Me 109, Squadron Leader Collins was seriously wounded. [1]

The 2nd of September was 85 Squadron's final day at Croydon, and although they carried out five patrols they made no contact with the enemy. The next day they were moved north to Castle Camps to begin training for night fighting. In fifteen days, three of the Squadron's twenty pilots had been killed and five wounded or burned. [2]

Returning to Croydon that same day was 111 Squadron from Debden. Their short recuperative period had not been as restful as anticipated. The previous day the Squadron had lost Sergeant Dymond during a dog-fight with Me 109s and Heinkel 111s. [4]

A pilot from 72 Squadron, Robert Deacon-Elliott, wrote of September 3rd:

Still at Croydon waiting on the airfield by our aircraft listening to the constant wailing of the air-raid sirens. As the raids came and went it was difficult to differentiate the distant 'all clear' from the adjacent 'take cover' warnings, and vice versa. Other than rapidly constructed slit trenches we had no other form of protection at Croydon - anyway, by now we were all getting a little blasé with the whole affair. 5

In action that day 72 Squadron were under the command of their new C.O., Squadron Leader R.B. Graham, and flying with the squadron was a previous C.O., Squadron Leader Lees, who was shot down and wounded.

At 9 o'clock on the morning of 4th September seven Hurricanes of 111 Squadron took off for the first patrol of their second spell at Croydon. Directed to the Folkestone area, they encountered several large formations of enemy fighters, apparently flying singly or in pairs, stepped-up between 20,000 and 30,000 feet. Flight Lieutenant Giddings led Red section into a head-on attack and, finding two Me 109s at the rear of the formation making no effort to take evasive action, he fired his machine guns and shot them down. Flying Officer Bowring, Pilot Officer Simpson and Sergeant Wallace claimed an Me 109 each. Despite his success, Flight Lieutenant Giddings had to force-land at Staplecross, after enemy fire had pierced a vital oil pipe on his aircraft. Two other pilots failed to return to Croydon, and were assumed killed during the action. Nobody, apparently, witnessed the fate of Flight Lieutenant Bruce; but Pilot Officer Maccinski was seen to bale out over the sea, and to be shot at by enemy aircraft despite the efforts of Bowring and Sergeant Wallace to protect him. 4

On September 4th, 72 Squadron received a telegram of congratulations from No. 13 Group. Deacon-Elliott, reviewing 72's successes and tragedies, wrote:

Apart from one M.E. 109 destroyed by P/O 'Dutch' Holland, I have no record of other claims. Our losses once again were tragic. P/O 'Snowy' Winter was shot down, tried to bale out but left it too late and was killed. Sergeant 'Mabel' Gray was seen to catch a terrific packet from a M.E. 110, apparently being killed instantly, his aircraft dived vertically into the 'deck'. Sergeant Gilder's aircraft was a write-off from enemy fire, but he managed to get away with it. F/O Desmond Sheen was wounded once again and taken off to hospital in Sidcup. 5

The next day Deacon-Elliott had to bale out of his machine after an encounter with an Me 109 over Marden in Kent.

He saw the German machine crash, and then realised that holes had been torn in the wings of his own Spitfire. A few moments later the engine cowlings flew off and the aircraft caught fire. He parachuted out from 800 feet and landed in a hopfield, only to be accosted by a member of the Local Defence Volunteers armed with a shotgun. Things were then sorted out and the hop-pickers offered him their last bottle of beer. Marcel Jullian in *The Battle of Britain* continues:

Then as they sat on the ground waiting for the army lorry to come and collect him, the conversation turned to the weather and above all the battle. The hop-pickers were not happy about the way things were going. They wanted to see more Huns shot down and fewer RAF boys. Elliott finished his beer and said how sorry he was to have disappointed them. 5

That same day, September 5th, eight 111 Squadron Hurricanes were scrambled from Croydon at 9.50 a.m.; and were placed in position six miles north of Biggin Hill. Here they met two blocks of enemy bombers, of twenty-four aircraft each, together with their fighter escort. 'Blue 1' had to dive away owing to oxygen trouble, and was followed down by the rest of his section, together with Green section. This left Red section, under Bowring's command, to press home the attack. Bowring's Hurricane was damaged on the wings and fuselage by machine gun and cannon shell but, after diving out of control from 15,000 feet to 1,500 feet, he chased an Me 109 out to sea and destroyed it ten miles south-south-west of Dungeness.

The Squadron log then recalls an incident involving Bowring: "He twice caught up with an Me 109 and beckoned the pilot to land, as he was obviously in a bad way, but each time the enemy pilot shook his fist, throttled back and opened fire." Sadly the log does not record the outcome of this encounter.

The only pilot from 111 Squadron to suffer injury during this dog-fight was Sergeant Silk, who force-landed at Lullington Castle with a wound to his forearm.

The 6th of September saw the Squadron in action twice during the day. In the morning, five Hurricanes under the leadership of Flying Officer Bowring intercepted a formation of Junkers Ju 88s between Kenley and Maidstone. Bowring managed to shoot down one Ju 88 before a bullet smashed his windscreen and forced him to land. Sergeant Tweed was also forced to make a crash-landing after sustaining injuries.

At 5.30 p.m. the Squadron was scrambled again and ordered to Thameshaven, to intercept an approaching enemy formation. Unfortunately, due to the smoke and haze created by the fires in London, the squadron lost contact with the enemy. Three He 113s had their sights on Red section, and shot down Flying Officer Bowring who, although wounded in the arm, managed to crash-land successfully near Dartford. The squadron log makes a particular point of noting that the 'He 113s' "were coloured silver all over with black crosses under the wings".

The 7th of September was to be 111's final day at Croydon, and their last encounter with the enemy took place in defence of their base. Three large formations of enemy bombers passed over Croydon and headed north-east towards London, whilst their escorts of Me 109s circled the aerodrome to await their return. 111 Squadron had been on patrol at Maidstone; and, returning to Croydon, Squadron Leader Thompson led the Hurricanes into the attack. The squadron appears not to have had any successes. Their only casualty was Sergeant Wallace who, having chased an enemy bomber out to sea, was himself damaged by an Me 109. His engine finally gave out, and he attempted to glide back to shore, but finally baled out over Ashford. He returned to Croydon with slight injuries to his legs and head.

The next day 111 Squadron was posted to Drem in Scotland to reform, and the squadron log ends its entries for Croydon with a list of successes and losses for the Battle of Britain. It claims that 111 Squadron destroyed ninety-four enemy aircraft for the loss of fifteen of its own pilots.

It was just over a year since war had broken out. The Battle of Britain was reaching its climax.

The weekend of September the 7th and 8th saw the beginning of the 'Blitz' on London; the period of nightly punishing raids by one hundred, two hundred, three hundred; even, on the 15th October, four hundred bombers in a night. It continued throughout the winter of 1940-41 and took in other major cities. In the first months, until November the 13th, there was only one night (that of November 3rd when weather held back the bombers) that German raiders did not pound the capital.

The Blitz at first took the public by surprise, as everyone was still assuming that the Germans would continue to concentrate on airfields. Colin Perry bicycled out into Surrey on the afternoon of the 7th to watch the RAF machines taking on the Germans:

Suddenly I thought to make Croydon, and remembered a marvellous viewpoint overlooking the 'drome from a hilltop some miles distant. I got every ounce of speed from the old bike, and simply flew down Chipstead Hill. I kept skidding to a standstill every so often and I picked out fresh tangles of aircraft, but they were always British. I had just passed the bottom of the deep valley between Chipstead and Woodmansterne when from a hole in the ground an air-raid warden told me to take cover. I conveniently ignored him, and bent hard on my pedals to climb the very steep hill. I was no more than half-way up, and already overlooking the whole of the district south of Croydon, when masses of planes roared above me . . . It was the most amazing, impressive, riveting sight. Directly above me were literally hundreds of planes, Germans! The sky was full of them. Bombers hemmed in with fighters, like bees around their queen, like destroyers round the battleship, so came Jerry. My ears were deafened by bombs, machine-gun fire, the colossal inferno of machine after machine zooming in the blue sky . . . It came home to me that in all probability it was the greatest massed raid the country had ever known, and I guessed they would be after Croydon.

He saw the fighters from Croydon going up to meet them, whilst he stood in the garden of a cottage with a group of farm workers and watched through binoculars:

Together we shared my glasses and scanned the numerous British machines, with which the air seemed infested, some came low, others so high even the glasses failed to locate them. Planes continuously kept landing and taking off from Croydon - so I concluded the airport was not the main objective. The men said they had seen smoke on the horizon and as we looked so it happened - the densest, biggest cloud of smoke I have ever seen formed itself on the skyline of London. [6] [The target was, in fact, specifically the East End of London and the London docks.]

September 7th also saw the arrival at Croydon of 605 "County of Warwick" Squadron, under the command of Squadron Leader Walter Churchill. His eyesight was reportedly weak and - perhaps because of this - he handed the squadron over on September 11th to Archie McKellar, a five-foot-three-inches tall Scotsman, whom Walter Churchill used to describe as the 'pocket Hercules'. He was also known as the 'pocket battleship'.

A book published in 1941, *So Few* by David Masters, reports a conversation between Churchill and McKellar on September 9th at Croydon after a battle in which Churchill had been able to see only a small proportion of the enemy formations visible to McKellar:

When he [Churchill] got back to base, he found his pilots at the dispersal point chattering like a lot of magpies, with Archie McKellar, who had knocked down a Messerschmitt 109 on the way home, telling them all about it. To destroy four enemy aircraft in one sortie was indeed a triumph for the fighter pilot, a feat which cost him 1200 rounds of ammunition. His leader was able to confirm the destruction of the three Heinkels in one burst of fire. But unhappily the triumph was marred by the loss of a friend during the fight, and Archie McKellar never referred to it again.

'I'm sorry I made such a mess of it', said [Squadron Leader] Churchill apologetically. 'Your sight is no good. You are too old - you're an old man!' exclaimed Archie McKellar - which must have been rather a shock for a young man of thirty-two. 'I'm going on flying', the commander replied. 'You'll simply be shot down', was the Scotsman's blunt reply. 'All right. I'll let you lead', was the rejoinder, and the next day and thereafter Archie McKellar led No. 605 Squadron most brilliantly. Keen sight to the fighter is as important as it is to the peregrine falcon. Without it, neither can detect the prey. The fighter risks being shot down and the falcon risks starvation, so defective sight threatens death to both. Archie McKellar knew this and used to lie upon his bed with pads of cotton wool, soaked in a special lotion, over his eyes in order to preserve his sight. 7

By the time Walter Churchill met his death, later in the war, over Malta, he had acquired a DSO and a DFC, and the rank of Wing Commander.

Archie McKellar, born in Paisley in 1912, had joined the City of Glasgow Squadron of the Auxiliary Air Force in 1936, and, after seeing action with this squadron in the early months of the war, was moved to 605 Squadron.

Mr. Robert Hall, now of Kelso, Roxburgh, was a member of the Squadron in 1940, and remembers that when they first arrived at Croydon the aerodrome was still in a mess from the recent bombing raids:

I remember treading and climbing over debris in the foyer of the hotel amongst which were hundreds of 20mm shells, scattered over quite a wide area - I never discovered where they came from, or how they got there, but assumed they were intended for defence of the hotel originally, as 20mm cannons were being used on some airfields against German raiders.

There was a very strong smell of perfume all around and the grass and everything around seemed impregnated. We heard that a perfume factory manufacturing 'Soir de Paris' on the edge of the aerodrome had been hit during the raid and several girl employees had been killed - several days passed before the air cleared. 8

Mr. Hall was evidently under the impression that the scent-smell and damage came from the big August 15th raid in which the girls were killed, but it seems unlikely that it would have lingered for so long, and more probably he was smelling the effects produced by the lone bomber of August 26th. He recalls being billeted in a local house:

Foresters Drive had been evacuated on both sides [not all, in fact, of the road had been requisitioned] and airmen moved into the empty houses after being issued with a 'Macdonald' folding bed and 3 'biscuits' which formed the mattress for the same - and 3 smelly blankets and no sheets.

The sergeants' and officers' messes were on the other side of the road.

The airmen's cookhouse and mess was a bungalow situated at the southern end of Foresters Drive not far from the airmen's billets. [Mr. Haimes remembers this cookhouse as just round the corner from The Newlands.]

The bungalow we were told belonged to a doctor, who I'm sure would have been petrified to see the transformation perpetrated by the R.A.F. cooks. Food was stacked in the garage and electric boilers to heat water and cook the food were all over the place, even up one side of the driveway and on the lawn - benches and tables had been put in every room and meal times had to be staggered to cope with approximately 150 mouths.

The diet consisted mainly of soup with lashings of potatoes and cabbage and rock-frozen kidneys which were chopped up with an axe from wooden cases. The wood often became mixed up with the kidneys which I'm sure improved the flavour.

'Bully Beef' was an alternative, rounded off with huge loaves of bread, butter and jam - what a wonderful feast it was after a full day on the airfield with only a snack, which was brought out to us on the aircraft dispersal point - pilots and groundcrews were at full readiness from dawn and did not move from the airfield, whilst aircraft were scrambled sometimes 8 to 10 times during this period to engage enemy aircraft approaching London.

The main hangars at Croydon were used by 605 Squadron for aircraft major inspections and repairs - daily inspections and maintenance was carried out by the ground crews on dispersal points. Material such as aluminium sheeting was in very short supply, and damaged wings were often patched with metal from 'bully tins' and empty fruit tins from the cook-house and a 'pop-rivetter'.

The operations room was a 4 wheeled caravan, as used by Montgomery I believe, and nicknamed 'The Elephant House' for some unknown reason - this was protected by a high wall of sandbags. 8

Another member of 605 Squadron's ground staff at this time was Mr. Albert Hodson, then Leading Aircraftman Hodson. Mr. Hodson was parachute packer for 605: responsible for the maintenance of the pilots' parachutes; a vital job at a time when recourse to baling-out was no remote possibility but an everyday likelihood and a matter very literally of life or death. Parachutes had to be unpacked for forty-eight hours each month to 'breathe' and then had to be carefully repacked. Mr. Hodson was billeted at No. 21 Foresters Drive, and discovered that the depth of the stairwell was just right for a parachute to hang its full length if suspended from a batten in the ceiling. Additionally, the back bedroom floor, suitably covered in the linoleum left by the peacetime inhabitants of the house, was just right for the refolding, diagonally, of the parachute for repacking. No. 21 Foresters Drive also housed 'the Armourers, gun repair, stripping and overhaul section'. In relation to their occupation of Foresters Drive, Mr. Hodson writes:

We were self-contained, all sections and staff needed for the repair, re-fuelling, re-arming and servicing of the Hurricane aircraft were housed in Foresters Drive. Stores, spares, rations and equipment were drawn from Kenley.

During our stay at Croydon we received wonderful support and generosity from the local people which was a great boost to our morale. Among their many kind gestures was the provision of a drum kit, from cash collections made locally, to enable us to complete the formation of a Squadron Dance Band. The Southern Railway Company generously allowed us to use the fine Club Room and Dance Hall which was the home of the Southern Railway Sports Club, and, by making the whole Squadron honorary members of the Club, ensured that we could all attend our dances with our local friends when time permitted. All the members of the band were groundstaff members of the Squadron and we enjoyed playing for the 'boys and girls' in off duty hours. I could not leave the subject without reference to the Steward of The Southern Railway Club and his wife, Mr. and Mrs. George Boto. I wonder if they are still alive? They were wonderful and did so much to make those evenings enjoyable, even to finding a supply of beer for the occasions.

We were also entertained at the Social Evenings of the Carshalton Tennis Club and again found a great welcome there from the members. 9

The fighters that young Colin Perry had seen taking off from Croydon on the afternoon of September the 7th included the Hurricanes of 111 Squadron and the Spitfires of 72. Flying Officer Edson of the latter squadron was shot down in this action, and was wounded in the knee by an incendiary bullet.

The Germans inflicted considerable damage on London that night and again on Sunday: the docks, parts of the City, a good deal of the East End and parts of South London were badly hit. Over the next few days such London landmarks as Leicester Square and Buckingham Palace were to receive bombs.

On the Sunday (September the 8th), 111 Squadron, which had now been in the front line of the battle for a long period, was posted to Drem, in East Lothian.

It was from this aerodrome that 605 Squadron had come. They had arrived at Croydon in the evening of the 7th and their log notes:

Pilots refuelled at Stringdon [sic: i.e. Abingdon] and arrived Croydon at 19.30. 605 Squadron were taking the place of 111 Squadron. Heavy bombing of London Docks in particular, commencing in the evening and continuing all night. Large fires from Docks and (?) Peckham gas works could be seen from Croydon. [10]

One of the pilots was Pilot Officer Bob Foster - later to become a Wing Commander; and, after the war, an aviation manager for Shell Mex and BP. Now living in Sutton, he recalls:

We flew from Drem to Abingdon, just near Oxford, before coming to Croydon. The main reason for that was to refuel. There had been a lot of air battles over the capital that day, so nobody knew if there would still be any action going on and we obviously didn't want to arrive over Croydon with no fuel. So we refuelled and flew in, and got to Croydon, as far as I can remember, in the early evening, and the first sight of London was the burning - we could see it all, a pall of smoke. And that was our first sight of the battle, because we'd been in Scotland up until then. As far as I was concerned, I couldn't have done much if we had met any enemy because I'd lost all air pressure, which meant that I couldn't use my brakes on the ground, and I couldn't fire my guns in the air. So I was flying into Croydon absolutely helpless. It was just an air leak, but the point was that with no air pressure you simply couldn't fire your guns. [11]

Also arriving with 605 Squadron was Pilot Officer (later Squadron Leader) Christopher 'Bunny' Currant. He, too, in 1983, remembers the drama of arriving from Scotland to a burning London.

. . . they set London ablaze the first night we got there, and that was a very unnerving experience, to see these fires burning all night, and all day, and the bombing going on all night; and we thought: 'My God, we really are in the thick of it, we're really up against it.' [12]

The Squadron log for September the 8th records how they went into action on their first day at Croydon, with eight aircraft from 253 at Kenley commanded by Flight Lieutenant Edge, against a large enemy formation between Maistone and Tunbridge Wells.

'B' Flight (F/Lt. McKellar D.F.C.) attacked Ju 88's and leading Do 215's 'A' Flight (P/O. Currant) attacking port side of leading Do 215 formation, who were themselves dived upon by Me 109s. Result was to turn formation completely: they disappeared East without dropping bombs. 1 Me 109 destroyed and 1 Do 215 damaged by P/O. Cooper Slipper, 1 Do 215 probably destroyed by P/O. Ingle, 1 Do 215 and 1 Me 109 damaged by P/O. Currant and 1 Me 109 damaged by P/O. Humphreys. P/O. Fleming's aircraft was shot down in flames he bailed [sic] out but was badly burned and suffering from shock. German bombers came over London district again at night, dropping bombs apparently indiscriminately: raids did not cease till dawn. F/Lt. McKellar, P/O. Humphreys and P/O. Forrester stole or borrowed the Station Bedford truck which F/Lt. McKellar drove to enable them to enjoy the fleshpots of London - owing to the airraids they never slept a wink and returned in truculent mood having found no consolation for lack of sleep, whereas we at Croydon slept soundly! [10]

Flight Lieutenant Edge, commanding 253 Squadron at Kenley, was himself formerly a member of 605, of which he had commanded 'A' Flight. He had been posted to 253 on 5th September, only a few days before the move to Croydon. The log for that date had noted:

Gerry Edge will be a very great loss to "A" Flight which he commanded and to the Squadron, being much loved and respected by officers and men. Very rarely in the history of a squadron could an officer be so much missed by so many. [Surely an echo, here, of Winston Churchill's famous speech of August 20th!] [10]

On Monday the 9th, Pilot Officer G.M. Forrester from the squadron was killed, and Pilot Officer Humphreys was injured on baling out. The log reports that the squadron took off at 17.00 and:

> . . . intercepted 17 He 111's with large numbrs of Me 110, Me 109 and He 113 protection near Farnborough, Kent. By constant attack the enemy formation was broken up and was prevented from attacking London. Other attacks took place as far away as Farnborough, Hants. F/Lt. McKellar destroyed 3 He 111's and 1 Me 109, P/O Currant and Sgt. Wright destroyed a Me 110 and P/O. Currant had a share in destroying a Me 109 with another Hurricane Squadron. P/O. Humphreys baled out near Bordon with a small wound in his hand, and P/O. Forrester is missing. London bombed at night . . . [10]

It was on September 9th, as already noted in the quotation from *So Few*, that Archie McKellar destroyed three Heinkel IIIs with one burst of fire. This is the story as told in *So Few:*

> It was a beautiful day, with some cloud at 4,000 feet and a clear sky above. Heading south, the Hurricanes climbed steadily to intercept at 20,000 feet.
>
> They had reached 15,000 feet when the voice of Archie McKellar came to his leader over the radio-telephone. 'Enemy ahead, sir,' shouted the Scotsman as he caught sight of a cloud of thirty Heinkel IIIs with an escort of fifty Messerschmitt 109s about 4,000 feet above them and twenty Messerschmitt 110s to guard the flank.
>
> At that distance Wing Commander Churchill could see no more than six Messerschmitt 109s and at once went in to draw them off with his section in order to give the other fighters a chance to get at the bombers which Archie McKellar told him were present. Directly he had drawn off the first batch of Messerschmitts and seen them go flashing past, he saw six more and as he was forcing them away a bullet grazed his leg and sent him spinning down out of the flank.
>
> By the time he recovered, he had lost the bombers and his squadron, but he headed after them all out on the course they were following. To his amazement he soon observed the Heinkels still flying in the same direction as though unaware of the British fighters that were stalking them.
>
> As he flew to overtake them, he saw Archie McKellar's section of three turn up sun and swing round to the attack. At that very moment the Heinkels turned into the sun straight towards the Hurricanes which were concealed by the glare. The Germans were, in the parlance of the fighters, 'a piece of cake'. No deflection was necessary at all. Archie McKellar, seeing the leading Heinkel in front of him, just pressed the button on his control column and squirted at it, and Wing Commander Churchill watched it blow up in the air and knock the wing of the port Heinkel, which immediately went down just as the starboard Heinkel turned straight into Archie McKellar's stream of bullets and got what is known in the service as a 'gutser'. Black smoke began to pour from the engines, the nose of the bomber reared up for a moment, then the third Heinkel went down on its back. [7]

Christopher Currant, however, remembered the event somewhat differently in 1983:

> Archie McKellar attacked a formation of Heinkels head-on. He fired at the leading Heinkel of the vic of three. The leading Heinkel blew up and blew up the other two either side, so he got three Heinkels for one blast. [12]

As well as the Squadron's battle on the 9th September, 605's log also notes that Squadron Leader Harrison had been doing "great work in requisitioning houses adjoining the aerodrome for the comfort of officers and men". [10]

Christopher Currant, at the time of writing living near Berkhamstead, recalls:

> We lived in the houses in Forest Drive - or was it Forresters? [i.e. Foresters Drive] - with the back gardens abutting the airfield. In fact my own aircraft was always parked exactly opposite the house we lived and fed in so that I could run straight out of the house, down the garden and across the airfield grass a few yards and into the cockpit. I was always lazy and believed in organising in such a way that was of convenience to me. All the Hurricanes were parked fairly close to these gardens. [12]

September 10th was a day of domestic activity for 605 Squadron:

59. Aircraftman Leslie William Lloyd Penfold, 615 Squadron, RAF photographer, in about 1940. Leslie Penfold took a number of the photographs published for the first time in this book.

British NSF factory. This was the factory totally destroyed in the raid of August 15th, 1940, and the one whose staff suffered the major number of casualties.

60. *ABOVE:* The frontage.

61. *BELOW:* At work inside the factory before the war, producing switches for the radio industry. NSF began the production of electrical components for the RAF on the outbreak of war.

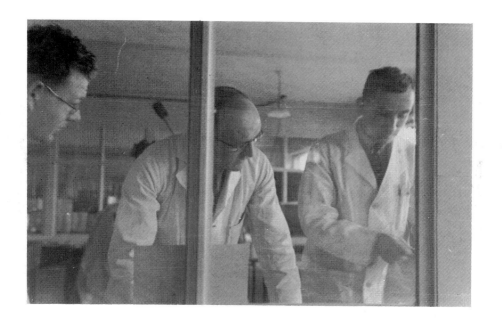

62. *ABOVE:* British NSF staff before 1940. Left to right: Victor J. Wood, injured in the air-raid; Hans Bitter, Chief Engineer, who returned to Germany just before the war; Bob Hutchings, killed in the air-raid.

63. *BELOW:* The demolished NSF factory from the damaged roof of Bourjois. Visible on the horizon, just left of centre, is the chimney of the Waddon Waterworks, and just to the right of that can be seen the rear of the damaged 'C' hangar, home of Rollasons, Redwing, etc. Left of the chimney is the Bowaters building on Purley Way.

64. *ABOVE:* Remains of the NSF factory looking towards Bourjois.

65. *BELOW:* The shattered Bourjois scent factory after the raid. This has now been rebuilt.

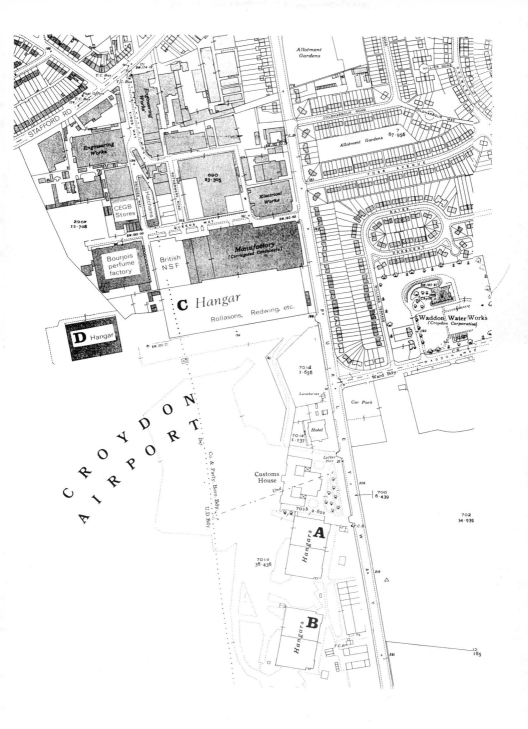

66.   Plan showing the factories in relation to the main aerodrome buildings.

67. Stafford Road, Wallington, after the raid of 15th August. Smoke rises from the factories beyond the camouflaged 'D' hangar block while cyclists stand on their bicycles for a view over the fence. One cyclist, however, with his friends, mends a puncture in his rear tyre. Note the trolley-bus lines overhead. Trolley buses replaced the trams from West Croydon to Sutton before the war.

Blackout letters

68. *ABOVE:* One of the raiders of Testing Group 210 which did not return home after the August 15th raid. This Me 110c was forced down by a Hurricane at Hooe, East Sussex, at 6.50pm. Lt. Koch and Uffz. Kahl, the crew, were captured. Note the censor's instructions before the photograph was published at the time.
Inset: Badge of Erprobungsgruppe 210, showing the British Isles as a target (with Eire omitted).

69. *BELOW:* Bomb crater in the garden of a house believed to be on the Waddon Estate.

70. *LEFT*: Pilot Officer Robert Wardlow Oxspring, of No. 66 Squadron, brought in by Kenley control to intercept the Croydon raiders on August 15th. Oxspring, with another Spitfire pilot, brought down at least one Me 110.

71. *RIGHT*: Squadron Leader, later Group Captain, G. R. 'Gerry' Edge. He was brought back from 253 Squadron to command 605 Squadron at Croydon after the death of Squadron Leader Archie McKellar in action on November 1st 1940, the day after the Battle of Britain is officially considered to have ended.

72. *LEFT*: Colin Perry, author of *Boy in the Blitz*, then a teenager living in Tooting, who observed the raids on Croydon. Here, he managed to get into the same newspaper photograph as Winston Churchill, who was on a visit to the City.

73. *RIGHT*: Flight Lieutenant Henry M. Ferriss, DFC, of 111 Squadron, who crashed near Marden in Kent in Hurricane R4193 after a collision with a Dornier on August 16th, 1940. (see p. 83).

Another lovely sunny day. No patrols by the Squadron to-day. S/L. Harrison takes chairs, tables, curtains, carpets, etc., from the Old Mess to put in our houses. 4 cooks and 4 batmen are engaged. Gas stoves are ordered. The food and crockery at the Mess continues filthy and we shall be glad to move from it. London bombed at night. 10

The next day, however, saw action against the enemy:

The Squadron took off at 15.45 and encountered near Addington a large formation of 40 He 111's protected by larger numbers of Me 109s and Me 110's. The engagement took place between Rochester and Eltham, the formation being turned south and west before reaching London. Before the formation turned P/O. Currant damaged 2 He 111's, P/O. Cooper-Slipper damaged another He 111, F/Lt. McKellar probably destroyed 1 He 111, P/O. Glowacki destroyed 1 Me 110 and Sgt. Budzinski destroyed 1 Me 109. After the formation turned south, those on the ground at Croydon saw P/O. Currant destroy 1 He 111 which crashed a few miles to the East, and he damaged 2 more He 111's. F/Lt. McKellar and P/O. Jones chased another He 111 to Beachy Head continuing feint attacks until after their ammunition was expended with the result that the crew bailed [sic] out and the He 111 crashed into the sea just off Beachy Head. S/L. Churchill received a slight flesh wound in his arm. Informed by Odiham Police that P/O. Forrester was shot in action and came down near Odiham. Terrific A.A. barrage all night round London. New tactics were adopted and no searchlights were used. This was apparently most effective in turning the enemy from their targets. The Squadron celebrated the day's work with an excellent dinner at the Greyhound in Croydon, going down in an open Bedford truck and returning running the gauntlet of the A.A. barrage. 10

That night, the aerodrome and its vicinity were repeatedly bombed: the station record describes the raids as being "intermittent throughout the night", and gives details of the bombing as:

Two oil incendiary bombs in vicinity of pavilion at North East corner of Trojan sports ground.
One H.E. bomb approx (100 kilo) about 30 yards south of No. 2 Hispano gun-post, near earthworks at south end of main line of buildings.
One D.A. bomb near No. 1 machine gun post at Plough Lane North.
Material damage: Crater 15' across by gun post - now being filled in. Portions of wooden fencing by Sports Pavilion burned. 13

This was a night when much of South London suffered. Colin Perry, living at Tooting, noted in his diary that the 'all clear' finally went at 6 a.m. 6

It may have been this night - with the trip to the Greyhound in Croydon and then a night of local bombing - remembered by 'Bunny' Currant in the following story:

We used to go to The Greyhound and have a jolly good nosh-up. We had a jolly good feast there one night, and there was bombing going on left, right and centre, and we were driving back to the Croydon Airport, and the gas holder was hit and went up just a few hundred yards from us - whoof! -and the top came off, and fell down inside, and the whole thing went off - well, I suppose gas would go up in one puff, wouldn't it? That was quite exciting. 12

Londoners were beginning to sleep in London Transport Underground stations at night; new jokes and catch-phrases abounded; and songs like *A nightingale sang in Berkeley Square* became evocative of a mood; and would, years later, bring back dramatic memories.

Robert Hall recalls the atmosphere at RAF Croydon at this time:

We had 2 Polish and 2 Czech sergeant pilots serving with 605 Squadron during this period and very skilled pilots they were, having served with 'Flying Circuses' before their countries were overrun.
Neither of them spoke a word of English and it was a miracle how they managed to find their way back to Croydon after combat in bad weather conditions with zero visibility.
After their numerous victories in combat with the German fighters, quite often they returned to Croydon with chunks shot off their propellers, shattered wings and fuselages, and under-carriages damaged beyond repair to make a perfect crash landing.

To see them drinking in the 'local' in the evening, with their infectious humour and high spirits, it was difficult to imagine how close to death they had been that day and what the impending future held in store for them. [8]

Christopher Currant confirms this memory of what he calls "those extraordinary stirring days". He writes:

It was a hectic time, very tiring physically as we were scrambled 3 or 4 times every day and then had disturbed nights from the night bombing. We had slit trenches at the end of the gardens on the airfield but I never even used them. I felt that if a bomb had to have my name on it then it could do its damnedest with my person, but I was damned if I was going to move from the warmth and comfort of my bed. I might as well be maimed or killed in bed rather than outside in a slit trench. [12]

Mr. Foster recalls the constantly interrupted meals:

We'd be at readiness, waiting, and nothing would happen and they'd say, 'Well, stand down and have lunch' and within fifteen or twenty minutes just as we were sitting down, the alarm would go and we'd have to rush off. It didn't happen every day, but I have memories of this - either at breakfast or lunch or some time. [11]

605's log for September 12th records:

Rather cloudy at last. We had our first complete day's meals in our mess at Dispersal. The cooks were excellent, and everyone was pleased to get away from the old mess. P/O. Currant, P/O. Cooper-Slipper and Sgt. Wright, as Red section, on patrol near Hastings encountered a Do 215 which they continuously attacked and brought down 8 miles S.E. of Cap Gris Nez. S/L. G.R. Edge, now commanding 253 Squadron at Kenley, came over to have dinner with us. 4 bombs (3 unexploded) landed 50 - 100 yards from our Mess about 21.00 in the back garden of a villa opposite doing no damage. [10]

On the 13th, Sergeant Peter McIntosh joined the squadron. He was a local man, having been brought up in Croydon.

Although that day in the air was generally quiet for the Squadron, Sergeant Wright damaged a Ju 88 in a chase from Tunbridge Wells to Hastings.

On the 14th of September, 72 Squadron went back to Biggin Hill in their Spitfire Is. With them went Pilot Officer Ernest E. Males who, whilst flying from Croydon, had destroyed an Me 109 on the 2nd of September, and claimed a half share in a Dornier Do 17 on the 10th. Return fire from this Dornier had brought him down at Little Hutchings Farm, Etchingham - unhurt but his Spitfire a write-off. He destroyed another Me 109 on the day his squadron returned to Biggin Hill, but was himself killed in combat on the 27th of September, his aircraft crashing at Shadwell Dock, Stepney.

The 15th of September is the day recognised as the most crucial day in the Battle of Britain. From Croydon, 605 Squadron took off at 11.25 a.m. to meet a formation of Dorniers in what was to become a running battle over Surrey and Kent.

In the course of that battle, Pilot Officer Mike Cooper-Slipper either deliberately rammed, or accidentally collided with, a Dornier. It is, perhaps, instructive to compare the different accounts to which a single incident can give rise.

Wilf Nicoll writes of the event saying Cooper-Slipper had been attacked and his machine was on fire:

As he prepared to abandon his Hurricane he discovered three Dorniers approaching him head-on and instead decided to ram them. At an impact speed of over 600 miles an hour he struck the centre bomber and, as he said later, 'things became a bit confused then.' Miraculously, he found himself swinging on the end of his parachute which had somehow opened and was undamaged. After numerous adventures, which included a near lynching by hop-pickers, he was returned to Croydon in an Army vehicle via a children's party and numerous pubs - he found on his arrival back at base that he had somehow acquired a rubber dinghy and two Luftwaffe Schwimmwesten! [German 'Mae Wests'] [14]

Robert Hall recalls:

Pilot Officer Cooper-Slipper came from Kinver in Staffordshire and his father was vicar of the parish - he was nineteen years of age, fair haired, thin and pale-faced.

Apart from being a 'natural' flyer with a DFC and Bar and 8 Kills to his credit whilst at Croydon, a mention should be made of his last 'spectacular' . . . After one of our busiest days, with hordes of Dorniers, Heinkels and Junkers 88s, supported by fighters, trying and sometimes succeeding to bomb London, on about his eighth encounter that day, having shot down two Dorniers and one Junkers 88 [the Squadron log credits him only with one Do 17 destroyed that day before this incident], he was engaging another Dornier when his ammunition ran out - not to be outdone, he crashed his Hurricane into the tail unit of the Dornier and managed to bale out safely, adding another Hun to his credit.

On this memorable day, in bright sunshine and a cloudless sky, with aircraft whirling and screaming whilst locked in deadly combat, with the victims plummeting to earth in a trail of smoke, not a soul stirred on Foresters Drive, and all that could be heard beneath the raging battle was the tinkle of thousands of cartridge cases as they fell from above, on to roofs of houses and the roadway. [8]

Christopher Currant, however, who was there in the sky with Mike Cooper-Slipper, disputes these versions of this incident. He is certain that the German aircraft involved was a Heinkel, not a Dornier (although the Squadron log talks of a Do 17). He also says that the collision was "accident, not design, a complete and utter accident."

This is his version of the story:

Now, Cooper-Slipper, he was a lucky chap. We attacked a formation of German bombers. I was leading the Squadron at the time, and I got there with plenty of height on the port side of the German aircraft which were coming this way, and we did a beam attack from above, and I led with Cooper-Slipper being my number two. I took the first Vic of bombers, fired at them, broke straight down beneath them, looked up, and when I looked up there was one Heinkel going round slowly with one wing off, and alongside it a Hurricane going round very, very much quicker, because it was a little aeroplane, also with one wing off; and then a parachute suddenly appeared. That was in the morning and when we got back, Cooper-Slipper was missing, and he was only eighteen at the time; and in the afternoon he rang up to say he was all right and was down in Kent somewhere, and he came back and brought me a German Mae West. What had happened was, he actually dived and hit the wingroot of the Heinkel, glanced off it upside down, into an inverted spin with one wing off. All he had to do was to open his hood, undo his straps and he was shot out, because of the inverted spin, like a cork out of a bottle, quite unhurt. He was very lucky.

Christopher Currant also says there was no question of Cooper-Slipper's aircraft being on fire. [12]

The Squadron log says:

During this engagement P/O Cooper-Slipper had a remarkable escape. His control was shot away and his aircraft hit a Do 17 amidships. P/O Cooper-Slipper's aircraft, minus port wing, spiralled down and he bailed [sic] out landing unhurt other than small bruises near Marden [it is, perhaps, unfair to the writer of the 605 log, who, on the whole, did rather well in comparison to other log writers, to speculate on how painful or otherwise 'small bruises near Marden' are]. He returned to Croydon later in the evening, apparently unshaken, with two German Mae Wests and complete rubber boat, given him by Maidstone police! [8]

After the war, Cooper-Slipper became test pilot for the de Havilland Canada Company.

September 15th was the climax of the Battle of Britain: the day that Hitler finally admitted that the invasion of England would have to be postponed indefinitely. The day's significance in history could not be known at the time, and the ferocious air-raids continued for the rest of the month; but the decision had been taken, and invasion was, in fact, no longer imminent. Effectively, the RAF had won control of the skies.

Before this, however, an official invasion warning brought 605 Squadron an anxious two hours of waiting. Bob Foster recalls:

> That particular day - I can't remember which day it was, but it was probably near the 15th, we had the Invasion Alert. We sat in our cockpits, on the airfield, from about an hour before dawn until an hour or so after dawn. In fact, we could see the dawn come up, we were facing that way. It was a beautiful day. And we sat there for about two hours waiting for this call, expecting that this was to be the invasion. And it never came: we just sat there and in the end we were stood down for what was called 'fifteen minutes readiness' - in other words, you didn't have to be in your 'plane but you had to get to it within fifteen minutes. So we could go back to the house or sit in the mess, or something. And there was quite a lot of tension there - just sitting there waiting, and then a bit of a let-down when nothing happened. 11

He recalls that it was possible - though officially not allowed - to tune in to the BBC on the 'R/T' and sit in the cockpit listening to music:

> You could just twiddle the dial and get the BBC music . . . now and again some one would just start his engines up to keep them warm. And that was it, we were just sitting there waiting. And then - nothing - though of course we went up again later that day, but not for what everyone was actually expecting. 11

On this occasion the Squadron - or Bob Foster's flight - was evidently on 'Standby'. Christopher Currant recalled that there was little 'time-off' during the Battle of Britain:

> Oh no, it was on all the while, unless you were released. You were on standby to sit in your cockpit; or readiness, sitting in the houses; or release, for half a day, never a day. There was A Flight and B Flight. It would be determined by the Sector Headquartrs at Kenley as to what they wanted on. Perhaps they would only want one flight on, and one flight released, or available. Standby, readiness, available or released: as far as I remember, the four states. 12

Risking one's life as a Battle of Britain pilot to ward off the German invasion did not earn one release from the minor irritations of life. Squadron Leader Currant recalled:

> I was driving back from Harpenden, one day, to go back to Croydon Airport, to rejoin the Squadron after having had forty-eight hours off. I went through London Colney. They had a police trap there, at *that* time of the war! - and they pinched me for doing thirty-seven miles an hour, and I was fined two pounds, I think, and my licence endorsed: for doing thirty-seven miles an hour through London Colney, and no other traffic on the road, at the height of the Battle of Britain. I felt very aggrieved about that. 12

On September 21st Croydon as a front-line station received a visit from the Secretary of State for Air, Sir Archibald Sinclair. On the night of September the 23rd/24th came another bombing raid. Nine incendiary bombs fell along Stafford Road and the northern half of Plough Lane. The old Redwing hangar along Stafford Road was occupied by "F" Company of the 12th Queen's Royal Regiment, but no one was injured or killed there despite the roof being damaged by fire. Two bombs fell on the south western corner of the airfield; one only 15 yards from the Bofors gun post, and the station log also noted: "1 D.A.

[delayed action] believed to have dropped in region of S.E. corner but not yet ascertained." One Hurricane had to be sent away for repairs, while two others were less seriously damaged. [13]

The next day (September 24th), 605 Squadron lost another pilot: Pilot Officer Glowacki, one of the Poles mentioned by Robert Hall, who failed to return after being intercepted by three Me 109s near the French coast.

On the loss of Glowacki, 'Bunny' Currant commented to one of us:

> Now that was a tragedy, dear old Glowacki, a young lad, very good-looking blond boy, and, like all Poles, he was so enthusiastic and so excitable; all they wanted to do was get at the Hun, and he flew off one day across the Channel to attack the Huns wherever he could find them, and he never did come back. Fine fellow, he was. [12]

Bob Foster recalls an unforgettable encounter during one patrol:

> The first trouble I had was on the 27th September when we went up to attack some Me 110s which were circling-in to the south. As we went in to attack, I thought I'd been hit, because everything blew up and there was a lot of glycol pouring out . . . but I didn't bale out because I wasn't on fire, so I glided down. The engine was making a noise like an old rusty car . . . I picked a big field, which in fact turned out to be Gatwick Airport, which was lucky for me . . .
>
> When I landed - I just managed it, gliding, because the engine was dead - I got out. One of these 110s had just crashed at Gatwick and was all in flames and some bright airman came over with - ugh! - a hat and an ear and asked if I would like these as a souvenir . . . I didn't. It just shows the horror, the tension - this chap not seeming to think anything of it. And there was this thing blazing away, just by the old Beehive building at Gatwick. [11]

He also recalls another occasion, watching from the sky as bombs fell on South London:

> My parents lived in Clapham then, just near Clapham Junction. When we were scrambled we were climbing up to get height when these bombers came over, and dropped their bombs in a stick all along Lavender Hill and Clapham Junction way. Looking down all I could see was this cloud of dust and so on, coming up, obviously within half a mile of Clapham Junction. And I thought, 'This isn't very pleasant' because it could have been my home, quite easily. And in fact when I got back I rang up, and they told me the windows had been blown in and so on - they hadn't actually been blown up but it was a near miss. [11]

Bob Foster's story about being offered an ear and a hat as souvenirs, reminded Christopher Currant of an equally gruesome experience of his own, flying from Croydon:

> We were sent up in twos, when it was very cloudy, and I intercepted a Ju 88, just before it went into the clouds, diving straight down to get away from me. I opened fire on it, and then we were in cloud; and then I came back. I'd no idea what had happened to it, but when the fitters started examining my Hurricane there were bits of blood on the cowling underneath the nose of the aeroplane, bits of blood and bits of flesh, which must have come from the rear gunner; but I've still no idea what happened to the bomber . . .
>
> Another incident which may or may not be in the log was, again, I set off with Milne, a Canadian, as my number two, and it was very cloudy. We entered cloud - I should think at about 800 feet, and we climbed up and were in about 15,000 feet of cloud before we could get out of it; and we were vectored on to an aircraft, and I saw it going south above the cloud, and I was way above it; and it was just one of those things where everything worked perfectly. I did an absolute beam attack straight down onto it, and I had one little burst and the whole front half of the cockpit just came away as though I'd opened a door or something and it had flown off - it just cut through it like butter and the thing just flew off: and then that went into cloud and went straight down and came out near Dungeness somewhere, and I found it again and I got my number two to come up and finish it off, and it went into the sea near Dungeness - and that was an incident that happened flying from Croydon. [12]

605 Squadron's log has, typed in to it, a letter introduced thus:

EXTRACT from a letter written by F/O. R. Hope to his family, relative to his parachute descent on Saturday 28th September 1940, and forwarded with the request that it may be inserted as Appendix to this Unit Summary of even date - 'F/O Hope was shot down, baling out on top of an oak tree near Ticehurst - unhurt' (See Appendix)

The letter graphically conveys Flying Officer Hope's experience - one which happened to many in the Battle of Britain, and often in far worse circumstances -and we quote here, in full, all of the letter which appears in the log:

. . . Saturday was not quite such a success from my point of view, as on our third patrol I lost my aircraft. We were at about 21,000 ft when we got involved with a squadron of Me. 109s. They got me before I even saw them, which is very annoying. I first felt a kind of funny bump, and as I turned to see what was up, my controls suddenly felt funny, and lots of red sparks and black smoke appeared round my feet and a cloud of white smoke, probably glycol, began streaming back from the engine. The aircraft began going downhill fast. I slid back the hood and began to get out, my goggles were stripped off and my helmet began to lift up in the slipstream; I realised I hadn't undone my straps so I pulled out the retaining pin and stood up, standing on anything which came handy (the seat,, the instrument panel or the stick: I don't know really). The air seized hold of me and there was a wrench as my oxygen tube snapped off (I had forgotten to undo it) and I shot out into the sky. The aeroplane disappeared. It was nice and cool falling. I was head down of course, but found the position quite comfortable; there was no sense of speed or feeling of falling. I had a look at the clouds below (they were about 4,000 - 5,000 feet) and then collected the odd bits of my helmet and had a look round. My parachute was still on my seat, both my boots were on, and I did not seem to have lost anything except my goggles, and a handkerchief and map which must have fallen out of the pockets in my knees when I first went upside down. After a while I thought about pulling the rip cord. 'What about giving the old "brolley" a try out?' I thought. I seemed to have fallen a goodish way, so I pulled. The canopy streamed out, there was a hard jerk, and there I was right side up, quite comfortable and floating slowly. Oh! so slowly earthwards. I was about 9 to 10,000 ft. so I had fallen free for about 8 or 9,000ft (from about 18,000ft) and might have fallen further with advantage. When I looked up I could see a shining white canopy above me, and little silver specks having no end of a dog-fight in the clear blue above me. A Spitfire dived down past me with a high pitched whine, but that was the only disturbance. The parachute began to swing me about and it wasn't long before I felt sick, very sick indeed in fact by the time I landed. It was fun going into the Clouds, as the sun played a sort of 'Spectre of the Brocken' effect on my shadow as I approached them. When I emerged the countryside looked pleasantly open, and after drifting quite a way I thought I saw where I should land. Two farm hands had the same idea. We were all wrong as in spite of attempts on my part to avoid it, I came down in a spinney of young oak trees, pulling up short about 20 feet from the ground, hanging in my harness. I managed to get hold of a trunk, pull myself over to it, get out of the parachute harness and climb to the ground, where I remained quite still until I was found. The Army soon took charge of me, gave me a drink and some lunch, and drove me back to Croydon. The only damage I sustained was a hefty bruise on my right shoulder from hitting the tail as I jumped, and a bruise on my leg, and a torn trouser from the some- what unceremonious descent through the upper branches of the oak tree. Now I go about with my arm in a sling, feeling particularly good as I have been given a week's sick leave. [10]

On September 25th a local resident who had special links with Croydon Airport was killed by a bomb at his home in Coulsdon. He was Mr. Philip Mighell, who had farmed the land at New Barn Farm on which the original aerodrome, then called Beddington Aerodrome, was constructed for the Royal Flying Corps in 1917. Mighell - born in 1867 - had retired from farming during the 1930s and had gone to live at The Wend, Coulsdon. He was killed when a delayed-action bomb which had fallen on his house exploded just after he entered. He is buried in Beddington churchyard.

On the last day of September, 605 lost Flying Officer P.G. Crofts, a new-comer to the Squadron.

October began with a bombing raid - a lone German bomber carried out a breakfast-time attack. At 6.47 a.m. it dropped two high- explosive bombs on the playing field close to the Bofors gun emplacement and then machine-gunned over the main terminal block. But there were no casualties. That after-noon came a rather different visitor - Air Marshal H. R. Nicholls from Fighter Command, visiting this Battle of Britain station.

Hitler may have decided to postpone the invasion of Britain, but the Luftwaffe attacks still continued. On October 4th, Flight Lieutenant Currant and Pilot Officer J.A. Milne from 605 claimed a Ju 88 just off Dungeness.

On October the 7th a massed formation of German machines was seen heading for London. Pilot Officer C.E. English from 605 Squadron lost his life in this battle, while Squadron Leader McKellar claimed three Messerschmitts, and Pilot Officer Bob Foster one. Mr. Foster recalls English as "a quiet chap who came from Brighton". They shared a room in one of the requisitioned houses in Foresters Drive for the short time English was with the Squadron.

We went up fairly early that morning, and it was a nice day, with a big sun. There was this saying, 'Beware of the Hun in the sun', which meant that you should never allow the enemy to get between you and the sun, because then you could not see. We were on patrol and no one could see a thing - and we were really 'jumped' in the classic way by 109s who came straight out of the glaring sun . . . and this was where he [English] got it. The rest of us got away, but he was shot down. That was the same battle that I got a 109 - shot it down. [11]

On October the 12th, Sergeant Peter McIntosh was shot down and killed. As mentioned he was a Croydon man: he had lived in Lower Addiscombe Road and had been educated at Woodside Primary and Whitgift Middle schools. He had enlisted in the RAF's volunteer reserve in February 1939, and gained his wings as a pilot in May 1940. Colin Brown, a member of the Croydon Airport Society, currently tends McIntosh's grave in St. John's churchyard, Shirley, and notes that the McIntosh family were notified originally only that their son was missing, and last seen going down in the Romney Marsh area. Peter's father and elder brother went there to investigate, and, after making enquiries, located the body, still in the aircraft. A press letter from Peter's father criticising the lack of care taken in establishing the fate of such pilots was never printed; doubtless for the sake of 'public morale'. [15]

On October 14th Flying Officer Hope was killed chasing an He III into London. He is believed to have struck a barrage balloon cable over Inner London defence zone: the Squadron log says: "F/O. Hope, losing his way flew into the I.A.Z. where [he] was either shot down or ran into a cable at South Norwood." It then pays him a tribute, which, judging from his letter quoted earlier, was not an empty formula:

Apart from being the only original 605 Squadron auxiliary still in the Squadron, his charming personality and quiet sense of humour and stability will be much missed by everyone in the Squadron. [10]

Or, as Christopher Currant said in 1983: "Hope - now, he was a nice chap." [12]

Next day, October 15th, Flight Lieutenant I.J. Muirhead died: killed over Kent. As Wilf Nicoll put it:

With the onset of winter, the strain normally imposed by combat flying in near perfect conditions was increased tenfold by the additional hazards of deteriorating weather. It became almost a daily feature of life to enter Croydon's messes and find some familiar face missing. [14]

Christopher Currant, asked about his feelings at this time and whether he felt then that he had any future, said:

You always felt that it would always be the other chap, and this is typical of the combat life. You were always very tense and apprehensive until you got into the aircraft and started to take off, and then that went. There was then the exhilaration of what was coming, which was quite a different feeling from when you were sitting around waiting to be told to take off; and that went through the whole of the war, that feeling . . . One was always very frightened, but you just carried on in spite of it.

I had no personal animosity against any particular individual German: I just hated those black and grey things which were flying over our country and trying to defeat us, and I was always only too anxious to get in amongst this metal and stop it. It wasn't really against people; you didn't think about people, you thought about those bloody aeroplanes which you'd got to knock out of the sky somehow or other. It's rather like if a burglar is on your property, you get very angry and you probably do things you would not do if you'd thought about it later on, don't you, and it was that sort of feeling I think we had.

I think, had we known at that time of what was to follow in Germany, with the concentration camps, and the awful, terrible things that went on, we might have felt very much more personally antagonistic . . . but we didn't know anything about that at that time. I think the Poles did, and that's why they were so anxious to get at them - they'd seen their own country over-run. 12

On October 15th Croydon had another lone bomber attack, in which a high-explosive bomb created a 50-yard crater on the Purley Way playing fields, but there were no casualties. A similar attack was to take place on the 19th. On the 20th, the Royal Artillery inadvertently caused damage; with two anti-aircraft shells destroying the aerodrome's Link Trainer Building. 13

On October 20th Squadron Leader McKellar claimed another Messerschmitt 109, in a battle over Ashford in Kent.

Two days later there was a further local bombing raid. This time it did not affect the aerodrome itself, but damaged homes in the vicinity. The station record for October the 23rd notes:

During night 1 high explosive bomb dropped in grounds of Great Woodcote House. No. 23 Ridge Park very badly damaged. One apparently unexploded bomb in Sports Ground 80 yards from junction of Plough Lane South and Foresters Drive. 13

This was the old Imperial Airways Sports Ground now, at the time of writing, owned by the John Fisher School.

October 21st saw Archie McKellar score "his last official victory, an Me 109, which crashed near Redhill to bring his bag to twenty-one destroyed, three probably destroyed and three damaged." 16 In the space of his month at Croydon he had been awarded the DSO, and DFC and bar. He met his death only a few days later, on November the 1st, when his Hurricane crashed into a Kent garden. As a Messerschmitt 109 also crashed nearby, it can be assumed that they were engaged in a dog-fight.

Bob Foster remembers that this was during a period when small groups of Germans would come over, more to harrass the RAF than to achieve any specific objective:

He and I and others took off early in the morning to intercept these chaps and we were somewhere down over the Kent side of the Thames estuary . . . and there was a general sort of dog-fight. I didn't get anything, and I lost Archie, we all lost him, didn't know where he had gone. We all went home in dribs and drabs . . . and he didn't.

When they did find him, he was further down towards the Kent coast, a long way down, so I think he was chasing some of these chaps, and was probably jumped or bounced by some others . . .

and that was it. He was a long way from Croydon and must have been chasing one of them. [11]

'Bunny' Currant took temporary command of the Squadron. On 6th November, McKellar was buried with full military honours in his native Glasgow. The Squadron log notes:

Owing to an unfortunate [mis]understanding the aircraft which was being sent to Croydon to take two representatives of the Squadron to Glasgow, never arrived until too late. This was most disappointing. The Squadron was, however, represented by S/Ldr R.C. Longsdon, our former adjutant and now Squadron Leader Admin. at Turnhouse, who acted as pall bearer. [10]

McKellar had been an extremely popular commanding officer. Squadron Leader Gerry Edge was later brought back from 253 Squadron to 605 to replace him.

October 31st 1940 was later to be regarded by the British as the final day of the Battle of Britain - after this the onset of winter weather prevented further daylight German attacks.

On 8th November the Duke of Kent visited 605 Squadron. Currant was presented with a bar to his DFC, Cooper-Slipper with a DFC; and Sergeant E.W. Wright with a DFM.

Wright was later to be commissioned, acquire a DFC, and serve in the Far East, where he became a prisoner of the Japanese. He remained in the RAF after the war and had a distinguished career, becoming an Air Commodore.

The Luftwaffe were now organising 'hit and run' raids; and on November the 15th, 605 Squadron claimed three Me 109s destroyed, during an action in which Pilot Officer Gauze lost his life.

The next day saw a happier occasion: the Squadron log notes that "P/O Hayter was married at the Parish Church, Harrow-on-the-Hill." There were further domestic notes - on the 17th Lord Willoughby de Broke visited the squadron and, on the next day there is news of the Welfare and Comforts Committee: "under the chairmanship of Sgt. Shakespeare, 54 Foresters Drive has been turned into 'rest rooms' and was opened today." [10]

A few days later, on the 22nd, Air Vice Marshal Keith Park came to Croydon to congratulate the squadron. It was one of his last duties with No. 11 Group - he was shortly to be replaced by Leigh Mallory. Air Marshal Dowding, who had been in charge of Fighter Command throughout the Battle of Britain, was also summarily removed in November: on the 17th he was sent to the Ministry of Aircraft Production, being replaced at Fighter Command by Air Marshal Sholto Douglas.

On November 29th came the good news for 605 Squadron of 'Gerry' Edge's return. The log noted:

Cold and rather foggy. No patrols flown. S/L. G.R. Edge arrives in the evening, to take over Command of the Squadron, after having satisfactorily passed his C.M.B. The whole Squadron is delighted that he should return to us, and we now await formal posting. [10]

Edge was to be shot down the following year, and very badly burned. After recuperating, he went on to fight in the Western Desert, ending the war as a Group Captain. In the post-war years he became a farmer in Kenya. He is now living in Worcestershire, and is President of the 605 Squadron Association.

December 1940 opened with a battle over Canterbury on the 1st, in which 605 Squadron lost three Hurricanes; although all three pilots parachuted to safety.

126

There was time for more homely activities. The Squadron log for the 4th noted:

We make ourselves more comfortable in the Officers Mess. Instead of having the two down-stairs little rooms only in our semi-detached surburban villa, we move into the two upper rooms in the house - one as a games room and the other as a card and writing room. No patrols. Capt. Bennett - of MI - gave us a most interesting talk on his own and other people's experiences and tips for escaping from German Internment Camps. Sgt. Kestler (Czech) posted to us.

There were further visits from Lord Willoughby de Broke; a 'smoker' at Kenley for the officers; cold weather and mist to prevent flying; and various postings. These last were not always popular. On December 18th there is a sharp comment in the log:

F/O. Passy and Sgt. Jones posted to R.A.F. Station Cranage for night flying duties. We are all sad to lose them after having been with the Squadron for so long. We have been constantly - and in increasing intensity - been bothered with pin pricks like this. We have been down here nearly four months, doing fine teamwork in the air and on the ground, and yet they pick upon front line Squadrons with requests to denude themselves of their better pilots, often receiving in exchange pilots with very little experience indeed. No operational flying.

Two days later there was further cause for disquiet:

A considerable flap caused in the Squadron when we were told we should be moving to Heston very soon after Christmas. This is the last thing we want to do. We are well 'dug in here', have made ourselves very comfortable in our own little Mess, and are a happy family by ourselves as a Squadron. The idea of the move is to make one flight operational and the other experimental with Hurricane IIIs.

Happily this was soon sorted out:

21.12.40. After constant telephone conversations S/L. Edge has arranged that we may stay here during our half operational and half experimental period. Much relief all round. Two patrols flown -the first for a considerable time - but no enemy encountered.

Christmas brought many festivities, thanks to the hard-working Sergeant Shakespeare:

24.12.40. Cold and grey again. We had previously obtained permission from the Southern Railway Co., to use their pavilion almost adjoining the aerodrome for the men's Christmas Dinner, so that all might be seated at once. Much work, under the guidance of Sgt. Shakespeare, has been put in to make the place look gay, and final touches were made to-day, with splendid result. No air raid warning to-night (a most unusual event) nor over the whole country. The Officers celebrate Christmas Eve with dinner at the Greyhound Restaurant, Croydon - and afterwards in our Mess, till a late hour.

25.12.40. A grand day, thoroughly enjoyed by everybody. Wing Commander Prickman calls in to see us in the morning. We are very fortunate in that our half day release, i.e. after 13.30 hours falls to-day. The Officers have their dinner 13.30 hrs the men, 1800 hrs and the Sergeants 19.30. Officers and senior N.C.O.s waited on the men as usual, and everyone thoroughly enjoyed themselves. 162 sat down to dinner, and congratulations are due to Corporal Lines and the other cooks who turned out a first class meal. No enemy aircraft over this country by day or by night.

A few days later came a new arrival for the squadron:

29.12.40. A fine day, but nothing doing. P/O. Thompson brings us a Squadron mascot, Timothy the goat. Unfortunately it is a billy, and smells awful. It will have to be moved about considerably, and always tethered down wind. A very heavy air raid early in the evening, and enormous fires started in London, its relfection [sic] being shown in our own windows here. 10

Was the goat Timothy the same as a goat remembered by Robert Hall as Willy? Mr. Hall wrote:

At that time we had two squadron mascots in the shape of "Raff" a mongrel stray terrier and "Willy" a mischievious billy goat. Both wore coats, resplendent with R.A.F. roundels on each side. Both had the freedom of Foresters Drive, and during hours of darkness in the blackout, many screams and shouts could be heard as "Willy" stealthily stalked his prey and prodded them gently in the rear.

During the night, whilst most of us were sleeping, "Willy" would go on a tour of inspection from house to house, where most of the front doors were left open - you would hear him sniffing around the hall, then up the bare wooden stairs he would go to investigate further - unfortunately "Willy" found it impossible to walk down again, and would fall with a clatter of hoof and horn from top to bottom, pick himself up and continue on his way - he never seemed to injure himself, and would return on following nights to go through the same routine.

On the few occasions that "Willy" was led up in front of the band on parades, he had a rotten habit of doing a 'sideways-pee' down the trouser leg of whoever was leading him, so volunteers to accompany him in pomp and splendour were few and far between. [8]

Squadron Leader Currant remembers only one goat - but not its name.

There was a disappointment for the Squadron as the year ended; the log notes:

Sgt. Budzinski ill with meningitis. This was diagnosed overnight and unfortunately meant that the Squadron Dance over which so many, especially Sergeant Shakespeare, took so much trouble, had to be cancelled. This was a great disappointment to everybody. It is hoped that this is merely a short postponement. [10]

It occurred to us at this point to hope also that our account of the rest of the war at Croydon, and indeed the rest of the Croydon story, would also be the subject of 'merely a short postponement'.

The year 1940 had been a momentous one in Croydon Airport's - as in the nation's - history. Four more years of war were yet to come, but the end of 1940 saw more or less the conclusion of the aerodrome's 'front line' role.

It is perhaps worth pausing to reflect that Croydon was the only British airfield to have been a front-line, defensive airfield in both World Wars. Its fame as London's inter-war airport has overshadowed this unique distinction.

The rest of the war was to see Croydon's function revert to something more approaching its peacetime one. In 1943 came the return of BOAC, which then ran the aerodrome in harness with the RAF as represented by 110 Wing Transport Command, which itself set up scheduled European services to the continent as liberation proceeded and was to become, at the end of the war, BEA. Thus much of the post-war pattern of British civil aviation was established at Croydon before VE Day, and this whole period, like post-war Croydon, deserves detailed treatment which we look forward to providing in due course. In the meantime, however, we leave Croydon Airport in a Christmas respite from activities of attack or defence as 1940, the most violent year of its life, comes to an end.

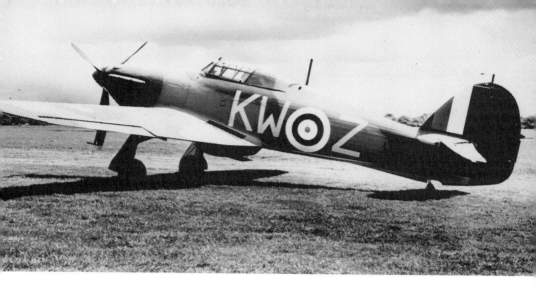

"Looker's Hurricane". Pilot Officer David Looker of 615 Squadron, who had been at Croydon at the beginning of the war, and was now at Kenley, crashed at Croydon on August 18th, 1940, trying to land his damaged Hurricane (see p. 86). .

74. *ABOVE:* His Hurricane, KW-Z.

75. *BELOW:* The Hurricane, now restored, in the Science Museum.

76.   *LEFT*: Sergeant Pilot Glendon Booth of 85 Squadron lived for five months after baling out of his Hurricane over Selsdon with a damaged parachute, before dying from his injuries in February 1941 (see p. 101).

77.   *RIGHT*: Pilot Officer Geoffrey "Sammy" Allard, DFC, DFM and bar, of 85 Squadron; fighter 'ace' who destroyed ten enemy aircraft and was credited with three probables in nine days in August 1940 whilst flying from Croydon. He was killed in an accident in March 1941 (see

78.   *ABOVE:* 85 Squadron on patrol in 1940.

79.   *BELOW:* Living by their aircraft: three pilots of 85 Squadron with a caravan at a dispersal point, ready to take-off in a few minutes at any time of day or night. This photograph was not taken at Croydon, but at a northern station, probably Church Fenton, Yorks.

80. Squadron Leader Peter Townsend with his N.C.O. pilots. Squadron Leader Townsend has a stick to help him walk with his bandaged foot after the amputation of his left big toe in Croydon Hospital when his foot was hit by a cannon shell whilst he was defending his Croydon base against German raiders on 31st August, 1940.

Pilot Officer (later Squadron Leader) Christopher 'Bunny' Currant of 605 Squadron.

81.   *ABOVE:* In September 1940

82.   *BELOW:* In Spring 1983 at home near Berkhamstead, talking about the Battle of Britain and his memories of Croydon.

84. Archie McKellar, later Squadron Leader of 605 at Croydon, and Christopher Currant, at a wedding in Edinburgh in 1940. Left to right (men): Christopher Currant, Cyril Passy, Flying Officer Paul Edge (Bridegroom), Archie McKellar.

83. Christopher Currant's Hurricane, K4186 at Kenley in August 1940. 'Bunny' Currant (with pipe) stands behind at the right. The name of the boat, painted on the fuselage, is 'Mizzen' and refers to a ribald 605 Squadron verse.

Pilot Officer, later Wing Commander, Robert (Bob) Foster of 605 Squadron.

85. *LEFT*: In 1940.

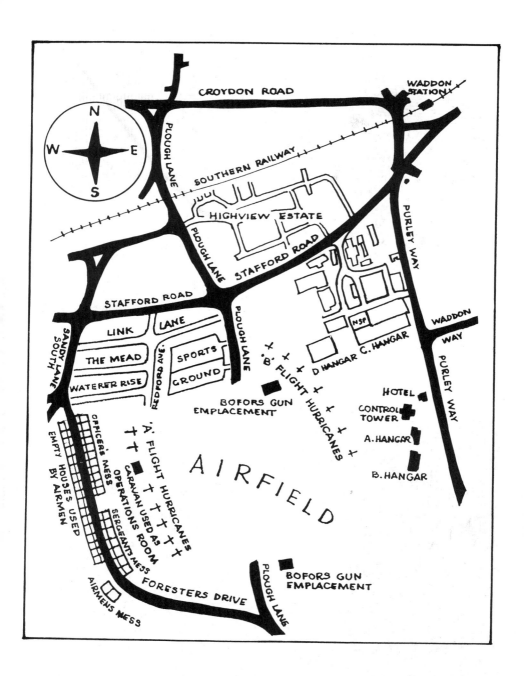

87. Plan of Croydon Airport in September 1940, showing the position of gun emplacements, billets, dispersal points, etc., as remembered by Mr. Robert F. Hall, then of 605 Squadron.

88. *LEFT*: Sergeant Pilot Peter McIntosh, a local boy who served with 605 Squadron at Croydon and was killed on October 12th, 1940 (see p. 124).

89. *RIGHT*: Pilot Officer Ernest E. Males who flew from Croydon with 72 Squadron. Whilst there he had one lucky ecape from a crashed Spitfire, but was later killed (see p. 119).

90. *ABOVE:* Ralph Reader of 'Gang Show' fame (fourth from left in the middle row) brought a concert party to Croydon during the Battle of Britain. Christopher Currant remembers being astonished at Reader's surprise at the small audience, which demonstrated his ignorance of the demands of a front-line Squadron. Comedian Dick Emery (second row, right) was amongst the entertainers.

91. *BELOW:* 605 Squadron's dance band, pictured in the Southern Railway Clubhouse on the edge of the aerodrome. Leading Aircraftman Albert Hodson (see p. 107) is the saxophonist, front row, left. The pianist was the dance band leader, Cliff Hughes, who was later to volunteer for air duties, become a Flying Officer and an air gunner in June 1943, and be killed on Christmas Eve of that year over Berlin with No. 50 Bomber Squadron.

92. *LEFT* and 93. *RIGHT*: The first picture shows Flt. Lt. I. J. Muirhead, left, and P/O C. E. English, right, of 605 Squadron. Flt. Lt. Muirhead was killed over Kent on October 15th 1940; P/O English (also shown in the portrait, 93, right) died on October 7th, 1940, intercepting German raiders heading for London. P/O English was with 605 Squadron in September, and was probably the only pilot to serve with two squadrons at Croydon in the Battle of Britain (see pages 99—100 and 124).

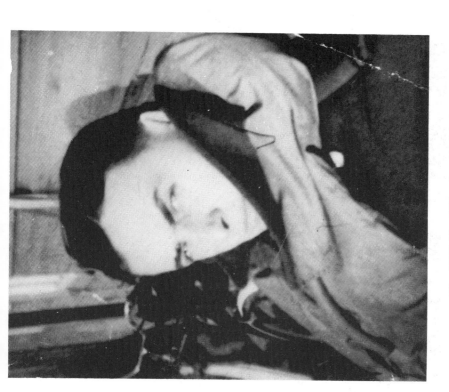

94. *LEFT*: Pilot Officer Oswald Pigg of 72 Squadron killed over Tunbridge Wells on September 1st, 1940.

95. *RIGHT*: Flight Lieutenant Stanley Connors of 111 Squadron, killed over Kenley, August 18th, 1940.

141

REFERENCES

NOTE: Material printed from RAF Croydon station log, the squadron logs, and other documents in the Public Record Office (as listed below) is Crown Copyright, and is reproduced here by permission of the Controller of HMSO

CHAPTER ONE

1. Not August 27th, as we stated on p.190 of *Croydon Airport: The Great Days.*
2. Curtis, Lettice. *The Forgotten Pilots: Air Transport Auxiliary 1939-45,* 1971. 2nd edition (paperback), the author, 1982.
3. Moss, Peter W. *Impressments log (Volume 3). 4 Vols and index.* Air Britain, 1962-66. Note: the Taifun's German registration was D-IJHW. It flew for the RAF as E.5955 and survived the war to become G-AFZO; until it was sold to a Swiss purchaser, Albert Valli, in April 1950. This aircraft is also mentioned on P.191 of *Croydon Airport: The Great Days.*
4. Information from Norman Griffiths, given to British Airways' magazine, *Touchdown*, 1982, and in conversation with the authors, 1983.
5. Brian Haimes: tape recording of conversation with Douglas Cluett and Joanna Bogle, November 1981. Sutton Central Library.
6. See *Croydon Airport: The Great Days*, pp.71-75
7. Information from Mr. E. J. H. Crawforth.
8. Lumsden, Alec. *Wellington Special*, Ian Allen, 1975; and information from Mr. Norman G. Parker in a letter to Douglas Cluett, 1983.
9. A. Deverell: letter to Mr. Norman Parker. Copy in Sutton Central Library.
10. Ken Steel: letter to the authors, 1983. Sutton Central Library.
11. Ramsey, Winston G., editor. *The Battle of Britain: Then and Now.* After the Battle magazine, 1980. Section: *Croydon* by Wilf Nicoll.
12. Late Leslie Penfold: letter to the authors, 1982. Sutton Central Library.
13. Keith Belcher: tape recording made by Mr. Derek Card for Croydon Airport Society, 1980, (copy in Sutton Central Library); and conversation with Douglas Cluett, 1984.
14. Operations Record Book: 615 Squadron R.A.F. Public Record Office (Kew). Ref. AIR 27/2123 XC/A024267.
15. Operations Record Book: 17 Squadron R.A.F. Public Record Office (Kew). Ref. AIR 27/233 XC/A/46415
16. Wood, Derek. *Attack Warning Red: The Royal Observer Corps and the Defence of Britain 1925 to 1975*, Macdonald and Jane's, 1976.
17. Eric Wheatley: conversation with the authors, 1983.
18. David J. Looker: conversation with Douglas Cluett, 1984.
19. Basil Peacock was later to become a prisoner-of-war of the Japanese and to write a number of books including *Prisoner on the Kwai.* He still lives in Wallington in 1984.
20. *Wallington and Carshalton Times*, September 21st, 1939.
21. Information from Mr. Colin Brown; *Croydon Advertiser*, 8th June 1945; Operations Record Book, 17 Squadron (see 15. above).
22. Operations Record Book: 3 Squadron R.A.F. Public Record Office (Kew). Ref. AIR 27/32 038822.
23. *The Times*, September 13th and 22nd, 1939.
24. Operations Record Book, R.A.F. Croydon. Public Record Office (Kew). Ref. AIR 28/178/9806.
25. Sayers, W.C. Berwick. *Croydon and the Second World War: The Official History of the War Work of the Borough and its Citizens from 1939 to 1945.* Croydon Corporation, 1949.
26. Operations Record Book: 145 Squadron R.A.F. Public Record Office (Kew). Ref. AIR 27/984/9814.

CHAPTER TWO

1. Public Record Office (Kew). Ref. AVIA 2/2089 21361.
2. Moss, Peter W. *Impressments Log.* 4 vols and index. Air Britain, 1962-66.
3. Bruce, Mrs. Victor. *Nine Lives Plus: Record Breaking on Land, Sea and in the Air*, Pelham Books, 1977.

4. Arthur Quin-Harkin, O.B.E.: tape recording of conversation with the authors. Sutton Central Library.
5. Norman Griffiths: information supplied to British Airways' magazine *Touchdown*, 1982; and conversation with the authors, 1983.
6. Pudney, John. *The Seven Skies: A study of BOAC and its Forerunners since 1919*, Putnams, 1959.
7. *Memorandum on the suggested revision of policy governing NAC*. Public Record Office (Kew). Ref. AVIA 2/2304 21390.
8. *Keesing's Contemporary Archives, 1938.*
9. *BOAC: Financial Matters Requiring Attention Between Passing of Act and the Appointed Day.* Public Record Office (Kew). Ref. AVIA 2/2109.

CHAPTER THREE

1. Operations Record Book: 615 Squadron R.A.F. Public Record Office (Kew). Ref. AIR 27/2123 XC/A/024267.
2. Operations Record Book: 607 Squadron R.A.F. Public Record Office (Kew). Ref. AIR 27/2093 XC/A/027936.
3. Peter G. Cooksley. Manuscript notes, Sutton Central Library.
4. Viscount Whitelaw, then Mr. William Whitelaw: letter to Joanna Bogle, following a radio broadcast mentioning his war service at Croydon. A similar letter was sent to Mr. Ewart Sanders, then Secretary of the Croydon Airport Society, following a similar enquiry.
5. Brickhill, Paul. *The Great Escape*, Faber, 1951.
6. Forrester, Larry. *Fly for your Life: The Story of R.R. Stanford-Tuck*, Muller, 1956.
7. Operations Record Book: 92 Squadron R.A.F. Public Record Office (Kew). Ref. AIR 27/743/021/237.
8. Operations Record Book: 145 Squadron R.A.F. Public Record Office (Kew). Ref. AIR 27/984 9814.
9. *Daily Mirror*, February 26th, 1940.
10. Bateman, Dennis C. *Night Solo to Eternity*, After the Battle Magazine no. 40, 1983.
11. Whiteing, Eileen. . . . *Some Sunny Day . . . : Reminiscences of a Young Wife in the Second World War*, London Borough of Sutton Libraries and Arts Services, 1983.
12. Operations Record Book: R.A.F. Croydon. Public Record Office (Kew). Ref. AIR 28/178 9806.
13. Information quoted by Mrs. Evelyn Boyd, Air Historical Branch, Ministry of Defence, from 11 Group Routine Orders, No. 7, 9/4/1940.

CHAPTER FOUR

1. Operations Record Book: 92 Squadron R.A.F. Public Record Office (Kew). Ref. AIR 27/743/021/237.
2. Operations Record Book: R.A.F. Croydon. Public Record Office (Kew). Ref. AIR 28/178 9806.
3. Operations Record Book: 2 Squadron R.A.F. Public Record Office (Kew). Ref. AIR 27/19.
4. Operations Record Book: 607 Squadron R.A.F. Public Record Office (Kew). Ref. AIR 27/2093 XC/A/027936.
5. Ken Steel: letter to the authors, 1983. Sutton Central Library.
6. Operations Record Book: 271 Squadron R.A.F. Public Record Office (Kew). Ref. AIR 27/15 74 38466.
7. Ifould, Lloyd C. *Immortal Era: The Birth of British Civil Aviation*, Adanar Press, Montreal, 1948.
8. Brickhill, Paul. *The Great Escape*, Faber, 1951.
9. Lloyd C. Ifould: letter to Douglas Cluett, 1983.
10. Operations Record Book: 501 Squadron R.A.F. Public Record Office (Kew). Ref. AIR 27/1949 028825.
11. Bishop, Edward. *The Battle of Britain*, Allen and Unwin, 1960.
12. Middleton, Drew. *The Sky Suspended*, Secker and Warburg, 1960.

13. Sands, R.P.D. *Treble One*, North Weald, 111 Squadron, 1957.
14. Cooksley, Peter G. *1940: The Story of No. 11 Group Fighter Command*, Robert Hale, 1983.
15. Information from Colin Brown: notes at Sutton Central Library.
16. *Wallington and Carshalton Times*, July 1940.
17. Daily Diary of 401 Squadron, R.C.A.F. Public Record Office (Kew). Ref. AIR 27/1771 024225.

CHAPTER FIVE

1. Operations Record Book: 111 Squadron R.A.F. Public Record Office (Kew). Ref. AIR 27/866.
2. Margaret Cunningham: written account for the authors. Sutton Central Library.
3. Brian Haimes: tape recording of conversation with Douglas Cluett and Joanna Bogle, November 1981. Sutton Central Library.
4. Leslie Penfold: letter to the authors. Sutton Central Library.
5. Quoted in: Jullian, Marcel. *The Battle of Britain*, Jonathan Cape, 1967.
6. Quoted in: Masters, David. *So Few . . . The Immortal Record of the R.A.F.*, Eyre and Spottiswoode, 1941.
7. Bill Whitehead: taped interview with Bob Learmonth, 1983. Sutton Central Library.
8. Ernest Jones: conversation with Bob Learmonth, 1983.
9. Printed notes accompanying a letter to Bob Learmonth from Mr. Alan E. le G. Gillett, Sales Promotion Manager of N.S.F. Ltd., May 1983. Sutton Central Library.
10. Victor J. Wood: letter to Bob Learmonth. Sutton Central Library.
11. Joss G. Spiller: letter to Bob Learmonth, 1983. Sutton Central Library.
12. Mrs. Phyllis Lane: letter to Douglas Cluett, 1983. Sutton Central Library. Partly based on information supplied by Mr. Cyril Smith, a Redwing employee at the time.
13. McKee, A. *Strike from the Air*, Souvenir Press, 1960.
14. List compiled by Mr. Colin Brown. Copy in Sutton Central Library.
15. Sayers, W.C. Berwick. *Croydon and the Second World War: The Official History of the War Work of the Borough and its Citizens from 1939 to 1945*, Croydon Corporation, 1949.
16. Rosalind Prest: letter to Douglas Cluett. Sutton Central Library.
17. Arthur W. Bridger writing to Valary Murphy, 1984.
18. *Hansard*, 20th August 1940.

CHAPTER SIX

1. Battle of Britain. Croydon 1940. Casualties. Manuscript list compiled by Colin Brown. Copy in Sutton Central Library.
2. Operations Record Book: 111 Squadron R.A.F. Public Record Office (Kew). Ref. AIR 27/866.
3. Price, Alfred J. *The Battle of Britain: The Hardest Day, 18 August 1940*, Macdonald and Jane's, 1979.
4. Burden, Philip. *A Hurricane's Day*; article in the *RAF Flying Review*, Vol. XVIII, No. 11; other information from conversation with David J. Looker in 1984.
5. Public Record Office. File AIR 38/153.
6. Townsend, Peter. *Time and Chance: An autobiography*, Collins, 1978.
7. Ramsey, Winston G., editor. *The Battle of Britain: Then and Now*, After the Battle magazine, 1980. Section: *Croydon* by Wilf Nicoll.
8. Perry, Colin. Boy in the Blitz, Leo Cooper, 1972. Illustrated edition, Colin A. Perry Ltd., 1980.
9. Operations Record Book: R.A.F. Croydon. Public Record Office (Kew). Ref. AIR 28/178 9806.
10. Operations Record Book: 85 Squadron R.A.F. Public Record Office (Kew) Ref. AIR 27/703 9806.
11. Manuscript notes on Glendon Booth compiled by Colin Brown. Sutton Central Library.

CHAPTER SEVEN

1. Operations Record Book: 72 Squadron R.A.F. Public Record Office (Kew). Ref. AIR 27/624.
2. Operations Record Book: 85 Squadron R.A.F. Public Record Office (Kew). Ref. AIR 27/743.
3. Manuscript notes on Glendon Booth by Colin Brown. Sutton Central Library.
4. Operations Record Book: 111 Squadron R.A.F. Public Record Office (Kew). Ref. AIR 27/866.
5. In Jullian, Marcel. *The Battle of Britain July - September 1940.* Jonathan Cape, 1967.
6. Perry, Colin. *Boy in the Blitz,* Leo Cooper, 1972. Illustrated edition, Colin A. Perry Ltd., 1980.
7. Masters, David. *So Few . . . The Immortal Record of the Royal Air Force,* Eyre & Spottiswoode, 1941.
8. Robert Hall: letter to Douglas Cluett, 1978. Sutton Central Library.
9. Albert Hodson: letter to Douglas Cluett, 1983 (at Sutton Central Library), and subsequent conversations.
10. Operations Record Book: 605 Squadron R.A.F. Public Record Office (Kew). Ref. AIR 27/2088.
11. Robert Foster: taped conversation with Joanna Bogle and Douglas Cluett, 1982. Sutton Central Library.
12. Christopher Currant: taped conversation with Douglas Cluett and Colin Brown, 17th March 1983. Sutton Central Library.
13. Operations Record Book: R.A.F. Croydon. Public Record Office (Kew). Ref. AIR 28/178 9806.
14. Ramsey, Winston G. *The Battle of Britain, Then and Now,* After the Battle magazine, 1980. Section: *Croydon* by Wilf Nicoll.
15. Colin Brown: letter to the authors. Sutton Central Library.
16. Baker, E.C.R. *The Fighter Aces of the R.A.F. 1939-45,* William Kimber, 1962.

RAF SQUADRONS AT CROYDON, SEPTEMBER 1939 to DECEMBER 1940 (in chronological order of arrival)

Squadron No.	Commanding Officer	Aircraft with which equipped	Arrived	Departed	Code Letters
615	Sqdn Ldr Arthur Vere Harvey	Gloster Gladiators Mks I & II	2.9.39 (1030 hrs approx.)	15.11.39	KW
17	Sqdn Ldr C. Walter	Hawker Hurricanes Mk I, plus 2 Miles Magisters	2.9.39 (Air party arrived 1110 hrs - ready to operate by 1200)	9.9.39	YB
3	Sqdn Ldr H.H. Chapman	Hawker Hurricanes Mk I	2.9.39 (time not recorded but believed to have arrived third)	12.10.39	QO
607	Sqdn Ldr L.E. Smith	Gloster Gladiators Mks I & II	13.11.39	15.11.39 (2 days only)	AF
3 (return)	1. Sqdn Ldr H.H. Chapman 2. Flt Lt Patrick Gifford (from 19.11.39 - promoted Acting Sqdn Ldr from 11.12.39 Awarded DFC 29.11.39)	Hawker Hurricanes Mk I	15.11.39	28.1.40 ('A' Flight at Hawkinge from 18.12.39)	QO
145 (re-formed at Croydon, after disbandment in 1919)	Sqdn Ldr J.D. Miller	1. Bristol Blenheims Mk I F 2. Hawker Hurricanes Mk I (conversion began on 6.3.40 - completed 30.3.40)	10.10.39	9.5.40	SO
92	Sqdn Ldr Roger Bushell	1. Bristol Blenheims Mk I F 2. Vickers-Supermarine Spitfires Mk I (conversion began 5.3.40 - completed 30.3.40); plus one Miles Master.	30.12.39	8/9.5.40	GR
2 (Army Co-Operation)	Wing Cmdr A.J.W. Geddes OBE	Westland Lysanders Mks I & II	20.5.40 (2100 hrs)	21.5.40 (1230 hrs)	

RAF SQUADRONS AT CROYDON, SEPTEMBER 1939 to DECEMBER 1940 (in chronological order of arrival)

Squadron No.	Commanding Officer	Aircraft with which equipped	Arrived	Departed	Code Letters
607 (return)	Sqdn Ldr J. A. Vick (Sqdn Ldr L. E. Smith reported missing in France)	Gloster Gladiators Mks I & II	22.5.40	4.6.40	AF
111	Sqdn Ldr J. M. Thompson, DFC	Hawker Hurricanes Mk I	4.6.40	19.8.40	JU
501	1. Sqdn Ldr M. V. M. Clube 2. Sqdn Ldr H. A. V. Hogan (from 29.6.40)	Hawker Hurricanes Mk I	21.6.40	4.7.40	SD
401 (= No. 1 Squadron RCAF)	Sqdn Ldr E. A. McNabb, DFC (This squadron was training - under battle conditions - with 111 at Croydon. It was declared operational on moving to Northolt.)	Hawker Hurricanes Mk I	5.7.40	16.8.40	YO
85	Sqdn Ldr Peter W. Townsend, DFC	Hawker Hurricanes Mk I	19.8.40	3.9.40	VY
72	1. Sqdn Ldr A. R. Collins (wounded 2.9.40) 2. Sqdn Ldr E. Graham (from 2.9.40)	Vickers-Supermarine Spitfires Mk I	1.9.40	12.9.40	RN
111 (Return)	Sqdn Ldr J. M. Thompson, DFC	Hawker Hurricanes Mk I	3.9.40	8.9.40	JU
605	1. Sqdn Ldr Walter Churchill, DSO, DFC 2. Flt Lt Archie A. McKellar, DSO, DFC and Bar (from 29.9.40 - promoted Sqdn Ldr 2.10.40 - killed 1.11.40) 3. Flt Lt Christopher F. Currant, DFC and Bar, from 1.11.40 (temp.) 4. Sqdn Ldr G. R. Edge, DFC (from 29.11.40)	Hawker Hurricanes Mks I & II	7.9.40	25.2.41	UP

With the departure of 111 Squadron on 8th September 1940, 605 was the squadron in sole possession of Croydon until the end of the Battle of Britain, and the end of the year.

APPENDIX B

Specimen aircraft movements at Croydon on afternoons of

> (a)   August 28th 1939
>
> (b)   March 30th 1940

Movement logs of Croydon Airport unfortunately (with one late exception) cannot be traced, and are presumably destroyed. It is therefore all the more valuable that we have been supplied with a record of some movements at Croydon on a number of days in 1939 and early 1940 by Mr. Geoffery A. Pott, who observed and recorded them as a schoolboy then. We publish here two of these, one of a week before the outbreak of war and one from March 1940. Compare the number of parked aircraft early in the last week of peace with the photographs at the beginning of Chapter Two. (Note: the record in each case is that of one afternoon, not a whole day's operations.)

CROYDON MONDAY AUGUST 28TH.1939.

WIND:- Calm.
CLOUD:- Cumulus and Cirrus. LOW CLOUD:- 3,000 ft.
SKY:- ¼ covered.
SUN:- Very strong.
VISIBILITY:- 6 miles.
RAIN:- Nil.
TEMPERATURE:- 72 degrees F.
BAROMETER:- 29.80 inches.

DEPARTURES.

Time	Reg.	Aircraft	Operator
14.52	G-ADWY	D.H.85. Leopard Moth.	Air Taxis.
14.56	G-ABUT	D.H.83. Fox Moth.	Surrey F/S.
14.57	G-AFDL	D.H.91. Albatross. "Fingal"	I.A.L.
15.03	F-AOHC	Bloch 220. "Guyenne"	Air France.
15.16	G-AFEP	D.H.89A. Dragon Rapide.	N.E.A.
15.26	G-ADUF	D.H.86B. Express. "Dido"	I.A.L.
15.28	G-AFSP	D.H.82A. Tiger Moth.	Thanet Aero Club.?
15.29	G-AEPW	D.H.89A. Dragon Rapide.	Olley A/S.
15.30	EI-ABK	D.H.86B. Express. "Eire"	A.L.T.
15.35	G-ACVY	D.H.86. Express. "Mercury"	R.A.S.
15.36	G-ADUF	D.H.86B. Express. "Dido"	I.A.L.
15.37	G-ADSS	A.W.27. "Egeria"	I.A.L.
15.38	G-ABUT	D.H.83. Fox Moth.	Surrey F/S.
15.39	G-AFET	Miles M.14A. Hawk Trainer III.	Ipswich Flying Club.?
15.48	PH-ALH	Douglas D.C.3. "Hop"	K.L.M.
15.51	G-AFNC	D.H.89A. Dragon Rapide.	?
16.04	F-AQNO	Bloch 220. "Alsace"	Air France.
16.05	G-AEVY	Stinson SR.9D. Reliant.	D.J.R.Bryans.?
16.17	G-ACYR	D.H.89A. Dragon Rapide.	Olley A/S.
16.20	G-ABSO	D.H.80A. Puss Moth.	?
16.29	G-AENN	D.H.89A. Dragon Rapide.	Olley A/S.
16.30	G-ABBJ	D.H.60G. Gipsy Moth.	Surrey F/S.
16.31	G-ADUF	D.H.86B. Express. "Dido"	I.A.L.
16.43	G-ABBJ	D.H.60G. Gipsy Moth.	Surrey F/S.
16.49	G-ADSY	A.W.27. "Empyrean"	I.A.L.
16.50	G-AFDJ	D.H.91. Albatross. "Falcon"	I.A.L.
16.51	G-AFDK	D.H.91. Albatross. "Fortuna"	I.A.L.
17.01	F-AOHH	Bloch 220. "Savoie"	Air France.

ARRIVALS.

14.47	G-AFSP	D.H.82A. Tiger Moth.		Thanet Aero Club.?
15.00	G-ABUT	D.H.83. Fox Moth.		Surrey F/S.
15.10	PH-ALH	Douglas D.C.3. "Hop"		K.L.M.
15.25	F-AQNO	Bloch 220. "Alsace"		Air France.
15.33	G-ADUF	D.H.86B. Express. "Dido"		I.A.L.
15.34	K3791	Hawker Demon I.		R.A.F.
15.59	G-ABUT	D.H.83. Fox Moth.		Surrey F/S.
16.00	G-AFDK	D.H.91. Albatross. "Falcon"		I.A.L.
16.06	?	Bristol Blenheim IF.	RO-K	R.A.F. (29 Sqdn).
16.12	G-ACYR	D.H.89A. Dragon Rapide.		Olley A/S.
16.15	OY-DEM	Focke-Wulf Fw.200. Condor. "Jutlandia"		D.D.L.
16.23	G-ADUF	D.H.86B. Express. "Dido"		I.A.L.
16.26	F-AOHH	Bloch 220. "Savoie"		Air France.
16.27	G-ABSO	D.H.80A. Puss Moth.		?
16.36	G-ADUF	D.H.86B. Express. "Dido"		I.A.L.
16.40	G-ABBJ	D.H.60G. Gipsy Moth.		Surrey F/S.
16.44	G-AFND	D.H.89A. Dragon Rapide.		?
16.45	PH-ASK	Douglas D.C.3. "Kemphaan"		K.L.M.
16.54	G-ABBJ	D.H.60G.Gipsy Moth.		Surrey F/S.
17.00	G-AEVY	Stinson SR.9D. Reliant.		D.J.R.Bryans.?
17.06	PH-ALI	Douglas D.C.3. "Ibis"		K.L.M.

PARKED AIRCRAFT.

G-AASP	Avro 618 Ten. "Achilles"	I.A.L.
G-AAUD	H.P.42W. "Hanno"	I.A.L.
G-AAXC	H.P.42W. "Heracles"	I.A.L.
G-ADSR	A.W.27. "Ensign"	I.A.L.
G-ADST	A.W.27. "Elsinore"	I.A.L.
G-ADSW	A.W.27. "Eddystone"	I.A.L.
G-ADSZ	A.W.27. "Elysian"	I.A.L.
G-ADTA	A.W.27. "Euryalus"	I.A.L.
?	3 A.W.27s.	I.A.L.
G-AAZX	D.H.80A. Puss Moth.	Charles S.J.Collier.?
G-ACIU	D.H.84. Dragon I.	Surrey F/S.
G-ACEK	D.H.84. Dragon I.	Air Dispatch.
G-AEKZ	D.H.84. Dragon I.	Air Dispatch.
G-AEMI	D.H.84. Dragon II.	Air Dispatch.
G-ADNI	D.H.89A. Dragon Rapide.	Air Dispatch.
G-AECX	D.H.90. Dragonfly.	Air Dispatch.
G-AESW	D.H.90. Dragonfly.	Air Taxis.
G-ACLT	Airspeed AS.5. Courier.	Air Taxis.
G-AERX	Junkers Ju.52/3M. "Jupiter"	British A/W.
G-AFAP	Junkers Ju.52/3M. "Jason"	British A/W.
D-AHMS	Junkers Ju.52/3M. "Martin Zander"	D.L.H.
OO-AGP	Savoia Marchetti S.73.	Sabena.
K4410	Hawker Hart(Special) Trainer.	R.A.F.
?	Hawker Hart (Special) Trainer.	R.A.F.

<u>CROYDON SATURDAY MARCH 30TH.1940.</u>

```
WIND:- Fairly strong, N.W.
CLOUD:- Cumulus and Cirrus.
SKY:- ½ covered.
SUN:- Fairly strong to strong.
RAIN:- Nil.
TEMPERATURE:- 55 degrees F.
BAROMETER:- 29.82 inches.
```

DEPARTURES.

Time	Serial	Aircraft	Code	Sqdn.	Service
14.48	L5937	Miles Magister.	(Uncoded)		RAF.
15.00	K7387	Hawker Audax.	(Uncoded)		RAF.
15.10	?	Hawker Hurricane I.	SO-S	145 Sqdn.	RAF.
15.10	?	Hawker Hurricane I.	SO-O	145 Sqdn.	RAF.
15.10	?	Hawker Hurricane I.	(Code ?)		RAF.
15.20	?	Hawker Hurricane I.	SO-K	145 Sqdn.	RAF.
15.24	?	Hawker Hurricane I.	SO-?	145 Sqdn.	RAF.
15.26	?	V.S.Spitfire I.	GR-S	92 Sqdn.	RAF.
15.28½	?	Bristol Blenheim IF.	SO-N	145 Sqdn.	RAF.
15.29	?	V.S.Spitfire I.	GR-A	92 Sqdn.	RAF.
15.29	?	V.S.Spitfire I.	GR-B	92 Sqdn.	RAF.
15.29	?	V.S.Spitfire I.	GR-G	92 Sqdn.	RAF.
15.42	L5937	Miles Magister.	(Uncoded)		RAF.
15.47	P9373	V.S.Spitfire I.	GR-H	92 Sqdn.	RAF.
15.47	?	V.S.Spitfire I.	GR-M	92 Sqdn.	RAF.
15.47	N3249	V.S.Spitfire I.	GR-P	92 Sqdn.	RAF.
15.48	L5937	Miles Magister.	(Uncoded)		RAF.
15.54	?	V.S.Spitfire I.	GR-D	92 Sqdn.	RAF.
15.54	P9374	V.S.Spitfire I.	GR-J	92 Sqdn.	RAF.
15.54	N3290	V.S.Spitfire I.	GR-U	92 Sqdn.	RAF.
16.04	?	Hawker Hurricane I.	SO-H	145 Sqdn.	RAF.
16.04	N2712	Hawker Hurricane I.	SO-?	145 Sqdn.	RAF.
16.04	?	Hawker Hurricane I.	SO-?	145 Sqdn.	RAF.
16.05	L5937	Miles Magister.	(Uncoded)		RAF.
16.07	?	Hawker Hurricane I.	SO-?	145 Sqdn.	RAF.
16.07	?	Hawker Hurricane I.	SO-H	145 Sqdn.	RAF.
16.07	?	Hawker Hurricane I.	SO-E	145 Sqdn.	RAF.
16.45	L5937	Miles Magister.	(Uncoded)		RAF.

ARRIVALS.

Time	Serial	Aircraft	Code	Sqdn.	Service
14.45	?	V.S.Spitfire I.	GR-L	92 Sqdn.	RAF.
14.45½	?	V.S.Spitfire I.	GR-M	92 Sqdn.	RAF.
14.46	?	V.S.Spitfire I.	GP-S	92 Sqdn.	RAF.
15.14	K7387	Hawker Audax.	(Uncoded)		RAF.
15.19	?	Hawker Hurricane I.	SO-H	145 Sqdn.	RAF.
15.23	?	Hawker Hurricane I.	SO-?	145 Sqdn.	RAF.
15.25	?	Hawker Hurricane I.	SO-?	145 Sqdn.	RAF.
15.25½	L5937	Miles Magister.	(Uncoded)		RAF.
15.28	?	Hawker Hurricane I.	SO-E	145 Sqdn.	RAF.
15.35	?	Hawker Hurricane I.	SO-?	145 Sqdn.	RAF.
15.45	L5937	Miles Magister.	(Uncoded)		RAF.
16.00	L5937	Miles Magister.	(Uncoded)		RAF.
16.15	L5937	Miles Magister.	(Uncoded)		RAF.
16.15¼	?	Hawker Hurricane I.	SO-E	145 Sqdn.	RAF.
16.15½	?	Hawker Hurricane I.	SO-?	145 Sqdn.	RAF.
16.19	?	Hawker Hurricane I.	SO-O	145 Sqdn.	RAF.
16.28	?	V.S.Spitfire I.	GR-O	92 Sqdn.	RAF.
16.29	?	V.S.Spitfire I.	GR-A	92 Sqdn.	RAF.
16.29	?	V.S.Spitfire I.	GR-S	92 Sqdn.	RAF.
16.30	?	V.S.Spitfire I.	GR-B	92 Sqdn.	RAF.
16.35	?	Hawker Hurricane I.	SO-K	145 Sqdn.	RAF.
16.38	N3290	V.S.Spitfire I.	GR-U	92 Sqdn.	RAF.
16.38	?	V.S.Spitfire I.	GR-D	92 Sqdn.	RAF.
16.38	P9374	V.S.Spitfire I.	GR-J	92 Sqdn.	RAF.
16.40	P9373	V.S.Spitfire I.	GR-H	92 Sqdn.	RAF.
16.40	N3249	V.S.Spitfire I.	GR-P	92 Sqdn.	RAF.
16.40	?	Hawker Hurricane I.	SO-?	145 Sqdn.	RAF.
16.41	?	V.S.Spitfire I.	GR-M	92 Sqdn.	RAF.

PARKED AIRCRAFT.

```
Hawker Hurricane I.    SO-P    145 Sqdn.    RAF.
2 Hawker Audaxes.      (Uncoded)            RAF.
Miles Magister.        (Uncoded)            RAF.
```

N.**B.** Miles Magister L5937 reliably reported on the strength of No.145 Squadron.

APPENDIX C   NO. 615 (CS) SQUADRON, R.A.F., CROYDON.

ORDERS FOR LOCAL NIGHT FLYING PRACTICE ON 22/9/39   -   22/9/39.

1.   Night Flying will be controlled by Officer i/c, Night Flying from the Control Tower, and not from the Taxiyng Post.

2.   Aircraft will taxi to the Taxying Post (2 orange glim-lamps) and signal to the Control Tower for permission to take off.

3.   On permission being given by the usual method, aircraft will take off down a line approximately 100 yads. to the right of the glim lamp flare path.

4.   The Chance light will <u>not</u> operate during the take off, but, the Pilots will be guided by a white light shining at an angle of 75 ° upwards. This white light will be situated in the same line as the flare path and will be about 1,000 yds. past the end flare.   It will be extinguished as soon as the aircraft has passed over. This light will be manned by one Officer and one airman.   The signal for this light to come on, will be 5 (five) greens flashed from the Control Tower to the Officer i/c white light.

5.   Permission to land will be given again from the Control Tower.

6.   Pilots are to keep a good look out for signals not only from the Control Tower but also from the flare path.

7.   If after having received the green light from the Control Tower they see a Red Aldis Lamp shone at them, from the Flare Path. this denotes that they must not land or take off until they have obtained fresh permission from the Control Tower.

8.   Pilots must not confuse with thier identification letter the 5 (Five) Green lights which are solely intended for the Officer i/c white light.

9.   Before giving Aircraft permission to land the Control Tower will signal to the Flare Path to enable Chance lights and Landing "T" to be switched on immediately.

                                    Flying Officer
                      for   Squadron Leader Commanding,
                             No. 615 Squadron,

The night-flying orders reproduced in facsimile on this page, and details on the next, were originally pinned on a notice-board, and left behind when 615 Squadron departed from Croydon. (Originals loaned by Brian Haimes.)

NIGHT FLYING DETAIL 20/9/39 - 21/9/39.

Pilot.	Aircraft No.	Call Sign.	Detail.	Time Up.	Time Down.
W/Cdr. A.M. Wray, M.C. D.F.C. A.F.C.	N.2314.	"M".)	Dusk and Dark	19.30.	20.15.
P/O. R.D. Pexton.	N.5581.	"K".)	Landings.	19.30.	20.15.
P/O. D.W. Gillen.	N.5582.	"S".)			

2nd. Detail.

F/O. P. Collard.	N.5578.	"D".	Local Flying.	19.20.	20.00.
P/O. D.J. Looker.	N.5580.	"H".	" "	19.20.	20.00.
P/O. G.B. Cobeden.	N.5587.	"J".	" "	19.20.	20.00.

3rd. Detail.

F/Lt. M-Neale.	N.2314.	"M".)	Patrol as	20.30.	21.30.
P/O. D.W. Gillen.	N.5582.	"S".)	Detailed by Kenley	20.30.	21.30.
P/O. R.D. Pexton.	N.5581.	"K".)	(Line Astern)	20.30.	21.30.

4th. Detail.

F/O. J.R.H. Gayner.	N.5580.	"H".	Local Formation.	20.20.	21.20.
F/O. J.R. Bradford.	N.5578.	"D".	" "	20.20.	21.20.
P/O. D.S.H. Bury.	N.5587.	"J".	" "	20.20.	21.20.

5th. Detail.

F/O. E.C. Fieldsend.	N.2314.	"M".	Local Formation.	21.45.	22.45.
P/O. P.G. Hancock.	N.5582.	"S".	" "	21.45.	22.45.
P/O. B.J.R. Brady.	N.5581.	"K".	" "	21.45.	22.45.

6th. Detail.

F/Lt. L.T.W. Thornley.	N.5587.	"J".)	Patrol as Ordered	21.35.	22.35.
P/O. D.J. Looker.	N.5580.	"H".)	by Kenley.	21.35.	22.35.
P/O. G.B. Cobeden.	N.5578.	"D".)		21.35.	22.35.

7th. Detail.

P/O. L. Bredman.	N.2314.	"M".)	Local 5 M. from	23.15.	00.15.
P/O. J.R. Lloyd.	N.5581.	"K".)	Croydon.	23.15.	00.15.
P/O. J.G. Hanbury.	N.5582.	"S".	Circuits & Landings.	23.15.	00.15.

Officer i/c. Night Flying and Control (from Control Tower):-
...... S/Ldr. A.H. Harvey.
(P/O. K.T. Lofts to assist in Control Tower)
Officer i/c. Flare Path.......................................P/O. W.O. Stern.
N.C.O. i/c. Leader Light.................................Cpl. Thackeray.

for,

Pilot Officer & Adjt.,
Squadron Leader, Commanding,
No. 615 (CS) Squadron,
R.A.F., Croydon.

APPENDIX D

Official report on the August 15th air-raid: this report forms Appendix A1 to the Operations Record Book of RAF Croydon (PRO: AIR 28/178 9806).

SECRET

From:	R. A. F. Station, Croydon.
To:	Officer Commanding, R. A. F. Station, Kenley.
Date:	16th August, 1940.
Ref:	CRO/S/405/Air.

<u>REPORT ON ATTACK BY ENEMY AIRCRAFT ON
R.A.F. STATION, CROYDON
15th AUGUST, 1940</u>

<u>Time of Attack:</u>

Station Warning............1830 hrs.
First bomb dropped.........1859 hrs.

<u>Duration of Attack:</u>

Five to ten minutes.

<u>Number of Aircraft:</u>

A minimum of twenty five to thirty.

<u>Type of Aircraft:</u>

Me. Jaguars, Heinkels 113. Me 109 (Number of Jaguars estimated at 15 minimum)

<u>Type of Attack:</u>

H.E. armour piercing bombs; incendiary bombs and machine gun fire. Dive bombing in waves.

<u>Extent of Damage:</u>

(a) <u>Terminal Block</u> badly damaged on southern wing by H.E. armour piercing bombs and incendiary bombs. Extensive damage to windows and walls.

(b) <u>Armoury</u> - direct hit scored, completely burnt out.

(c) <u>Control Tower</u> showed evidence of machine gun fire.

(d) <u>"A" Hangar</u> - windows damaged.

(e) <u>"D" Hangar</u> - badly damaged by explosion and showed evidence of machine gun fire.

(f) <u>"C" Hangar</u> - used by Rollason Aircraft Services Ltd.,

Extent of Damage (continued)

(g) One Hispano gun - in car park by Officer's Mess put out of action by jambing.

(h) Officer's Mess - glass shattered by blast, window frames forced out, etc., internal damage to doors, woodwork, etc.

(i) M.T. Petrol installation - one fuel pipe out.

(j) Blockhouse outside Officer's Mess slightly damaged by blast.

(k) Shelter trenches (2) in car park slightly damaged.

(l) Two sports Grounds adjoining aerodrome - pavilions rendered useless.

Types of bombs used:

7 500 lbs. H.E. bombs.

2 Medium H.E. bombs.

A number of incendiary bombs.

For positions of bomb craters on aerodrome, see plan attached.

Craters in aerodrome - typical heavy bomb craters - 28' diameter by 10' deep with parapet 2' 6".

Gas:

Nil.

Casualties (R.A.F. Personnel)

	Fatal		Injured	
	Officers	Airmen	Officers	Airmen
S.H.Q. Personnel		1		
No. 111 Squadron		5		4 (taken to hospital)
No. 1 Canadian Squadron				1 (taken to hospital)

Casualties: (Civilians)

	Fatal	Injured
Civilian Telephone Operators		2 (taken to hospital)

Time: 1900 hours.

Date: Thursday, 15th August, 1940.

APPENDIX E

111 Squadron's gains and losses, recorded on leaving Croydon: page from their Operations Record Book (PRO: AIR 27/866 XC/AO27936).

Place.	Date.	Time.	Summary of Events.	References to Appendices
		8/9/40	out over Ashford at 1,000', and returned to base with slight injuries to his legs and head.	
			Squadron posted to Drem to reform. The following table of squadron and individual successes against enemy aircraft may be of interest, with the exception of 6 destroyed at Wick, they were all destroyed from the commencement of the campaign in France on the 16th of May until the Squadron was moved out of the line on the 7th September 1940.	

		Destroyed.	Probably destroyed.	Damaged.	
Killed in action	18/8/40	S/Ldr. Thompson. D.F.C.	6		4
" "	16/8/40	F/Lt. Powell. D.F.C.	5	1	2
" "	4/9/40	F/Lt. Connors D.F.C.& Bar	10½	1	6½
" "	4/9/40	F/Lt. Ferriss. D.F.C.	9	2	1
" "	10/7/40	P/O. Maccinski			1
		P/O. Bruce.	1		3
		P/O. Higgs,	6	1	1
		F/O. Walker D.F.C.	6		3
Killed in action	11/8/40	P/O. Simpson.	3½	1	3
" "	11/8/40	P/O. Copeman.	2	2	2
" "	19/5/40	P/O. Wilson.			
" "	2/9/40	P/O. Bury.	1	1	5
		Sgt. Dymond. D.F.M.			7
		Sgt. Craig. D.F.M.	4½	4	4
		Sgt. Carnall.	4½		5
		Sgt. Robinson.	2		
		Sgt. BROWN	1		1
		P/O. McIntyre.			
		F/O. Hardman.	1		1
		F/O. Fisher. B.	6		7
Killed in action	15/9/40	P/O. Fisher A.	1	3	1
		Sgt. Newton.			1
		Sgt. Wallace.	6		4
		Sgt. Deacon.	1		
		S/Ldr. McNab	3		1
		F/Lt. Giddings	3		1
Killed in action	18/5/40	F/O. Bowring.		2	4
" "	19/5/40	Sgt. Ritchie.			1
on active service	19/6/40	Sgt. Hampshire.			1
Killed in action	11/8/40	Sgt. Ekins.	1	1	
" "	11/8/40	F/Lt. Darwood,			
		P/O. Moorwood,			
		Sgt. Pascoe	1		
					3 probably destroyed with 615 S'qdn

ENEMY CASUALTIES.

		Destroyed.	Probably destroyed.	Damaged.
P/O. McKenzie.		9	1	1
Sgt. Sim.				
Squadron Generally		94	18	59

(Plus 1½ destroyed
(1 damaged with 64 Sdn

Page numbers in **bold** type refer to illustrations

Abingdon aerodrome, Berks, 107
Acklington aerodrome, Northumberland, 34
Addington Surrey, 118
Aerodrome Hotel, Croydon, vi, **ix**, 3, 5, 7, 16, **25**, 46, 86, 105, 166
Aeroplane, The, 79
'Air Armada', 13, 14, 19, 33, 45, **61, 62, 63, 64**
Air Britain, 16
Air Commerce, 20
Air Defence Cadet Corps, 2, 8, 11, 79
Air Despatch, 16
Air France, 7, 11
Air Ministry, 15, 16, 18, 20, 68, 79
  Accident Investigation Branch, 39
  Air Historical Branch, 86
Air Navigation (Restriction) Order, 1939, 16
Air-raids on Croydon Airport
  Principal, 15th August 1940, 69 *et seq*, 110, **111, 112, 114, 115, 116**
  Other, 85, 96, 98, 105, 121, 132
Air Transport Auxiliary, 1
Aircraft Disposal Company, 76
Allard, *Pilot Officer* Geoffrey ('Sammy'), 96-97, 99, **130**
Amiens, France, 8
Anderson, *Major-General,* 67
Anderson, *Sir* John, 41, 81
Andover aerodrome, Hants, 68
Anti-aircraft posts, **58, 59,** 95, 118, 121, 124
Armstrong Whitworth Ensign, 8, 18, **22,** 33, 34, 48, 49, 50, 51, **55, 61, 62, 63, 64,** 94
Army detachments at Croydon, 41, 43, 67, 166
  Essex Yeomanry, 41
  Honourable Artillery Company, 6, 11
  London Rifle Brigade, 2nd Battn., 41, 44, 67
  Middlesex Regt., 67
  Royal Artillery, Light A.A. Battery, 44, 67, 97
  Royal Horse Artillery, 43
  Scots Guards, 35, 38, 41
  Tower Hamlets Rifle Brigade, 67
  12th Queen's Royal Regt., 41, 67, 121
Ascot Concentration Camp, 37
Ashford, Kent, 103, 125
Associated Airways Joint Committee (AAJC), 20
Aston Down aerodrome, Glos., 12, 40
Audax (aircraft), 4, **21**
Audry au Bois, 47
Avro aircraft
  Lancaster, 77
  Ten, 33, 34
BEA, 128
BOAC, 18, 20, 33, 48, 50, 94, 128
Balfour, *Capt.* H. H. *(Lord Balfour of Inchrye),* 9, 20, 68
Barraclough, *Sergeant Pilot,* 43
Bartley, *Pilot Officer* Tony, 37, 40, 43
Barton aerodrome (Manchester), 17
Battle, Sussex, 96
Battle aircraft *see* Fairey Battle
Battle of Britain, 67 *et seq*
  Official dating of, 67
  Star: qualification for, 67
Bazin, *Flying Officer* J. M., 34
Beachy Head, 96, 118
Beacon, landing (civil) at Croydon, **23**
Beacon, neon (civil) at Croydon, 11
Beard, Georgie, 73

Beddington aerodrome, 68, 74, 123
Beddington churchyard, 123
Beddington Lane, **53**
Bedminster, Bristol, 18
Bekesbourne aerodrome, Kent, 46
Belcher, Keith, 5-6, 11
Benenden, Kent, 97
Bennett, *Captain* (MI), 127
Bensham Lane, Thornton Heath, 77
Benson, H. J. V. (pilot), 13
Benson aerodrome, Oxfordshire, 8, 37
Berck-sur-Mer, France, 8
Bergman, *Unteroffizier* Franz, 87
Berkhamstead, Herts., 108, 133
Bertram Mills' Circus, 37
Bert's Café, Stafford Road, 74
Bethune, France, 34, 46
Beudel, *Leutnant,* 78
Biarritz (ship), 47
Biggin Hill aerodrome, Kent, 7, 39, 68, 70, 72, 83, 85, 99, 10, 103, 119
Birkenhead, 101
Bishop, Edward *The Battle of Britain,* 51
Bitter, Hans, 75, **111**
Blackadder, *Flying Officer* W. F., 34, 51
Blackburn aircraft
  Roc, 66
  Skua, 46, 66
Blake, *Flight Lieutenant* Minden Vaughan, 10, 52
Blenheim aircraft *see under* Bristol aircraft
Blenheim Conversion Flight, Hendon, 12
Bletchingley, 10
'Blitz, The', 104 *et seq*
Blomeley, *Pilot Officer* D. H., 40
Blue Barns aerodrome, Colchester, 76
Bombay (aircraft) *see under* Bristol aircraft
Booth, *Sergeant Pilot* Glendon, 98, 100, **130**
Boto, Mr. and Mrs. George, 106
Boulogne, France, 12, 47, 48
Boulton and Paul Defiant, 66, 77
Bourjois factory, 59, 73, 74, 80, 83, 95, 105, **111, 112, 113**
Bowaters building, Purley Way, **111**
Bowen, *Flying Officer* C., 13
Bowling, *Pilot Officer* F. G., 6
Bowring, *Flyint Officer,* 102, 103
Box Hill, Surrey, 36
Boyd, *Flight Lieutenant* A. H., 13, 40
Bradford, *Flying Officer* J. R. T., 34
Brenchley, Kent, 83
Brewers' Society, 67
Brickhill, Paul *The Great Escape,* vi, 35, 48
Bridge, Doris, 38, 39
  Jack, 38
  Jill, 38, 39
  Montague, 38, 39
Bridger, Arthur, 81
Brighton, Sussex, 37, 124
Brigstock Road, Thornton Heath, 77
Bristol, 3, 18
  Bedminster, 18
  Filton aerodrome, 45
  Grand Spa Hotel, 17-18
  Stoke Bishop (NAC HQ), 17
  Whitchurch aerodrome, 3, 17, 18, **55**
Bristol aircraft
  Blenheim, 12, 32, 35, 36, 37, 38, 39, 40, 41, 42, **88, 89, 90, 91,** 92, **94**
  Bombay, 34, 47, 48

Bristol Flying School, Filton, 95
British Airways Ltd., 3, 9, 15, 17, 18, 19, 20, 33, 47, 55
See also British Overseas Airways Corporation
British European Airways, 128
British N.S.F. Ltd., 59, 74, 76, 77, 83, **110, 111, 112, 113**
British Overseas Airways Corporation, 18, 20, 33, 48, 50, 94, 128
Act, 1939, 20
Brockley County School, 100
Brooke, *General Sir* B. S., 67
Brown, *Sergeant Pilot,* 65
Brown, Colin, 124
Bruce, *Flight Lieutenant,* 102
Bruce, *Mrs.* Victor, 16, 17, 19
Bryson, *Pilot Officer* John, 35, 40, 42, 43
Buchanan, Jack, 11
Buckingham Palace, 106
Budzinski, *Sergeant,* 118, 128
Burden, Philip, 86
Burnett, *Sir* Charles, 11
Burpitt, Ronald (guardsman), 38
Bury, *Pilot Officer* D. S. H., 11
Bushell, *Squadron Leader* Roger, vi, 13, 35, 37, 39, 40, 43, 48-9, 94
Butterick, *Sergeant Pilot* A. F., 10
Buxton, *Captain* (Imperial Airways/BOAC pilot), 48, 49, 50
Byrne, *Flight Lieutenant* Vincent, 36, 38, 39, 40, 41, 42
'Cadman Report', 3
Calais, France, 66
Campbell, *Wing Commander,* 68
Campbell, *Sir* Edward, 11
Canada-Croydon links, 68
Canadian 2nd Infantry Brigade, 68
Cannock Chase, Staffs., 43
Canterbury, Kent, 126
Cap Gris Nez, 119
Cardiff aerodrome, 39
Carleton Avenue, Wallington, 11, 86
Carnall, *Sergeant Pilot* R., 83
Carr's Autos, Croydon, 77
Carshalton, 1, 70, 100
Carshalton Council Chamber, 39
Carshalton Hall, 9
Carshalton Road, Sutton, 81
Carshalton Tennis Club, 107
Carshalton War Memorial Hospital, 38
Caseley, *Flight Engineer,* 18
Caslaw, *Pilot Officer* J. A., 34
Castle Camps aerodrome, Cambs., 101
Caterham, Surrey, 100
Catterick, Yorkshire, 39, 40
Cazenove, *Flying Officer* Peter, 43
Central Electricity Generating Board stores 74, 77, **113.**
Chamberlain, Neville, 5, 7, 45
Channel, The, 2, 8, 48, 66, 67
Channel Islands, 51
Chapman, *Squadron Leader* H. H., 7, 13
Chatham, Kent, 101
Cheam, 81
Cherbourg, France, 51
Chipstead, Surrey, 104
Chipstead Hill, Surrey, 104
Chislehurst, Kent, 83
Church Fenton aerodrome, Yorkshire, **131**
Church Hill, Purley, 86
Church Street, Croydon, 77
Churchill, *Wing Commander* Walter, 104-105, 108, 118
Churchill, *Sir* Winston, 8, 9, 12, 45, 51, 87, 96, 107, **117**

Civilian Repair Organisation, 77
Clapham Junction, 122
Clark, *AC2* A., 47
Clifford and Snell, 81
'Cliff's Crochets' (605 Sqdn's dance band), 139
Clube, *Wing Commander,* M. V. M., 51
Cobb, *Colonel* (RASC), 44
Colchester, Essex, 76
Colgate, Sussex, 37
Collard, *Pilot Officer* P., 34
Collins, *Squadron Leader* A. R., 99, 101
Collyer Avenue, Beddington, 34
Comely, *Pilot Officer* P. W., 13, 37
Connors, *Flight Lieutenant* Stanley D. P., 69, 70, 72, 84, **141**
Control tower, Croydon Airport, ii, ix, 9, 54, **63**, 73, **136**
Cooksley, Peter G., 34, 54, 60
1940: The Story of No. 11 Group . . . , 67
Cooper, *Flight Lieutenant* Geoffrey A. B., 2, 3, 6
Cooper-Slipper, *Pilot Officer,* T. PM., 107, 118, 119, 120, 126
Cosford aerodrome, 40, 91
Coulsdon, Surrey, 123
Craig, *Flying Officer* G. D., 34
Craig, *Sergeant Pilot* J. T., 69, 70, 72, 83
Cranage aerodrome, Cheshire, 127
Crofts, *Flying Officer* P. G., 123
Cromie, *Flying Officer* R. S., 6
Crossley, *Squadron Leader* Michael N., 72, 85
Crowe, *ACI* C., 37, 42
Croydon (town and County Borough), 12, 77, 80
Council, 81
ARP Committee, 81
Town Hall, 81
Croydon Advertiser, 12, 79, 81
Croydon aerodrome (RAF Croydon)
Operations Record Book (Station log) 6, 33, 41, 45, 47
Croydon Airport: The Great Days 1928-39, 2, 3n, 76
Croydon Airport Society, 43, 124, 165
Croydon Gas Co. Sports and Social Club, 5, 72
Croydon General Hospital, 76, 80, 97, 132
Croydon Police Station, 38
Croydon Power Station, **53**
Cumnor House School, Croydon, 86
Cunningham, Margaret, 70
Currant, *Squadron Leader* Christopher, 107, 108, 118, 119, 120, 121, 122, 124, 125, 126, 128, **133, 134, 135,** 139,
Curtis, Lettice, 1, 21
Cuthbert, *Flying Officer* G. I., 47
Daily Mail, 39, 54
Daily Mirror, 38, 78
Dampier, Claude, 6
Dampier, *Flight Lieutenant* E. P., 6
Dartford, Kent, 103
Davis Theatre, Croydon, 5
Day and Night Café, Stafford Road, 74
de Havilland aircraft
Albatross, **55**
84 (Dragon), 47
86, 18, **22,** 33, 34, 47
89 (Dragon Rapide/Dominie), 47, 68
Leopard Moth, 46
Mosquito, 77
91, 18
de Havilland, Canada, 120
Deacon, *Sergeant Pilot* Harry, 85
Deacon-Elliott, Robert, 102

Debden aerodrome, Essex, 10, 87, 96, 100, 101
Defence posts, Croydon aerodrome, **23, 29, 58, 59,** 79, 95, 118, 121, 124
Defiant (aircraft), 66, 75
Degaussing rings (on Wellington bombers), 4, 31
Demon (aircraft), 4
Derwent Works, 77
Desures, France, 47
Deutsche.Luft Hansa, **x,** 1, 2
Deverell, A., 4
Digby aerodrome, Lincs., 34
Directional Wireless Installation (DWI), 3
Dixon, *Pilot Officer* H. P., 34
Doncaster aerodrome, 19, 20, 48
Donibristle aerodrome, Fifeshire, 19, **56, 57**
Dorking, Surrey, 11
Dorman, *Flight Lieutenant* Geoffrey, 79, 80
Dornier aircraft, 83, 101, 117
   Do 17, 67, 83, 84, 85, 99, 119, 120
   Do 215, 66, 69, 95, 98, 100. 117, 119
Douai aerodrome, France, 46
Douglas, *Air Marshal* Sholto *(Lord Douglas of Kirtleside),* 126
Douglas aircraft, 48
   Havoc, 96
Dover, 12, 66, 69, 99
Dowding. *Air Chief Marshall Sir* Hugh *(Lord Dowding),* 11. 39, 99, 101, 126
Dragon (aircraft), 47
Dragon Rapide/Dominie, 47, 68
Drem aerodrome. East Lothian. 103, 106 107
Drewey, *Major,* RCAF, 68
Drive, The, Wallington, 38, **89**
Dungeness, Kent, 83, 96, 97, 103, 122, 124
Dunkirk, France, vi, 48
Duxford aerodrome, Cambridgeshire, 37
Dymond, *Sergeant Pilot* W. L., 69, 72, 101
'Eagle Day', 82
Eastchurch, Kent, 95
Eddystone (A.W. Ensign), **22**
Edenbridge, Kent, 41
Edge, *Group Captain* G. R., 107, **116,** 11ь, 126, 127
Edge, *Flying Officer* Paul, **135**
Edgehill Road, Purley, 165
Edinburgh, **135**
Edson, *Flying Officer,* 106
Edwards, *Pilot Officer* 'Eddie', 36, 43
Egeria (A.W. Ensign), **55**
Ehekercher, *Feldwebel* Richard, 78
Elcombe, *Mrs.* D., 81
Electra (aircraft), **55**
Ellis, *Sergeant Pilot* J. H. M., 100
Elmers End cemetery, 100
Elson, *Pilot Officer* A., 37, 89
Eltham, Kent, 118
Elysian (A.W. Ensign), 48, 50
Emery, Dick, **139**
Emney, Fred, 11
Empire Agreement, 17
Empyrean (A.W. Ensign), **22, 55**
Endymion (A.W. Ensign), 51
English, *Pilot Officer* C. E., 99-1G0, 124, **140**
English Channel, 2, 8, 48, 66, 67
ENSA, 68
Ensign aircraft *see under* Armstrong Whitworth (and individual names)
Enterprise (A.W. Ensign), 50
Epps, Bernard, 77

Ereminsky, *Flying Officer* L., 34
Erprobungsgruppe (Test Group) 210, 70, 73 77. 78. 82. **115**
Essex Yeomanry, 41
Etchingham, 119
Ettrick (A.W. Ensign), **22,** 49-50, 94
Euryalus (A.W. Ensign), 48
Evans, *Sergeant,* 100
Exmouth, HMS, 54
Explorer (A.W. Ensign), 8, 33
Eyles, *Sergeant Pilot,* 40, 43
Eyre, *Wing Commander* Anthony, **24,** 34
Fairey Battle, 3, 8, 77
Farnborough, Hants. Royal Aircraft Establishment, 74, 108, 165
Faversham Cottage Hospital, 10
Ferriss, *Flight Lieutenant* Henry M., 69, 83, **117**
Fidler, *Acting Squadron Leader,* 47
Fiedeler, *Oberleutnant,* 78
Field (Consolidated) Aircraft Services Ltd. 3n, 4
Filton aerodrome, Bristol, 45
Fire Brigades
   Beddington & Wallington, 45
   Croydon, 45
First Croydon Airport 1915–1928, The, 3, 74
Firth of Forth, 13
Fisher, *Pilot Officer* A., 70
Fisher, *Flying Officer* B., 70
Fleming, *Pilot Officer,* 107
Fleet Air Arm, 66
Fletcher, *Air Commodore,* 17
'Flight Shed' (Hangar 'D'), 4, 6, **30, 52**
Fokes, *Sergeant Pilot,* 40, 43
Fokker F.XII, 33, 34, **63, 64**
Folkestone, Kent, 67, 96, 102
Ford Tri-Motor aircraft, 20
Foresters Drive, Wallington, 6, 9, 11, 23, 26, **27,** 38, 39, 86, 87, **90,** 95, 105, 106, 108, 124, 125, 126, 128
Forrester, *Pilot Officer* G. M., 107, 108, 118
Forrester, Larry. *Fly For Your Life,* 35, 42
Forster, *Pilot Officer* A. D., 34
Foster, *Wing Commander,* Robert. 107, 119, 121, 122, 124, 125
Foulness, Kent, 95
Fowler, *Flying Officer* H. N., 34
Fox, *Squadron Leader,* 2
Foxley Lane, Purley, 86
Frant, Kent, 78
Fraser, *Lt. Commander Sir* Malcolm, 11
Fredman, *Pilot Officer* L., 34
'Gang Show', **139**
Gas Company Sports Club, 5, 72
Gatwick aerodrome, Surrey, 36, 37, 41, 76, 122
Gauze, *Pilot Officer,* 126
Gayner, *Flying Officer* J. R. H., **23,** 34
George VI, *King,* 86, 87
George, *Duke of Kent,* 96, 126
Geschwader 76 (Luftwaffe), 85
Giddings, *Flight Lieutenant* H. S., 34, 102
Gifford, *Squadron Leader* Patrick, 13, 40
Gilder, *Sergeant Pilot,* 102
Gillies, John (pilot), 43
Glasgow, 126
   Renfrew aerodrome, 17
Gloster Gladiator, 5, 10, 11, **26, 27, 28,** 33, 34, **60, 63, 64,** 96
Glowacki, *Pilot Officer,* 118, 122
Goodman, *Sergeant,* 99
Gordon-Wilson, *Pilot Officer* C.D., 40
Gore, *Flying Officer,* W. E., 34, 51
Gossage, *Air Vice Marshal Sir* Leslie, 11

Government Training Centre, Stafford Road, 77
Gower, *Flying Officer,* 100
Graeme, *Flying Officer* N. S., 34
Graf, *Herr,* 75
Graffiti panel with squadron and army detachment numbers, 166
Graham, *Squadron Leader* R. B., 102
Gray, *Sergeant Pilot* "Mabel", 102
Grand Theatre, Croydon, 36
'Great Escape', 13
Great Western & Southern Air Lines, 20
Great Woodcote House, Wallington, 125
Great Woodcote Park, Purley, 86
Green, *Flight Lieutenant* Paddy, 36, 39, 40, 43
Greyhound Hotel, Croydon, 118, 127
Grievson, Frankie, 72
Griffiths, Norman, 2, 18
Group of Independent Operators (private airlines), 19
Guinness. *Hon.* A. E., 20
Gun emplacements, **58, 59,** 118, 121, 124
Habisch, *Oberleutnant,* 78
Hackbridge House, 9
Hadrian (H.P.42), 19, 20, **56**
Haigh, *Sergeant Pilot,* 36
Haimes, Brian, 2, 3, 4, 5, 7, 8, 11, **23,** 29, 38, 71, 77, 79, 105
Hall, Robert F., 105, 118, 120, 122, 128, 137
Halton (No. 1 Apprentice Wing, RAF), Bucks., 95
Hamilton, *Flight Lieutenant* H. R., 96
Hamilton Way. Wallington, 71
Hanbury, *Pilot Officer* John C. M., 11
Handley Page aircraft
  H.P. 42, 3, 18,19, **21, 22,** 39, **56**
  Harrow. 34
Hangars, Croydon Airport, **113**
  'A' (Imperial Airways), 7, 73, 85
  'B' (Air France, Sabena, KLM, DLH etc.), 2, 7, 11
  'C' (Rollason's, Redwing, etc.), 4, 73, 76, 97, **111**
  'D' (Flight Shed), 4, 6, **30, 52,** 73, **88, 114**
  'Glove Hangar', **88**
Hannibal (H.P. 42) 19
Hannow (H.P.42) 18
Hanworth, 13
Hargreaves, *Flying Officer,* 43
Harkin, Arthur Quin-, 17, 18
Harpenden, Herts., 121
Harper, *Pilot Officer,* 10
Harrison, *Squadron Leader,* 108
Harrow (aircraft), 34
Harrow-on-the-Hill, 126
Hartley, *Sir* Harold, 20
Hartnall, Charles, 18
Harvey, *Squadron Leader* Arthur Vere *(Air Commodore Lord Harvey of Prestbury),* 5, 6, **24,** 34
Harvey, *Wing Commander* G., 12
Harwell, Berkshire, 12
  aerodrome, 31, 35
Hastings, Sussex, 96, 119
Hatcham Rubber Company, 74, **113**
Havercroft, *Sergeant Pilot* 'Tich', 41, 43
Havoc aircraft, 96
'Haw Haw, Lord', 12
Hawaiian Air, 7
Hawker aircraft
  Audax, 4, **21**
  Demon, 4
  Hurricane, **ix,** 6, 7, 10, **32,** 40, 45, 46, 51, **52, 60,** 66, 67, 68, 69, 70, 71, 72, 78, 79, 81,

83, 84, 85, 86, **92, 93,** 95, 96, 97, 98, 99, 100, 102, 103, 106, 108, 115, 117, 119, 120, 122, 126, 127, **129,** 130, **131, 132, 134, 135,** 137. **cover**
Hawkes, *Flying Officer* J. R., 34
Hawkhurst, 78, 97
Hawkinge aerodrome, Kent, 13, 46, 48, 69, 70, 83
Hawley's Corner, Biggin Hill, 100
Hayes, *ACI,* Leslie J., 37, 41, 42
Hayter, *Pilot Officer,* 126
Heakes, *Group Captain,* 68
Healey, *Flight Lieutenant,* 40
Heinkel aircraft, 13, 97, 99
  He 111, 101, 108, 118, 124
  He 113, 66, 103
Helena, (H.P.42), 19, **56, 57**
Henderson, *Sir* Neville, **x,** 1
Hendon aerodrome, 12, 37, 45, 47, 48, 68
Hengist (H.P.42), 19
Henley-on-Thames aerodrome, Berkshire, 68
Heracles (H.P.42), 18
Herne Bay, Kent, 101
Herner, *P.C.* J., 38
Heston aerodrome, Middlesex, 1, 34, 47, 127
Higgs, *Flying Officer* T. P. K., 67
Highview Avenue, Wallington, 5
Hildreth, W. P., 17, 19
Hill, Howard (pilot), 43
Hillcrest Road, Purley, 71
Hitler Adolf, 1, 66, 75, 101, 121, 124
Hodgson, *Pilot Officer* W. T., 96, 98
Hodson, *LAC* Albert, 106, 107, **139**
Hogan, *Squadron Leader* H. A. V., 51
Hogg, *Pilot Officer* R. N., 13, 37
Holland, Bob (pilot), 43
Holland, *Pilot Officer* 'Dutch', 102
Honourable Artillery Company, 6, 11
Hooe, East Sussex, 78, **115**
Hope, *Flying Officer* R., 123, 124
Horatius (H.P.42), 19, **21, 22**
Horley, Sussex, 78
Hornchurch aerodrome, Essex, vi, 48
Horsa (H.P.42), 19
Horsham, Sussex, 40
Howell, *Sergeant* F., 10
Howes, *Sergeant,* 100
Hudson (aircraft), 18, **55**
Hughes, *Flying Officer,* Cliff, **139**
Humpherson. *Flying Officer,* J. W. B., 34
Humphreys, *Pilot Officer,* 107
Hunt, *Pilot Officer* W. E., 40
Hunting Group of companies. 3n
Hurricane aircraft *see under* Hawker aircraft
Hutchings, Bob, 76, **111**
Ifould, Bill, 50
Ifould, Lloyd C., 48, 49-51, **94**
Ightham, Kent, 78
Imperial Airways, 2, 3, 5, 7, 15, 17, 18, 19, 20, 22, 25, 33, 39, 48, 55, 94
  Silver Wing service, 39
  Sports Ground, 125
  see also British Overseas Airways Corporation
Impressments Log. 2, 16
Ingle, *Pilot Officer,* 107
Irving, *Flying Officer* M. M., 34
Isle of Man (Ronaldsway) aerodrome, 17
Isle of Man Air Services, 20
'Ives, The', Kenley, 100
Jackson, *Pilot Officer* T. C., 34
Jacques, F. C. R., 19
Jarman, *ACI* A., 37
Jenkin aerodrome (Merville, France), 48
John Fisher School, Purley, 11, 125

Jones, *Pilot Officer,* 118
Jones, *Sergeant Pilot,* 127
Jones, Ernest, 74, 77
Joyce, William, 12
Jullian, Marcel *The Battle of Britain,* 102
Junkers aircraft
  Ju, 52/3m, x, 1, 2, 8, **55**
  Ju 87 (Stuka), 71, 81
  Ju 88, 65, 69, 82, 103, 107, 119, 120, 122
K.L.M., 7
Kahl, *Unteroffizier,* 115
Kaiserslautern, Germany, 49
Karachi, 19
Kayll, *Flight Lieutenant* J. R., 34
Keighley, Yorkshire, 75, 76
Kelso, Roxburgh, 105
Kemble aerodrome, Gloucestershire, 12
Kenley, Surrey, 40, 100
  aerodrome, 3, 5, 8, 13, 39, 70, 72, 78, 80, 83, 84,
    85, 103, 106, 107, 116, 119, 121, 129, **135**
Kenley Lane, Kenley, 100
Kennards of Croydon, 9
Kent, *Duke of,* 96, 126
Kenya, 126
Kestler, *Sergeant,* 127
Kinver, Staffordshire, 120
Kirton-in-Lindsay aerodrome, Lincs., 96
Klipsch, *Sergeant Pilot,* 43
Knittel, *Leutnant* Werner, 43
Koch, *Leutnant,* 78, 115
Kretzer, *Obergefreiter,* 78
Lake, Jack, 76
Lancaster (aircraft), 77
Lane, John K., 76
Lane, Phyllis, 76
'Lascelle' (code word), 16
Laurie, *Colonel* (Essex Yeomanry), 41
Lavender Hill, Battersea, 122
Le Bourget aerodrome, France, 2, 9, 45, 48,
  49-50
Le Brulle, *Flying Officer,* 47
Le Havre, France, 47
Le Treport, France, 34
Learmond, *Pilot Officer* Pat, 40, 43, 49
Lees, *Squadron Leader,* 102
Leicester Square, 106
Lewes, Sussex, 40
Light, Bill, 11, **29,** 71
Lines, *Corporal,* 127
Lines-Roberts, *Pilot Officer,* 10
Lingfield, 37
  racecourse ('near Edenbridge, Kent'), 41
Link Lane, Wallington, 86
Link Trainer Building, Croydon aerodrome,
  125
Lipperer, Hans, 75
Little Hutchings Farm, Etchingham, 119
Littleheath Road, Selsdon, 100
Liverpool, 101
  Speke aerodrome, 17, 20
Lloyd (airman barber), **28**
Lloyd, *Pilot Officer* J. R., 34
Local Defence Volunteers, 102
Lockheed aircraft
  Electra, **55**
  Hudson, 18, **55**
Lofts, *Pilot Officer* K. T., 34
London Colney, Herts., 121
London Docks, 107
London Electric Company, 100
London Rifle Brigade, 41, 44, 67
London Transport, 118
Longsdon, *Squadron Leader* R. C., 126

Looker, *Flight Lieutenant* David J., 9, 34,
  85-86, 129
Lower Addiscombe Road, Croydon, 124
Loughton, Sussex, 40
Lucas, *Pilot Officer* K. R., 13, 40
Ludgershall, Tidworth, Wilts., 47
Lufthansa *see* Deutsche Luft Hansa
Luftwaffe, 101
  Erprobungsgruppe (Test Group) 210, 70,
    73, 77, 78, 82, **115**
  Geschwader 76, 85
Lullington Castle, 103
Lyall, John (guardsman), 38
Lydd, 99
Lympne aerodrome, Kent, 46, 48, 99
Lysander (aircraft), 46
Maccinski, *Pilot Officer,* 102
McGrigor, *Sir* Charles, 44
McIntosh, *Sergeant Pilot* Peter, 119, 124, **138**
McIntyre, *Pilot Officer,* 70
McKellar, *Squadron Leader* Archie, 104, 105,
  107, 108, 116, 118, 124, 125, 126, **135**
Mackenzie, William (Guardsman), 38
McNabb, *Squadron Leader* Ernest A., 68, 69
McWilton, Gladys and Robert, 39
Magister (aircraft), 6, 21, 34
Magraten, *Miss* (British NSF), 76
Maidstone, Kent, 95, 103, 107, 120
Major Motors, Purley Way, 77
Males, *Pilot Officer* Ernest E., 119, **138**
Mallory, *Air Marshal Sir* T. Leigh, 126
Malta, 105
Manchester (Barton) aerodrome, 17
Manston aerodrome, Kent, 3, 10, 12, 13
Marden, Kent, 83, 102, 117, 120
Margaret, *Princess,* 87
Marshall, *Pilot Officer,* 97
Massey, *Hon.* Vinent, 68
Masters, David. *So Few,* 104
Measures, *Wing Commander* A. H., 20
Meredith, *Pilot Officer,* 10
Merville, France, 33, 34, 47, 48
Messerschmitt aircraft, 98
  Bf 108-1 Taifun (Aldon), 2
  Me 109, 43, 48, 66, 69, 70, 73, 78, 83, 96, 97,
    98, 99, 100, 101, 102, 103, 104, 107, 108,
    118, 119, 122, 123, 125, 126
  Me 110, 49, 70, 71, 72, 74, 97, 98, 99, 100
    101, 102, 108, **115,** 116, 118, 122
Middle Wallop aerodrome, Hampshire, 51, 68
Middlesex Regiment, 67
Middleton, Drew. *The Sky Suspended,* 66
Mighell, Philip, 123
Miles aircraft
  Magister, 6, **21,** 34
  Master, 40
Miller, *Squadron Leader* John D., 12, 39, 40
Miller, Temple, 17
Milne, *Pilot Officer,* J. A., 122, 124
Ministry of Aircraft Production, 76, 126
Ministry of Home Security, 81
Ministry of Information, 67
Mitcham Road Cemetery, Croydon, 80
Mitchell, *Air Marshal Sir* William G. S., 68
Montgomery, Bernard *(Field Marshal Lord*
  Montgomery), 106
Moore, *Dr.* William S., 38
Morgan, Eric, 50
Mosquito (aircraft), 77
Moss, Peter W. *Impressments Log,* 2, 16
Mottram, *Pilot Officer* Roy, 42, 43
Muirhead, *Flight Lieutenant* I. J., 124, 140

Murton-Neale, *Flying Officer* P. N., 6, 34
NAAFI (Navy, Army and Air Force Institution), 6
National Air Communications organisation (NAC), 7, 15, 16, 17, 19, 20
National Aircraft Factory No. 1, 3, 76
    Factory estate on site in 1940: map, **113**
Neale, *Pilot Officer* P. N. Murton-, 6, 34
New Barn Farm, 123
Newcastle-upon-Tyne, 69
Newlands, The, Wallington, 86, 105
Newling, *Pilot Officer* M. A., 13
News Chronicle, 79
Newton, *Sergeant Pilot* Harry S., 69, 84-85
Nicholls, *Air Marshal* H. R., 124
Nicoll, Wilf, *Croydon* in *The Battle of Britain: Then and Now,* 5, 87, 95, 119, 124
Noordwijk cemetery, Holland, 67
North Eastern Airways, 16, 19
North Weald aerodrome, Essex, 6, 12, 51, **93**
Northern Europe and South Atlantic Agreement, 17
Northolt aerodrome, Middlesex, vi, 13, 40, 43, 68, 83
Norwood, London, 39
Nuremberg, 75
Nuremberg Schraube Fabrik, 74
Nutfield aerodrome, Surrey, 78
Odiham aerodrome, Hants, **56**, 118
Old Sarum, Wilts. School of Army Co-operation, 46
Olley, Gordon, 20
Olley Air Service, 16, 20, 47
Oman, Gulf of, 19
'Operation Sealion', 67, 101
Oswald Boelcke (Ju 52/3m), x, 1
Oxford, 107
Oxspring, *Pilot Officer* Robert W., 78, **116**
Oxted, Surrey, 100
Paddock Wood, Kent, 83
Paisley, Scotland, 105
Palais de Dance, Croydon, 77
Palmer, Jane, 39
Palmer, Reginald, 39
Pampisford Road, Croydon, 12, 165
Paris
    Le Bourget aerodrome, 2, 9, 45, 48, 49-50, 94
Park, *Air Vice Marshal* Keith, 68, 126
Parker, *Mr.* (British NSF), 76
Parnell, Tony, **32**
Passy, *Flying Officer* Cyril, 127, **135**
Patterson, *Aircraftman,* 46
Payne, *Flight Sergeant,* 40
Peacock, *Major* Basil, 9
Peaks Hill, Purley, 11, 71
Pearson, *Colonel* (12th Queen's Royal Regiment), 41
Peckham Gas Works, 107
Penfold, *Aircraftman* Leslie W. L., 5, 23, **25**, 28, 72, **109**
Percival Vega Gull, 68
Perry, Colin, 104, 106, **117**, 118
    Boy in the Blitz, 96
Personal Airways, 78
Pexton, *Pilot Officer* R. D., 34
Philips factory, 81
Phillips, Ken, 76
Pigg, *Pilot Officer* Oswald, 99, **141**
Pine Ridge, Carshalton, 70
Playfair, *Air Vice Marshal* P. H. L., 67
Plough Lane, Beddington, 71, 86, 118, 121
Plough Lane, Purley, **32, 53**, 125

Plymouth, 39, 66
Pocock, *Sergeant Pilot,* 99
Police Station, Croydon, 38
Pond Hill Gardens, Cheam, 81
Portland, Dorset, 66
Potts, *Brigadier* Arthur, 68
Prest, Rosalind, 80
Prestcott, *Flying Officer,* 12
Prestwick aerodrome, Ayrshire, 86
Price, Alfred J. *The Battle of Britain: The Hardest Day,* 84
Prickman, *Wing Commander* Thomas, 84, 127
Progress Way, Croydon, 77
Prosser, Fred, 6
Propeller Inn, Purley Way, 77
Pudney, John. *The Seven Skies,* 18
Pumphrey, *Flying Officer* R. E. W., 34, 47
Purfleet, Essex, 98
Purley, 32, 71, 86
Purley War Memorial Hospital, 10, **52**, 99
Purley Way, Croydon, 7, 12, 58, 71, 72, 77, 79, 85, 86, 97, **113**
    gates across, **165**
    Open Air Swimming Pool, **58**
    Playing Fields, **58**
Putts, Johnny, 73
Quin-Harkin, Arthur, 17
RAF Flying Review, 86
Radcliffe, *Pilot Officer,* H. P. J., 34
'Raff' (dog - 605 Squadron mascot), 128
'Railway' and 'non-Railway' grouping of private airlines, 19, 20
Railway Air Services, 20
Rainier, *Pilot Officer* P. H. O'C, 13
Ramsey, *Sergeant Pilot,* 10
Randolph, Elsie, 11
Rapide/Dominie (aircraft), 47, 68
Reader, Ralph, **139**
Reading aerodrome, 40
Red Cross, **63**, 66, 80
Redford Avenue, Wallington, 86
Redhill, Surrey, 78, 125
Redwing Aircraft Ltd., 76, 97, 111, 121
Reith, *Sir* John, 17, 20
Renfrew aerodrome (Glasgow), 17
Ribbentrop, Joachim von, 2, 8
Richthofen squadron, Luftwaffe, 43
Ridge Park, Purley, 125
Roberts, *LAC* Albert, 12
Roberts, *Pilot Officer* Lines-, 10
Rochester, Kent, 118
Rochford aerodrome, 95
Rollason, W. A., 3n
Rollason Aircraft and Engines Ltd., 4
Rollason Aircraft Services Ltd., 3, 4, 31, 46, 47, 72, 73, 79, 111
Rolls Royce engines, 77
Romney Marsh, Kent, 124
Ronaldsway aerodrome (Isle of Man), 17
Rose, *Mr.* (of Vickers Supermarine), 40
Rose, *Pilot Officer* Anthony Ste. C., 10
    Mrs. F. H., 11
    Jean, 11
Ross, *Pilot Officer* W. A., 12-13
Rotherfield, Sussex, 78
Roundshaw Estate, Wallington, 95
Roundshaw Park, Wallington, 9, 26, 27, 95
Royal Air Force
    Auxiliary Air Force, 105
    Fighter Command, 17, 19, 67, 68, 82, 124
        No. 11 Group, 3, 5, 11, 40, 67, 68, 99, 126, 141
            Flying Training School, 13
            Pool (pilots), 13

No. 13 Group, 102
No. 110 Wing, 128
Maintenance Unit No. 9, Cosford, 40
Maintenance Unit No. 13, 86
Maintenance Unit No. 27, Shawbury, 40
Squadrons, 166, *see also* Appendix A
  2, 46
  3, **ix,** 7, 8, 10, 12, 13, 14, **32,** 40, **53**
  16, 46
  17, 6, 7, 10, **52**
  32, 72, 73, 85
  43, 100
  50, 139
  54, 65
  56, 7
  64, 84
  65, 13, 42
  66, 78, **116**
  72, 99, 101, 102, 106, 119, **138, 141**
  74, 68, 42
  81 (No. 1 RCAF, WWI), 68
  82, 78
  85, 86, 95, 96, 97, 98, 99, 100, **130, 131**
   140
  92, vi, 13, 35, 36, 37, 38, 39, 40, 41, 42, 34,
   45, 48, **88, 91,** 93, 94
  111, 51, 66, 67, 69, 70, 72, 73, 78, 83, 84,
   85, 87, 101, 102, 106, 107, **117, 141** *see*
   also Appendix E
  141, 66
  145, 12, 13, 35, 36, 37, 39, 40, 41, 42, 45,
   89, 92
  148, **31**
  222, 37
  235, 3
  242, 46
  253, 107, **116,** 119, 126
  257, 93
  271 Transport Squadron, 20, 47, 48
  401 (No. 1 RCAF), 68
  501, 51
  504, 46, 68
  600, 13
  601 (County of London), 36, 46, 66, 94
  604, 12, 13
  605 (County of Warwick), 33, 100, 104,
   105, 106, 107, 108, **116,** 118, 119, 120,
   121, 122, 123, 124, 126, 127, **133, 134,**
   135, 136, 137, 138, 139, 140
  605 Squadron Association, 126
  607 (County of Durham), 13, 33, 34, 45,
   46, 47, 51, **61, 63, 64**
  615 (County of Surrey; 'Churchill's
   Own'), 3, 5, 6, 8, 9, 10, 11, 12, 13, **23,**
   24, 25, 26, 27, 28, 30, 33, 34, 45, 46, **60,**
   61, 62, 64, 65, 66, 72, 84, 85, 86, **129**
  801 (Fleet Air Arm), 66
Technical Training Command, 42
Transport Command, 128
Volunteer Reserve, 100, 124
Royal Aircraft Establishment, Farnborough,
  74
Royal Army Service Corps, 44
Royal Artillery, 44, 97, 125
Royal Canadian Air Force, 68
  Squadrons
   1 (81 — WWI), 68
   1 (401 — WWII), 68, 69, 73, 83
   110, 46
Royal Engineers, 31st Regt., 9
Royal Flying Corps, 9, 68, 74, 123
Royal Horse Artillery, 43
Royal Observer Corps, 7, 78

Rubensdorffer, *Hauptmann* Walter, 70, 78
Russell, *Flying Officer* J. B., 47
SABENA, 7
Saemann, Hans, 75, 76
Saemann, Justin, 75
St. Athan, South Glamorganshire, 13, 39
St. Helier, Jersey, 51
St. Inglevert, 96
St. John's Church, Shirley, 124
Sample, *Squadron Leader* J., 34, 51
Samson, Tom, 165
Sanders, *Flight Lieutenant* J. G., 34
Sanders, *Pilot Officer* W. A., 13
Sanderstead, Surrey, 100
Sandy Lane South, Wallington, 6
Savoia-Marchetti aircraft, 48
Sayers, W. C. Berwick-. *Croydon and the*
  Second World War, 80
Scawen *see* Woods-Scawen
School of Army Co-operation, Old Sarum, 46
Schulz, Emil, 49
Science Museum, London, 86, **129**
Scots Guards, 35, 38, 41
Scott, *Pilot Officer* L. D. M., 13
Scottish Airways, 20
Scylla (Short L.17), 33, 34, **63**
Seelöwe (Operation Sealion), 67
Selsdon, Surrey, 130
Selsey, Sussex, 70
Sevenoaks, Kent, 73
Shadwell Dock, Stepney, 119
Shakespeare, *Sergeant,* 126, 127, 128
Shawbury aerodrome, Shropshire, 13, 40, 41
Sheen, *Flying Officer* Desmond, 102
Sheephurst Farm, Kent, 83
Shell Mex, 107
Shelmerdine, *Sir* Francis, 15
Sherbrook-Walter, *Colonel,* 66
Shoreham 8
  aerodrome, 17, 34
Short L.17, 33, 34, **61, 63, 64**
Shotgate, Essex, 98
Shrewsbury, *Pilot Officer* R. W., 13
Sidcup, Kent, 102
Siedenburg-Seymour, *Squadron Leader,* 3
Silk, *Sergeant Pilot,* 103
Silver Lane, Purley, 86
Simpson, *Pilot Officer* Peter, 84, 102
Sims, *Sergeant Pilot* P. A., 10, 12
Sinclair, *Sir* Archibald, 121
Slipper, *Pilot Officer* Cooper-, 107, 118, 119,
  120, 126
Smith, *Sergeant Pilot* F. R. Walker, 96
Smith, *Squadron Leader* L. E., 13, 34, 47
South Norwood, London, 124
Southampton, 51
Southern Railway Company, 106, 127
  Sports Club, 106, **139**
Spann, *Dr.* (Gestapo officer), 49
Speed, *Brigadier-General,* 66
Speke aerodrome (Liverpool), 17, 20
Spiller, Joss, 75, 76
Spitfire
  see under Vickers aircraft
Stafford Road, Wallington, 5, **52,** 59, 73, 74,
  77, **114,** 121
Stalag Luft III, 13, 49
Stanford-Tuck, *Wing Commander* Robert R.,
  vi, 42, 43, 45, 49, **93**
Stanmore Hospital, 66
Staplecross, Sussex, 102
Starke, *Herr,* 2
Steel, Kenneth, 4, 47

Stern, *Flying Officer* W.O., 34
Stewart & Arden's garage, Croydon, 77
Stoke Bishop, Bristol, 17
Stonrar, *Pilot Officer* J. E., 13
'Stuka', 71, 81
Sullivan, *Acting Flight Lieutenant* J. L., 47
Surrey Flying Services, 16, 79
Sutton, 107
Sutton, *LAC* J., 37
Sydenham, London, 100
Syrinx (Short L.17), 33, 34, **63**
Taberner, Ernest, 81
Taifun (aircraft), 2
Tangmere aerodrome, Sussex, 35, 36, 37, 51
Tatsfield Beacon, Surrey, 85
Templehof aerodrome, Berlin, 9
Terminal Building, Croydon Airport, ix, 5, 6, 48, **65**, 73, 86, **113**
Ternhill aerodrome, Shropshire, 12
Thames, River, 69, 71, 125
Thames estuary, 71, 98
Thameshaven, 98, 101, 103
Thompson, *Squadron Leader* John H., 51, 69, 72, 83, 103
Thompson, *Flying Officer* M. H. B., 34, 47
Thompson, *Pilot Officer* R. A., 'Happy', 99, 127
Thorney Island, Sussex, 70
Thornley, *Flight Lieutenant* L. T. W., 34
Thornton Heath, Croydon, 77
Ticehurst, Sussex, 123
Tideler, *LAC* A, 37
Tidworth army camp, Wilts., 46, 47
Times, The, 1, 10, 66, 78
Timothy the goat, 605 Squadron mascot, 127, 128
Tiverton, Devon, 19
Tizer Drinks Factory, Croydon, 77
Tooting, London, 87, 117, 118
Townsend, *Sergeant Pilot*, 47
Townsend, *Squadron Leader* Peter, 86-87, 95, 96, 97, 98, **132, cover**
Trenchard, Hugh *(Marshal of the RAF Lord Trenchard)*, 95
Trojan sports ground, 118
Trolley buses, 114
Tuck, *Wing Commander* Robert R. Stanford-vi, 42, 43, 45, 49, **93**
Tunbridge Wells, Kent, 83, 99, 10, 107, 119, 141
Turnhouse aerodrome, Midlothian, 126
Tweed, *Sergeant*, 103
Tweedie, *Wing Commander* Patrick, 39
Ungar, Guenther, 84
Usworth aerodrome, Co. Durham, 51
Van Vleit, *Wing Commander*, RCAF, 68
Vick, *Flight Lieutenant* J. A., 34
Vickers/Vickers Supermarine aircraft
  Aircraft Experimental Dept., Weybridge, 4
  Supermarine Spitfire, vi, 40, 41, 42, 48, 49, 66, 78, 81, **91**, 96, 97, 99, 101, 102, 106, 116, 119, 123
  Wellington bomber Mk.I, 3, 4, **31**, 77
Vickery, *Flying Officer*, 10
von Ribbentrop, Joachim, 2, 8
W. A. Rollason Ltd., 3n
Waddon, 74, 75, 86, 95, **115**
  Railway station, 18
Waddon Way, Croydon, **58**, 59, 73, 74, 86, 165
  Waterworks pumping station, **58, 59, 111, 113**
Wakeham, *Pilot Officer*, H. J. C., 13
Walker, *Pilot Officer* J. A., 83

Walker, *Colonel* Sherbrook , 67
Wallace, *Sergeant Pilot* T. J., 72, 83, 102, 103
Wallington, 1, 9, **32**, 38, 67, 86
  Town Hall, 9
Wallington and Carshalton Advertiser, 8
Wallington and Carshalton Times, 1, 67, 81
Walsh, *Air Commodore*, 68
Walter, *Squadron Leader* C., 7
Wandle river, 9
Warninglid, Sussex, 40
Warr, *Mr.* A. F., 77
Waterer Rise, Wallington, 27, 86
Watterston, *ACI* William, 38
Weatherill, *Flying Officer*, 47
Wellington (aircraft), 3, 4, **31**, 77, 165
Wellington (school), 35
Wells, *Flight Lieutenant*, 12, 13
Welsh, *Air Vice Marshal Sir* Wiliam L. 41
Wend, The, Coulsdon, 123
West Coast Air Services, 20
West Malling aerodrome, Kent, 69, 77
Western Isles Airways, 20
'Western Plan', 16
Westgate, Kent, 69
Westland Lysander, 46
Wevelghem, Belgium, 46
Weybridge, Surrey, 4
Weymouth, Dorset, 66
Wheatley, Eric, 7, 8
Whitchurch aerodrome, Bristol, 3, 17, 18, **55**
White, *Flight Lieutenant* G. C., 34
Whitehaven, Cumberland, 19
Whitehead, Bill, 73
Whiteing, Dennis, Eileen and Frederick, 39
Whitelaw, William *(Viscount Whitelaw)*, 35
Whitgift Middle School, Croydon, 124
Whitmarsh, *Pilot Officer* Reginald J., 38, 39, 90
Whittaker, *Pilot Officer*, 10
Whitty, *Pilot Officer* W. H. R., 34
Whyteleafe, Surrey, 40
Wicknem, *Pilot Offficer* S. N., 34
Willet Road, Croydon, 77
Williams, *Pilot Officer* Bill, 37, 43
Willoughby de Broke, *Lord*, 126, 127
Willy the goat, 605 Squadron mascot, 128
Wilson, *Pilot Officer* C. D. Gordon-, 40
Wilson, 'Tug', 11, **29**, 71
Wimbledon tennis courts, 66
Winchelsea, Sussex, 96
Winter, *Pilot Officer* 'Snowy', 102
Wolf, *Captain* (Scots Guards), 41
Women's Auxiliary Air Force (WAAFs), 3
Women's Voluntary Service, 70
Woodmansterne, Surrey, 104
Wood, Derek, *Attack Warning Red*, 7
Wood, *Sir* Kingsley, 11
Wood, Victor J., 75, 76, **111**
Woodcote Park, Epsom, 84
Woods-Scawen, *Flying Officer* Patrick, 100
Woods-Scawen, Tony, 100
Woodside Primary School, Croydon, 124
Woolworths, Church Street, Croydon, 77
Worrall, *Pilot Officer*, 97
Worrall, *Squadron Leader* J., 78
Wray, *Wing Commander*, 3
Wright, Allan (pilot), 43
Wright, *Sergeant* E. W., 108, 119, 126
Wrightways Ltd., 16
Yatesbury, 51
York aerodrome, 34
Young, *Pilot Officer* B. P., 34
Yule, H. D. (pilot), 13

96. An aerial photograph of Croydon Aerodrome taken in 1942, after the Battle of Britain had ended. The perimeter track and dispersal points can be seen clearly, as can craters from various bombing raids.

Iron gates 6ft. tall, topped with spikes and barbed wire, stood across Purley Way during the war. One pair was immediately south of Waddon Way and is just visible in the photograph; the other was just north of Edgehill Road, Purley. They are believed to have been there for most of the war; exact dates of erection and dismantling are not known. Traffic had to be diverted via Waddon Way, Pampisford Road, etc.

This photograph was taken from a converted Wellington bomber at 20,000ft. by Tom Samson of Handford Photography (who is still an aerial photographer, and a member of the Croydon Airport Society), when serving as an RAF photographer at Farnborough.

97. Burnt-in World War II graffiti on an overmantel panel in the Aerodrome Hotel, discovered some years ago during redecorations. It is now displayed in a frame in the 'Captain's Bar'. Note Squadrons (nos. 17, 92, 601, 615, etc.) and also army guard detachments — e.g. HAC (Honorable Artillery Company).